THE

RHETORIC OF CONVERSATION:

OR,

BRIDLES AND SPURS

FOR

THE MANAGEMENT OF THE TONGUE.

BY

GEORGE WINFRED HERVEY,

AUTHOR OF "THE PRINCIPLES OF COURTESY."

"If any man offend not in word, the same is a perfect man."—JAMES.
. . . . . *Dicenda tacendaque calles?*—PERSIUS.
"Knowest thou when to speak and when to hold thy peace?"

NEW YORK:
HARPER & BROTHERS, PUBLISHERS,
329 & 331 PEARL STREET,
FRANKLIN SQUARE.
1854.

Entered according to Act of Congress, in the year 1853, by
HARPER & BROTHERS,
In the Clerk's Office for the Southern District of New York.

PREFACE.

This work is the result of a purpose to write an original monograph on Conversation which should keep clear of all irrelevant matter, and at the same time contain all the instruction as to the art and ethics of talking that the most ambitious aspirant after colloquial excellence could reasonably desire. After some laborious research, the writer came to the conclusion that no complete work on this subject exclusively has ever been published in any country, not even in France, where Conversation is deservedly ranked among the arts. There are to be found, in several languages, short essays and chapters on this subject, some of which possess great merit, though many of them are vague and commonplace, some demoralizing, and all incomplete. Their incompleteness, however, should not keep any one from reading them, for though they are small, they all, except those that have an immoral tendency, help to cure the bad habits of talkers. The writer would apologise for them and for parts of his own work, in the well-known words of Galen, *In medicinâ nihil exiguum:* "In physic nothing is little."

We have a variety of works on Rhetoric, which teach the art of speaking in public, but not one sufficient treatise on the art of speaking in the sundry circumstances of private and social life. Hitherto we have sought to make orators of *the few*, rather than conversers of *the many ;* not duly considering that it is every way more desirable that the multitude of private citizens should talk well in their daily intercourse, than that a small number of orators should know how to address them on stated occasions. Even public speakers themselves would not find it amiss to acquire some skill in this art. Whatever design they would compass by their powers of utterance, they will, in the course of a life-time, make as many, if not as deep marks, on their generation by their frequent talks as by their few speeches; nor let them indulge the notion that the gifts and acquirements which make them orators do necessarily make them conversers also. The two characters are not often united in the same person; for this reason, among others, that the habit of addressing public bodies, though favorable in some respects, is unfavorable in others to excellence in conversation.

As all our great authorities in Rhetoric hold that the orator should be a good man, so we affirm, a little more explicitly, that the conversationist should be a man of evangelical piety. Whether the assertion of Theremin that "eloquence is a virtue," be true or untrue, depends on the meaning he attaches to the word *eloquence:* thus much, however, we do hazard, that the highest style of colloquial eloquence is the result of many virtues.

Possibly some readers will meet with a few observations in this work which seem so agreeable to common sense, that they may erroneously conclude that they had themselves previously made the like, or expressed in such simplicity and familiarity of style, that they may be ready to impute the same property to the thought. If they here read what their own observation had before taught them, they ought at least to cheerfully allow us the good sense to be of their own opinion. These coincidences will settle them more firmly in the conviction of their own wisdom, and prepare them to act upon its dictates with more freedom and boldness. Should they recollect to have seen, as possibly they may, the substance of a few of the following admonitions in the writings of others, let them only the more highly prize and diligently heed them, now that they find them still haunting them in a different garb, and supported by fresh sanctions.

Let no one suppose that the author sets up for a conversationist, or puts himself forth as an example in this particular. He knows better his own defects than to pretend to any such thing. While he can lay nò claim to skill in the art of talking—as he is grievously unskilled in the art of holding his tongue, for that matter—yet he could wish that few would thence conclude him incompetent to give useful hints to those who are in all respects his superiors. Phœnix, who was chosen the companion of Achilles to teach him how to speak, never became so distinguished for eloquence as his heroic pupil. It does not require brilliant parts to be a successful instructor or a just critic. Machiavelli is of opinion that a person must be one of the people in order to judge properly of a prince. Even so it is not he who sways the colloquial sceptre that is always best prepared to discourse of this kind of kingcraft, but he who in the character of humble subject has been gladdened by his clemency or troubled by his wrath.

May that God who caused the scroll of the prophet to outlive the fire on the hearth of Jehoiakim the king, and moved the men of Ephesus to burn their magical books, either command these pages to bear some humble part in teaching the art of conversing with propriety and profit, or speedily consign them to eternal forgetfulness.

CONTENTS.

CHAPTER I.

Page

Silence.......... 11

CHAPTER II.

Conversation in Private and Domestic Life.......... 25

CHAPTER III.

Conversation of Christians with one another.......... 43

CHAPTER IV.

Sunday Conversation.......... 67

CHAPTER V.

Conversation in General Society.......... 67

CHAPTER VI.

Interviews with the Unbeliever relative to his Spiritual Interests.......... 90

CHAPTER VII.

Page

Religious Conversation with Prejudiced Persons........... 123

CHAPTER VIII.

Discussions.. 132

CHAPTER IX.

Reproof 163

CHAPTER X.

Flattery and Praise 183

CHAPTER XI.

Detraction and Scandal.................................. 197

CHAPTER XII.

Interrogations 220

CHAPTER XIII.

Egotism and Boasting 227

CHAPTER XIV.

Anecdotes and Stories 243

CHAPTER XV.

Page
Wit and Pleasantry.................................... 256

CHAPTER XVI.

The Style of Conversation.............................. 269

CHAPTER XVII.

Physical Habits in Conversation........................ 390

CHAPTER XVIII.

Preparation for Conversation........................... 395

CHAPTER XIX.

Accompaniments of Conversation......................... 315

CHAPTER XX.

A History of Certain Conversation-Clubs, with Sketches of the Conversation of Johnson, Hannah More, Coleridge, and others.. 323

CHAPTER I.

SILENCE.

Harpocrates, the Egyptian god of silence, was represented holding one of his fingers on his mouth. He was almost the only heathen deity that ever and in the least degree deserved imitation; and those who paid him divine honors, idolators though they were, do not appear to have been wholly lost to the charms of virtue. But useful as the idol may have been to remind men of the general duty of silence, it was deficient in this, that it did not exemplify the duty in a variety of circumstances. It was fixed in one posture on all occasions. It is the privilege of the Christian to copy an Exemplar who, though he spoke a great deal, knew *when*, *where*, and *how*, to be silent. When the Scribes and Pharisees drew an adulteress into his presence, and began to ask impertinent and insidious questions, He made no reply, but stooped down and wrote on the ground, as though He heard them not. What wisdom, dignity, modesty, and tact! This was the eloquence, not of words, but of action. When at the grave of Lazarus, his groans were interrupted by silent weeping, the Jews, looking upon his tears, could not help exclaiming, "Behold how he loved him!" When He was accused by his enemies before the tribunal of Pilate, He answered not a word. This was the eloquence of silent meekness, and so powerful was it that it filled the Roman governor with wonder. In the silent look, which was such a pathetic rebuke to Peter, there was an eloquence that has found no match in the history of human oratory.

Great numbers have been ruined for the want of skill in the art of silence. Had Moses, the meekest of men, but suppressed his impatience in his own bosom, he might have been permitted to pass over to the land of promise. Had the children who met Elisha bowed before him in reverent silence, they would not have been torn in pieces. Had Michel abstained from a little persiflage, she might have been blessed with descendants. Had Peter been silent before his accusers, he might have saved himself tears of remorse. How many have closed their days in shame or sorrow because they lived long enough to say one word too many. How many who, had they the power, would warn us in the spirit of Sir Henry Wotten's lines, supposed to have been written by John Hoskins to his little child, Benjamin, from the Tower where he was imprisoned for having more volubility than the law allowed him ;

> "Sweet Benjamin since thou art young,
> And hast not yet the use of tongue,
> Make it thy slave while thou art free,
> Imprison it, lest it do thee."

"Be swift to hear, slow to speak," is the apostolical precept; and even the relative number of the organs of hearing and of speaking teach as much. It was a saying of Zeno, that men have one tongue and two ears, and should therefore hear much and speak little. If a person be moved by no other consideration than that of learning to talk well, he should not open himself too freely in new companies and among strangers. He should consider that every circle has its own tone, laws of decorum, and modes of thinking and talking, which he must learn by reserved observation, before he can safely take the lead of its conversations. It would do some people good if they could take a course of philosophy under the instructions of old Pythagoras. He enjoined silence on his disciples for the first two years, forbidding them during that period either to ask questions or make remarks. After they had thus learned to hold their tongues, he gradually permitted them to make inquiries, and finally to communicate their own opinions.

Laudable as a well-timed silence is, so much praise has been lavished upon it, as to lead some to say nothing, or next to nothing, in society. Taciturnity is not always an indication of wisdom; it may be the necessity of ignorance. Some who have been taught that wise men are not great talkers, seek a reputation for wisdom at the expense of affability. Cyrus once said to a person who was always speechless in his presence: "If thou art a wise man thou doest foolishly: if thou art a fool thou doest wisely." Men of solitary and studious habits too commonly take for granted that they are out of their element when they are in society, and carry themselves accordingly. Though no other class of men have a greater fund of thought, few are so much at a loss for a theme, or hold themselves less in readiness for talking. The modesty of some always draws a veil over their splendid intellects. The pride of others whispers to them that this is not the opportunity to set their talents in an advantageous light. Some have contracted habits of silent thinking which they cannot lay aside in seasons of recreation, else they have come from their studies with their thoughts so confused, their powers so fretted, and their nerves so sensitive, that they fear if they attempt to open their lips they shall torture themselves and all about them. Many a one has taken leave of circles in which there were men of letters, saying to himself, "I have lost my time in the company of the learned." When this distracted and absent manner is unfeigned—and we must always believe that it is, till we know it to be otherwise—it must be pitied and pardoned. While Thomas Aquinas was absorbed in controversies he was invited to dine with the king of France. He went, but was lost to those around him; at length suddenly dropping his knife and fork, with his eyes fixed, he struck his hand upon the table crying out, "I have confuted the Manicheans." For one who is not a student to maintain a long silence, or to break it only by irrelevant remarks, is to gain the reputation of a dullard. Certain literary characters must pardon us if we say, that in our humble judgment the greatest minds are free from this infirmity. The absent-*minded* are stumbling blocks in society, and ought not to appear there without making an apology for not being absent also *personally*.

In some, taciturnity is the dictate of a self-important spirit. They foolishly fancy that to speak to another is to admit him to an equal footing with themselves. Lacking the common sympathies of humanity, they cast a wondering and supercilious eye upon the generality of those who make bold to accost them.

Again, we meet with those who are taciturn from bashfulness. This is beautiful in young persons; and those who labor to remove all traces of it from their manners, are only preparing them to be impudent in later years. But though modesty is comely in all, bashfulness in men and women, whether it be real or affected, is very troublesome to themselves and to their neighbors. One can hardly be at ease in the society of such people. Sympathizing with their silly looks and awkward gestures, he is apt to lose his self-possession, and appear as timid as they.

The worst kind of silence is sullenness; and it is a fault of many kinds of taciturnity that they are apt to be mistaken for it. People that have much knowledge of the world very seldom manifest their ill nature, obstinacy, or enmity in this way; they are careful to cover their feelings beneath a more close and comely veil. The bare suspicion that there is a sulky person in a company, fills us with painful apprehensions. He appears to us as if he were laboring under a load of hatred, which he is ready every moment to roll off upon us; it is impossible for us in his presence to talk with freedom; he chills and petrifies us: he is akin to the Gorgons of classic fable, who are said to have had the power of converting into stone every object on which they fixed their eyes.

It must not be overlooked, however, that the most

affable and good humored persons have their silent moods, when it is equally tiresome to talk and to listen. A shrewd observer will readily detect this humor, and regulate his tongue accordingly.

Silence is, now and then, useful by way of reproof, more particularly when it is assisted by a corresponding look. When people are talking against their acquaintance, uttering profanities or obscenities, or wantonly taunting us, or on any other sufficient occasion, we may resume silence in a manner that will reprehend the talker. In such a case we must not only hold our peace, but avoid even a smile of seeming approval. Some have so very gay and jocular a way of rebuking, that one thinks them half delighted with the act of wickedness that called it forth. When people bring to our ears the slanders they have heard of others, or tell us of their own grievances on purpose to obtain our favoring judgment or to enlist us on their side, then silence is commonly the part of wisdom. A hubbub which is commenced by words, it is hardly in the power of words to hush. Slander-bearers take heart from those who deign to give ear to them. When a strife of tongues has once begun in a coterie or neighborhood, the example of one or two sealed mouths does marvels in settling commotions and restoring peace. Of such persons we may say what Ignatius declared concerning the bishop of the church of Philadelphia: "His moderation I admire; by his silence he is able to do more than others by all their vain talk."

Do not go off in raptures at the first sight of a work of nature or art, unless you mean to show your enthusiasm rather than your taste. You had better keep silence till you have formed some opinion. While Sir Joshua Reynolds was at Rome, studying the works of Raphael in the Vatican, he observed that most strangers who came to see them, began to praise them the moment their eyes fell upon them, whereas he was rather disappointed with them at first, and did not begin to appreciate them till he had made them objects of protracted study. Minds of sensitive and poetic mould are at first sight awed into silence when they contemplate natural scenery of great beauty, grandeur, or sublimity; while persons of less taste are talkative, and are apt to give the objects before them anything but their right names.

Do not talk in church either before or after service. Silence is a mark of reverence which is due to the place and the occasion. It is a good rule among the Scotch to be silent at the breakings up of congregations. Romaine used to reprove church gossips by knocking their heads together. Even the ancient heathens were wont to hold their peace when they supposed themselves in the presence of their gods. Neither talk at a concert or where people are listening to music. "Pour not out words," says the son of Sirach, "where there is music, and show not forth wisdom out of time."

Silence is also the proper language of grief. When we are overwhelmed with any calamity our words are few. The Psalmist David once said, "I am so troubled that I cannot speak." For this reason, when we pay a visit of condolence we should not talk a great deal. The expression of our compassion and fellow-feeling we shall find scarcely less acceptable to the bereaved, than urging motives of consolation. The friends of the afflicted patriarch of Uz behaved with singular propriety when they came to comfort him—"They lifted up their voice and wept; and they rent every one his mantle; and sprinkled dust upon their heads towards heaven. So they sat down with him upon the ground seven days and seven nights, and none spake a word unto him, for they saw that his grief was very great." After making every allowance for the customs of Eastern pastoral life, it may be questioned whether the talkativeness, which is somewhat customary among us on such occasions, is any improvement on the silence of these ancient orientals.

The fluent talker is oftener met with in society than the accomplished listener; for this reason, perhaps, that the latter must forego his own gratification for that of others. He is usually a greater favorite, and dispenses more pleasure to those around him than the talker. And it is a mistake to suppose that a good listener bears no part in conversation. He is, in truth, the only one that can shine without envy, and speak without interruption, impertinence, and tediousness. By an animated attention and an intelligent look, he can be eloquent even beyond the power of words. By a smile of assent he can show his approbation, his interest, his delight. By a question, he may indicate his curiosity or his humility. By starting a question for others to discuss, his deference and complaisance—by listening to tiresome prosing, his patience—by offering a doubt, or confirming an assertion, his appreciation—by calling out and encouraging the timid, his kindness. And yet his silence is devoid both of servility and stateliness;

he pleases without flattery, and though he says few things himself, his easy yet spirited attention incites others to outdo themselves. Heraclitus being once asked why he kept silence, replied, "That you may talk"—and this is the compliment that every good listener makes to those who are discoursing. Let any one bring to mind those whose society has afforded him particular pleasure, and if we are not mistaken, he will find them to have been those who seldom opened their mouths for any other purpose than that they might hear him more distinctly. People often complain of the trite and vapid talk that prevailed in companies from which they have just come, but we may be certain that engaging discourse is rarely wanting where there are good listeners.

More than a few pay so little attention to what is said, that they do not know how to make a suitable reply, or ask an apposite question. If they advance anything, it is alien to the matter in hand, and they say *yes* or *no* in the one place of all others the most improper. Failing to listen to one half of our remarks, they misunderstand the other half. They ask us to repeat, as they were thinking of something else just then. Rousing occasionally from their dreams, they cry out, "What was that you were saying, sir," "I did not understand that, sir." Some, especially in argumentation, will hold their peace till others have taken their turn indeed, but will not listen to a word they say. They are all the while employed in framing a reply, or inwardly felicitating themselves on a triumphant confutation as soon as occasion offers. Solely attentive to the premises, they are preparing to deny the conclusion, leaving the chain of argument that conducts to it quite out of the question. "Answer not," says the son of Sirach, "before thou hast heard the cause." And Solomon says, "He that answereth a matter before he heareth it, it is a folly and a shame unto him."

Interruption is *the habit* of the inattentive and the rude; but only the *accident* of the alert and the polite. Some persons have a way of making long pauses, so that, at the moment when you think they have done and begin to reply, they start off anew, saying, "Let me finish what I have to say." Such interruptions must happen to the best talkers. In friendly dialogue it is occasionally allowable to break in to finish a sentence or to improve an epithet —to clear up a remark which threatens to prejudice some absent person; and to check the talker when he is going to flatter us or say something to his own disadvantage.

Nothing is more provoking to a talker than to see a person spring up and leave the circle when he is saying something which he wishes to be appreciated. "I have known," says Sir Richard Steele, "a challenge sent to a person for going out of the room abruptly, and leaving a man of honor in the midst of a dissertation."

When you come into company while a topic is discussing, do not request a recapitulation, but speak to what follows. Yet it is sometimes the duty of the conversers, unasked, to explain the subject to a new comer. When a long story is being told, do not ask the narrator to stop and repeat for your benefit. It is apt to make them look foolish and awkward, especially if you are behind the time appointed for taking the chair. Conversers should sometimes behave as the Marquis of Abercorn did, who determined to teach his visitors punctuality by sitting down at dinner at the hour named in the card, which was worded "at 5 o'clock precisely." When the time arrived only one gentleman had come. However, they sat down to dinner and disposed of the first course. About six, visitors began to drop in. His lordship was at dinner, and made no apologies as they sat down to what remained. Others of the party arrived about seven, and, instead of dinner, were complimented with coffee.

There are occasions when it is not prudent to listen to a conversation, as generally when we are not addressed and the subject does not concern us, and particularly when persons are wrangling. In their calmer after-thoughts they may be mortified to recollect that we heard what they said; and besides, we may be tempted to take sides, and so involve ourselves in the contention.

There is one kind of silence that is almost too contemptible to deserve mention. We mean that silence which some ill-bred men are a long time breaking to those who ask of them a favor, or request their attention to some business which needs to be immediately despatched, and which requires but a moment, and not the slightest forethought, to transact. They like to keep people in suspense, and would seem to find self-satisfaction in the thought that they are like those princes whose palaces are thronged with subjects who are detained for weeks awaiting the answer to their petitions; or like the great English equity lawyer, Lord Eldon, for whose learned decisions, as tardy as they were profound, the client waited long in consuming anxiety, and starved while the chancellor mused.

It is no very courteous practice for people to maintain strict silence when they are unknown to each other, as when persons are brought together at a house before the master or mistress has appeared. I had rather have my ear-drums beaten all day long than to endure such a dumb-show for five minutes. This sort of silence is a most refined torture. It is wrong to suppose we cannot speak to people till we have learned their names.

We must not be loquacious in the hearing of those sly listeners who catch our words from our lips, and lay them up in their memories with the intent to report them to our disadvantage. They practise great reserve in their intercourse with strangers, but contrive to call them out and encourage them to lay open all their hearts to them. They will listen to you, and, if needs be, applaud you; but it is only when you speak your mind, and give them a clew to the weak points in your character. Some put on a seeming ignorance, that they may ascertain how much others know; or, under an air of indifference, hide an eager desire for secret and personal information. Others, more crafty still, compass the same object by great volubility, in order to embolden their victims to declare themselves without reserve. Without being suspicious, we should be on our guard against this kind of double-dealers.

To little purpose shall we attempt to master this difficult art unless we learn to rule our own spirit. The mind is the real source of most of the faults that are committed in conversation. Let this be in subjection to Divine Grace in all who would cultivate the proprieties of speech. A wise ancient remarks that it is the gods alone who inspire the wisdom of silence; and a wiser than he has said that "the preparation of the heart and the answer of the tongue are from the Lord."

We have little hope of effecting any durable reform in the conversation of those whose hearts are not undergoing the transformations of sanctifying grace. Moral precepts are all but lost upon those whose unrenewed nature is continually repelling them. In vain do we cleanse and whitewash the door of the sepulchre so long as the inner walls are reeking with corruption. Says the apostle James, "Every kind of beasts, and of birds, and of serpents, and of things in the sea, is tamed, and hath been tamed of mankind, but the tongue can no man tame; it is an unruly evil." Yet the same apostle would have Christians bridle the tongue. After Divine Power has subdued it, we may do something towards managing it. To our hands He resigns, not the *lasso*, but the *bridle.*

Whoever knows how to listen to a rude, tedious,[1] or conceited talker, with attention and civility, neither complaining of impertinences nor hinting to others that he knows what good breeding is, if they do not;

[1] Be not a button holder. One can easily ascertain when a person he meets wishes to talk. If he is walking with a hurried step, do not stop him; or if this is necessary, detain him but a moment; even then, it is better to turn about and hurry along with him till you have spoken your word. When a professional man is called from his office, or a student from his books, deliver your message with all possible despatch. Have not the vanity to think that great novelty of thought,

but, overlooking the untold irregularities of the tongue, and counting them as nothing—such a one, however ignorant and ungifted and ungainly he may be, shows that he is, at least, not wanting in meekness, a virtue which has no fellow in the whole circle of exterior graces—a virtue which is one of the most amiable peculiarities of the Christian, and a chief qualification for the society of fallible beings.

even though you can deliver it with great suaviloquence, will be gladly received by those whose minds are preoccupied. Long talks are never to be allowed, except among fast friends who have an abundance of leisure. In the Hindoo paradise two deities are represented as sitting engaged in eternal conversation. This may do very well for a heathen paradise, but it will never answer on this whirling planet.

CHAPTER II.

CONVERSATION IN PRIVATE AND DOMESTIC LIFE.

NUMBERS that can entertain the occasional assemblies of their friends and acquaintance, or the conversation clubs to which they belong, with the variety, grace, and brilliance of their discourse, do not know how to adapt their tone and style to the members of the family circle. They are not skilled in those cadences of kindness that soothe the dull ear of age and the sensitive ear of weariness, affliction, and pain. They have never learned to take part in the prattlements of children, and to attemper the light of instruction to their budding faculties. They cannot greet the poor and the dependent with those words of good will and encouragement which are more melodious than the chink of gold, and are laden with sympathies that are more precious than rubies.

Home, to those who are so happy as to have one, must ever be the principal scene of entertainment and vexation, moral conflict and victory, joy and sorrow. Over this spot must ever hover the dearest and holiest memories. Here the world search after the secret springs of action, and find a solution of the mysteries of our character and career, and thence the angelic recorder brings the chief items for the doomsday-book. To home are our destinies chained, from the morning dawn of life till its departing hour. That, then, is a most sterling accomplishment, which serves to gladden, instruct, and warn those who are wont to gather there. It matters little whether the fickle multitude applaud or hiss, bless or curse those who are on good terms with their relatives and domestics, and, by kind words and gentle acts, endear themselves to these. Unsuccessful though they be in the strife and tumult of the world, they still have it in their power to perform

> "Deeds
> Above heroic, though in secret done."
> *Milton.*

There is, perhaps, no fault more characteristic of modern conversation than an irreverence for age. The command, "Thou shalt rise up before the hoary head, and honor the face of the old man," would seem to be thought obligatory only on the people of a former dispensation. But neither time nor place can alter or abrogate this law. Were the aged no longer sensible of neglect and disrespect, then their might be some color of reason for the abolition of this statute; but the sensibilities of the aged pilgrim of this generation are the same with those of the gray-headed man of the olden time. How much soever the people of the world may be wanting in these assiduities to the aged, it ill becomes the Christian to deny them, in any instance, that reverence and kindness which both religion and nature require. Their petulance or childishness can never justify our impatience, disrespect, or inattention. Great deference should be felt for their opinion. When information is desired as to a matter that is familiar to them, they should first be consulted, always taking care, however, not to ask them any question which is likely to expose their ignorance, or the decay of their memory or other faculties. When a discussion is going on, our seniors must be attentively heard before we presume to put forth our own reasons. Young Elihu, the spirited opponent of Job, and his three friends, did not suffer his zeal for truth to encroach upon the honor that was due to years. He held his peace till all had spoken, because they were older than he, and did not begin to answer them till he perceived they had all concluded their remarks.

Old people like to be reminded of their age as associated with wisdom, experience, and virtue, but not as implying infirmity and dotage. Some, it is true, take a kind of pleasure in describing their diseases and complaining of their pains. But the greater number, though they like to have us sympathize with their infirmities, do not wish us to dwell at great length on the subject. Some one who called on Dr. Johnson, in his old age, says that he soon dispatched the inquiries that were made about his illness, by a short and distinct narrative; and then assuming a gay air, repeated from Swift:

"Nor think of our approaching ills,
And talk of spectacles and pills."

In conversing with sick persons, the attendant should suit his topics to their mood. When they are melancholic he should not, in general, talk in a lively or humorous strain. "As he that taketh away a garment in cold weather, and as vinegar upon nitre; so is he that singeth songs to a heavy heart." When they show a desire to forget their malady, he should transport their minds as far as possible from the sick bed, and especially keep clear of all gloomy and funereal considerations. He should praise their patience when they exercise it, return the mildest answers to their chidings, and listen to their groans as if they were the most plaintive melodies. In answer to their murmurs, he must not inform them that he was himself once afflicted with the same disease, except when it may serve to inspire them with the hope of a speedy recovery. He should be so attentive to their wants, and alive to their condition, as to forget his own indispositions which have been occasioned by watching and confinement. He should express joy and gratitude for any signs of recovery, and not call their attention to any change he may discover in their features, unless it is for the better, nor remark that it will be a long time before they are quite recovered.

When the sick person and the attendant are both pious, the work of consolation will, in most cases, be easy. A knowledge of the Scripture promises, skill in applying them, strong faith and habitual prayerfulness, are the principal aids to the performance of this duty. We must not omit to mention the efficacy of sacred music, in cases where the afflicted saint has any perception of harmony. The uses of music in the sick room have hitherto received much less attention than they deserve. The Scotch gipsies were wont to deem their songs of sovereign efficacy in diseases, and no doubt they were in some cases.

When the sick one is an unbeliever, the attendant

must, it is scarcely worth while to say, manage according to his temper, abilities, and principles. A nurse or other person, who is in constant waiting, can better administer to the spiritual wants of the sick, than a physician, whose calls must be brief, and perhaps at distant intervals, though the latter is by no means to be excused from a faithful performance of this duty. When the physician or the nurse has won the affection and confidence of patients, by many obliging attentions, he has prepared the way for the most successful appeals to their heart and conscience.[1] They will not be slow to believe that a person who shows such a benevolent care for their bodies, is equally solicitous for the welfare of their souls. The proper discharge of this duty demands wisdom as well as piety. Still, we must not be so lithe and circuitous in our address as to diminish the momentum of the truth. When the person is unconcerned, we must urge alarming considerations, and we should aim to startle him to a degree that will make him lose all thoughts of our manner, in an overwhelming anxiety about his relations to the Redeemer, and his preparation for eternity. Perhaps the patient confesses his ignorance of the gospel, and asks us to instruct him, but does not wish us to go beyond instruction. Nevertheless, we should go on to convince him that his very ignorance aggravates his guilt before God, asking him in the spirit of our Lord's question to Nicodemus, "Art thou a master of Israel and knowest not these things?" Another passively admits what we say, but does not feel its

[1] See letters of Dr. Burder to a Young Physician, annexed to "Memoirs of Dr. Hope."

force; then we must earnestly enlarge upon it, and set it home to the conscience. It will not be enough to rouse any sort of feeling; as to dissolve him in tears, to fill him with alarms, or provoke his opposition. We should not give over till we find him a true disciple of Christ. Some will resolutely withstand all our attempts to engage their thoughts on the side of their salvation. They either take ground against the Gospel itself, or attempt to keep us at a distance, by taunts and reproaches. Yet, though we should declare to them the whole counsel of God, we should receive their angry retorts with compassion and meekness. Such a behavior on our part will, in many cases, prove the most powerful rebuke to their consciences, show them their own depravity, and direct them to the Saviour.

As to those who would keep us back from serious addresses to the sick, by the plea that they would hasten the dissolution or delay the recovery of the patient, they are for the most part persons who are more tender of the bodies than of the souls of men. What if religious conversation should shorten his days; were it not better that this should result, than that his life being prolonged by an utter neglect of his soul, both his soul and body should be eventually swallowed up in hell? Whether such exhortations will be hurtful to the health of a patient, must often depend on the spirit and manner in which they are made. Where these are what they should be, few, very few will suffer physical detriment by conversation or prayer. So far from it, could facts bear testimony, they would, we doubt not, show that multitudes have owed their recovery to the faithfulness of their spiritual guides during their sickness.

Impressions made on the near prospect of death are not unfrequently effaced by returning health. The pious attendant should remind the convalescent of the vows he made in sickness, and entreat him to gird himself with the pious resolution of the psalmist: "I will go into thy house with burnt offerings. I will pay there my vows, which my lips uttered when I was in trouble."

Tact and address are of much service in comforting the mourner and the heart-stricken. Although a tender and sympathizing spirit is the first and the indispensable qualification, much depends on the use of expedients to lead away the thoughts of the afflicted from their troubles. In fact, so numerous and multiform are the diseases of the mind brought on by sins, follies, trials and reverses, it is surprising that medical men have not set themselves more earnestly to find out preventives and remedies for them, instead of suffering them to rage till their victims are prepared to end their days in lunatic hospitals. They must know that the keenest and most dreadful pains are those of the mind; and many of them, we trust, are feeling a growing interest in this department of mental science. We doubt not that the general prevalence of the principles of the gospel will scatter most of the noxious vapors that have now settled down upon the mental world, and are destroying some of the noblest sons of genius. Daily experience attests that divine grace is potent to drive from the soul remorse, doubt, fear, sorrow, and a long train of other disturbing feelings.

One of the highest excellences of human speech is its power to comfort, and that not merely the mourner, but the disappointed, the unfortunate, the perplexed, the wronged, and the oppressed. Within the circle of our own family we may find repeated occasion for this noble office of the tongue. How does a word of encouragement from the lips of friendship and love raise our sinking spirits, and nerve them for high undertakings; how does the word of hope support us in the exhausting and doubtful struggles of life; how do the promises of a faithful God, repeated to us at some difficult stage of our pilgrimage, carry us smoothly and quickly over it. When a concurrence of petty mishaps has brought the family circle into an irritable mood—or when it seems as if a ban of silence were laid upon the lips of all, or every heart is sad, it knows not why—how angelic is the voice that can revoke the edict, call up the memories of happier hours, and draw covenanted hearts into free and cheerful conference. It is commonly thought a great inconsistency that some of those who are accomplished in the art of pleasing a circle of acquaintance, show no skill in consoling the unhappy members of their own household, being affable and complacent in public, but morose and disobliging in private. But this seeming incongruity is explained the moment we reflect that the temper of such persons is naturally ungovernable, and that though they are able to manage it during an hour of general joyousness, they cannot hold it in check through all the days and years of private vexation and care. Passions that were swayed by admiration, flattery and hilarity, whilst around them, assert their native freedom as soon as they have passed the borders of the empire of those alien and controlling influences. In the world they found variety and novelty; in the domestic circle they find what is trite and monotonous. People of fashion appear to best advantage when they are removed from themselves and familiar scenes, and are lost in the parade and festivity of fashion's carnivals; whereas the people of God grow more and more lovely in our eyes, as we follow them into each smaller circle, and approach their hearts—those pure and perennial springs of satisfaction and peace.

The intercourse of private life calls into service a more active attention and a finer delicacy than the occasional concourses of general society. In the former, persons of an ungentle spirit are daily, if not hourly, disturbing the peace of a few; in the latter, they can appear but seldom, and he who has once suffered from their misbehavior can shun them for the future. In the latter, people meet for the express purpose of pleasing and being pleased; in the former, the turbulent are to be quieted, the vexed to be soothed, heart-aches cured, antipathies reconciled, foibles indulged, and an ardent and life-long affection to be fostered. He who makes levies on the patience of a whole party may easily be tolerated, since the tribute of each will be small, and will be required a few hours only; but when the same tax is laid on a single heart, it becomes most oppressive; especially when the exactions are made daily for years. Who can calculate the amount of pain which an unkind spirit thus inflicts on those who are bound to it by the inviolable ties of kindred.

"The hint malevolent, the look oblique,
The obvious satire, or implied dislike;
The sneer equivocal, the harsh reply,
And all the cruel language of the eye;
The artful inquiry whose venomed dart
Scarce wounds the hearing while it stabs the heart.
The guarded phrase whose meaning kills, yet told,
The listener wonders how you thought it cold;
Small slights, neglect, unmixed perhaps with hate,
Make up in number what they want in weight.
These and a thousand griefs minute as these,
Corrode our comfort and destroy our ease."

Mrs. H. More.

He who can talk to the entertainment and improvement of children, has mastered one of the last difficulties in the art of conversation. He ought to possess a vivid recollection of what he once was, much knowledge of human nature, a wide range of illustration, a ready command of Saxon and other simple words, and especially an acquaintance with the idioms and provincialisms that are current among children in certain places. If all this, it may be said, is required in order to talk with children, few people are equal to the duty. But allowing this and a great deal besides, we ought to make the best use we can of our abilities, and supply by study, reflection, and especially by practice, the deficiencies of nature.

In conversing with the young, living examples and ocular illustrations should often be brought forward. The Spartans showed their knowledge of human nature by bringing a drunken slave into the public place, that their children might look upon him and be so disgusted with the unseemliness of intoxication as forever afterwards to be on their guard against it. Horace holds his father in grateful remembrance for having kept him from vice by showing him the bad consequences of it in known examples. Cecil says he imprinted on the mind of his daughter the idea of faith at a very early age, by persuading her to throw some beads into the fire in reliance on his superior wisdom and tried goodness. We take for granted that the reader is familiar with the example which may be found in "Cecil's Remains." The incident is related in this great conversationist's most energetic style, and is replete with instruction. It shows not only how we may teach the intellect just notions of religion, but also how we may discipline the heart in the exercise of the trust, submission, and self-denial which are essential to the reception and practice of evangelical precepts.

There is much reason to fear that the Bible is allowed to take too little part in the religious instruction of children, and that pious parents do not often enough resort to it for matter of conversation with them. Catechisms and other religious books are made almost exclusively the starting points of religious remark. These are excellent in their place, but should never be allowed to engage more attention than the Bible. Nor should parental authority and example in religious matters be suffered to take the place of it. Few children will regard those religious obligations as very binding which they are not wont to trace to anything higher than the will of their parents; for they early learn that there is a higher authority before which all must bow equally low. Their own observation convinces them that the Bible—in Christian countries at least—holds the supremacy in all spiritual concerns. They see their parents, their neighbors, the clergy, legislators, laws, occupations, and even time itself, paying homage to the Word of God. If they respect one thing more highly than another, it must be that volume which is reverenced by those whom they revere, and commands those whom they obey. Parents should, therefore, habitually read and quote the lively oracles in instructing their children in religious knowledge, and read parts of them at the morning and evening devotions of the family. When the children are remiss, let the Bible correct them; when they do well, let it encourage them; when they are to be instructed, let it inform them; when they complain, let it teach them submission; when they are in trouble, let it comfort them; when they would argue a religious question, let it reason with them. Let Jehovah speak in his own pure and commanding voice. Not that parents should lay aside their own authority in bringing them to submit to wholesome moral discipline; for parental obedience is an important part of such discipline. Only let Holy Writ occupy the first place in the minds of children, and let them be taught to regard the divine law as paramount to human precepts. So shall they ever have an ever-present monitor, and still be reminded of duty when the instructions of their youth shall have faded from their memories as things long past.

Let parents also teach their children the lessons of creation and Providence as they are interpreted by the Sacred Word. They, and they only, can penetrate the mysteries that veil the world, who go forth to view the works of God, and study his dealings with their Bible open in their hands. Yet, with all these means of instruction, the parent may fail of his duty by neglecting to watch for opportunities to make and fix moral impressions on the tender heart. We saw this duty well illustrated not long ago, while we were passing some hours in the galleries of the Academy of the Fine Arts in Philadelphia. A member of the Society of Friends had brought in his little son to show him West's great painting of "Christ Healing the Sick." The day was cloudy and did not throw a good light upon the picture, especially on the benevolent countenance of our Saviour. They stood before it some time, till the boy grew impatient, but the father kept his own eyes still fixed on the work of West, his immortal friend. Suddenly the sun came out, and the father exclaimed, "*Now* look, my son!" as he pointed to the Great Healer's countenance, which was lit up with such a glory as helped to explain to us how it was that the votaries of pictured saints had seen them kindle up with miraculous smiles. There are times when the Holy Spirit does throw an unwonted radiance on the compassionate brow of the incarnate Redeemer, on human guiltiness and woe, on His power to regenerate and renew; and wise is the father or the mother that prayerfully and laboriously waits for such openings in the clouds, and, at the happy moment, exclaims, "*Now* look, my son!" Let him also improve times when a striking providence or a beautiful landscape flashes back truth, the light of God. Children may early acquire not only a love for the charms of nature, but alacrity in discerning the fingers of God busy upon all his works. Bryant, whose inspiration is the love of nature, tells us how he formed in the heart of a little girl of four years a like passion:

> "For I have taught her with delighted eye
> To gaze upon the mountains, to behold
> With deep affection the pure ample sky,
> And clouds along its blue abysses rolled.
> To love the song of waters, and to hear
> The melody of winds with charmed ear."

It may seem needless even to mention the detestable practice of objurgation, or to give its own fitting Saxon title, scolding. Would it were so; for we are loth to defile our page with the word. But we are compelled to say that not a few who plume themselves on their conversational powers, fail most grievously in the spirit and mode of their commands to their children. They would be very sorry to be accounted scolds, and scolds of the more infuriated kind they are not: only they do all the mischief of these creatures without incurring their odium. They may want their clamor, but have their rudeness. They may not equal them in cursing, but they do in teazing. When ordering their children or servants to do anything, they add, "Be sure not to do as I tell you," or, in sending them on an errand, "Mind what I say, and don't be in haste; be sure to stay all day." We should shun every way of addressing them that provokes resentment. The apostolic injunction is, "Fathers, provoke not your children to wrath." When a child is angry, it should be treated with mildness, and soothed by appeals to conscience and to reason. Commands should be well considered, never repeated, and always enforced. Strictness should be tempered with calmness and tenderness.

There can be no doubt that the difference between a scolding parent and one in whose lips is the law of kindness, has made the difference between a murderer and a philanthropist.

As to servants, we must not only, as just now intimated, never stoop to rave at them, but never dispute with them. Whether we gain the point or not, we are sure to lose their respect. We must address them in a firm yet mild tone. We must request them to execute our commands as if we left it to their own pleasure whether they would do us a favor or not; and when they have rendered us a service, we should give them some intimation of our gratitude, if not at least of our approbation. It is in general imprudent to make servants our confidants unless we have bound them to secresy by extraordinary liberality. We should not converse with the servants of our host, nor reprove our own in the presence of guests. Let us also avoid the common practice of entertaining others with accounts of the falsehoods, thefts, and insults of our domestics.

We cannot be too much on our guard against treating the poor with neglect or disrespect on account of their poverty. And this caution is as applicable to our behavior towards our poor domestics as towards those poor people who do not live under our roof; for there are those who spend half their time in visiting the cottages of the poor, and supplying their wants, and the other half in quarrelling with their own servants about their bad economy, and in contriving ways of paying them the exact amount of wages they have earned, and nothing beyond. Such is the prevailing sycophancy to pelf, that the Christian can never enough keep in mind that wealth cannot, of itself, confer personal worth, or make a man more entitled to our deference than his indigent servant or neighbor. It is this mean and blind devotion the poor everywhere behold paid to mammon, that makes them so jealous of their rights, and ever keeps alive their suspicion. Equivocal remarks are interpreted unfavorably to themselves. Slights and oversights are regarded as personal affronts. Counsels are interpreted as upbraidings, and pleasantry received as derision. They put forth an opinion tremblingly, and are wounded when it is disputed. They have too much cause to think that, were their own opinions put into the mouths of the rich, they would have been heard with applause and repeated as oracular.

Though most men are ambitious of the accomplishments which make them pleasing among their superiors or equals in wealth, they are very neglectful of the conduct that commends them to the poor. The etiquette of the cottage is less easily learned than that of the court. If it has not as much dignity, it has the more condescension; if not as much flattery, the more encouragement; if less ceremony, the more compassion. Let the disciple of the Nazarene be equally observant of the marks of respect towards the poor and the rich. It is a great reproach to the politeness of the world that its offices are chiefly intended for superiors and equals as to fortune; like the peculiar languages of some heathen despotisms, where a special phraseology is kept in use, to be employed only by the inferior in his trembling colloquy with a superior.[3] Our Lord was the first to teach an unselfish and humble courtesy towards the poor and the unfortunate. Said he to his host, the chief Pharisee: "When thou makest a feast, call the poor, the maimed, the lame, the blind." This precept forbids us to confine our social generosities to those only who can equally administer to our gratification, or for each mark of regard make a return in kind. Neither does the mere alms-receiver alone call for our benevolent attentions. The dependent, or the acquaintance, or the relative of the opulent, who is, it may be, domesticated in their families, are always hurt by a cold or reserved demeanor on the part of their benefactors. We should not remind them, or others in their presence, of their dependence, nor insinuate by our behavior that their dependence is any disparagement to them. It is not enough that we provide merely for the bodily wants of the needy, we must also show a solicitude for their mental tranquillity and ease; and do all in our power to keep them from gliding into solitude and neglect. A number of richly-dressed people were, one cold day, gathered round a stove in a ferry-house. An old man of shabby exterior, who sat shivering behind those who had crowded before him, made a civil remark, with a view to break the silence that oppressed him, and draw some one into conversation. There was no other reply than a leer at his rags. He spoke again, when a young man who had hitherto held his peace, manifestly from deference to his superiors,

[3] See "Bagster's Bible of Every Land," (Mexican language), p. 384; and "Transactions of Amer. Ethnolog. Society" for 1845, p. 28.

ventured a kind and respectful answer. Whereupon the old man smiled heartily, and seemed on a sudden to forget alike his poverty and his age in the thought that he was not yet cut off from all the sympathies of his fellow-mortals. He manifests a doubtful benevolence, who sends his coin to the needy, while he is too proud to speak to them. He does little more than remind them of their poverty and their increased obligations to him. He who never fancies that his own wealth adds to his worth, and that poverty takes anything from the worth of his neighbor, possesses a greatness of soul which the votaries of mammon despise, because they are too deeply degraded to appreciate it.

CHAPTER III.

CONVERSATION OF CHRISTIANS WITH ONE ANOTHER.

THE church is the oasis where the social virtues best thrive and mature. Her frequent occasions of bringing together the faithful, afford every facility for the commerce of brotherly affection, and the circulation of desirable thought. The people of the world are connected by selfish ties and transient interests. They generally assemble at wide intervals, and many of their friendships do not outlive a single season. With the people of God it is not so. They are bound together by ties that are benevolent, delightful, strong and ever growing stronger. They meet weekly, and many even daily. They assemble in circles rising in numbers from the private prayer-meeting to the great congregation.[4] Nor is this their intercourse limited to one congregation. Their more general interests collect them from all parts of states and nations. Thus are assembled the elements of a high-toned, liberal and improving conversation. And the effects of this intercourse are heightened by a divine agency, which is continually coöperating with the social principle. As the pebbles are assem-

[4] See "Principles of Courtesy," Part II., Chap. XIII.

bled on the beach, and mutually polished by the chafing waves, even so the souls of the saints are wrought into comely forms by being gathered into communion under the grace which moves upon them as it comes from the eternal world. And it is this grace alone that can prepare the social principle to polish and beautify our shattered nature.

And in proportion to the piety of professors, will be the desire to meet for religious conversation. It is the testimony of the sacred historian, that after the miraculous effusion of the Holy Spirit on the day of Pentecost, the disciples daily broke bread from house to house, and ate their bread with gladness and singleness of heart. The outpouring of supernatural gifts, attended with the appearance of a fountain of light, streaming forth upon each disciple a tongue of lambent flame, the general exultation that would naturally follow this dedication of the Christian temple, together with an ardent brotherly love and a faith unbeclouded by doubts, frequently drew the first formed church together in separate groups at different houses in the city, and supplied themes for joyful and open-hearted conversation. Besides these advantages peculiar to their condition, there was another in the gift of speaking in foreign languages, by the help of which the natives of widely-sundered regions, once strangers to each other, because they had no common mediums of speech, could now blend their minds and interchange the truths of revelation.

If there are any two qualities that make Christian society distinct from any other, they are the gladness and simplicity of heart which were so conspicuous in the primitive assemblies of the disciples. There is a joyousness in the circles of believers which is not often met with elsewhere. What disciple that ever went to an assembly of his brethren with a sad spirit, did not take leave of that sadness very soon after he had joined the happy company. On the other hand, how often has the man of the world, who had cherished bright anticipations of the next party, been overtaken with a sort of stupefaction the moment he entered the circle, and felt disappointment and disgust when he left it. This same gladness prevails in all their meetings, whether they come together to interchange the common tokens of fraternal affection, or to contribute their substance or service to the gospel cause, or are driven together as sheep by wolves. Their disinterested benevolence puts to flight all cold calculations and dark anxieties, and leaves the mind in a state of unconcern and abandonment, which is congenial with cheerfulness. When they are maltreated and maligned for Christ's sake, they are exceeding glad by reason of the assurance which persecution gives them of a great celestial reward. The sight of one suffering wrong with cheerfulness and rejoicing, is enough to send a gleam of light across the darkest soul. For my part, I can hardly ever figure to myself the scene of the primitive confessors taking joyfully the spoiling of their goods, without feeling a fellow pleasure; and though removed from them at the distance of eighteen centuries, I catch the sympathy of their transported hearts and gladsome countenances.

We must not, however, let this feeling degenerate into levity, as it is apt to do when it is not supported by other evangelical virtues. There are not a few professors who allow themselves to lay aside their spiritual weapons, and suffer all their sentinels to fall asleep whenever they are in Christian society. But let them not suppose they can safely be off their watch, because they are secure against the temptations of secular companies. Let them not dream that the assemblies of their brethren are protected by bands of armed angels. Let them remember that it was in Eden, that the tempter laid his first and most fatal snares. It is only the vigilant spirit that is able to hit upon that

"Mirth, which after no repenting draws;"

and it is singular, that though only a thread of gossamer separates cheerfulness from levity, the former is becoming to piety, and the latter is inconsistent with it.

After all, we must not commit the mistake of those who are afraid of all pleasant talk which is not directly improving or useful. Such people would find it hard to justify Job for saying, "Ye are the men and wisdom will die with you;" and Elijah for ridiculing the vociferations of the prophets of Baal. Nor could they quote with a good grace such scripture proverbs as these: "all the days of the afflicted are evil; but he that is of a merry heart hath a continual feast." "A merry heart doeth good like medicine; but a broken spirit drieth the bones."

Singleness of heart, the other quality which is peculiar to pious society, gives a kind of graceful negligence to the deportment which, while it cannot be exactly described, may be found in that medium which is as far from the studied ease of the courtier, as it is from the rude familiarity of the clown. It is akin to the unreserve we often witness in the young. It is the frankness of a child who is not sensible that there is in his mind a single faulty idea, and innocently speaks his uppermost thoughts. It is a conduct so transparent, that the heart may always be seen through it. It is imitated by those who, when they would appear pleased, torture their faces into a sardonic smile; when they would appear honest, are garrulous and bold. When they would demonstrate their frankness, they betray some vice or other that they ought to have kept concealed; or if they are more crafty, they make the openness of their demeanor throw their real character into the shade. This virtue, like every other, has its pretenders, who closely copy it, and for which the counterfeit is very frequently mistaken.

This cordiality sometimes engenders a freedom that greatly detracts from gravity and respect. This freedom, again, leads many to petulence and querulousness. Having admitted them to our confidence, they treat us as though we were no longer free agents, but solely the tools of their will. It is, to be sure, the bounden duty of brethren to "be subject one to another in love," but there ought to be some limits set to complaisant submission.

Another of the abuses of sincerity, is the confidential talk in which brethren are wont to indulge themselves; as the laying open of personal affairs, the dissecting of characters, and the handling of ecclesiastical difficulties. They think it not amiss to make remarks in an under-tone, which should not have been made at all. Brethren often talk with the expectation that nothing that is said in the circle, is to be reported out of it. How often is the expectation disappointed. In the most faithful band, there is almost always some one who seizes the first opportunity to betray the confidence reposed in him, and who, while his lips are yet wet with the sacramental cup, goes forth to defame those who sat with him around the sacred board; or if he has no evil intention, yet by misquoting our remarks, or repeating them out of their connection, and to malignant ears, he does us as great a mischief as the most insidious foe—an injury not a little aggravated by the thought that it was inflicted by a brother. As we muse upon it, we are forced to take up the satirical lament of David: "It was not an enemy that reproached me; then could I have borne it; neither was it he that hated me, that did magnify himself against me; then I would have hid myself from him; but it was thou, a man, mine equal, my guide and mine acquaintance. We took counsel together; and walked to the house of God in company."

Yet let not such betrayals of confidence make you suspicious. You will always gain more by relying on the integrity of others than by habitually holding it in distrust. There is no man I would sooner trust than the rogue whom I had detected, and who knew that I had detected him. "M. De Witt," says Sir William Temple, "told me he had been very suspicious when he first became pensionary; but had been so often deceived by it that he had cured himself of that quality." A friend of Sir Henry Wotton's, qualifying himself for the office of ambassador, requested of him some practical rule to guide him in diplomatic affairs. Sir Henry smiling, said, "To be in safety yourself, and serviceable to your country, you should always and upon all occasions, speak the truth; for you shall never be believed; and by this means you will secure yourself, if you shall ever be called to an account, and it will also put your adversaries to a loss (who will still hunt counter), in all their disquisitions and undertakings." Besides, your crafty and disguised characters almost always by some accident or other let drop their mask before their plot is executed. They make us close and taciturn. They provoke us to put their boasted sagacity and circumspection to the test, and to set ourselves to hoodwink them by taking advantage of their craftiness. Open-hearted and open-handed honesty inspires its like in all. I think it is Baron Knigge, who very wisely advises us to treat persons whom we have reason to suspect of artifice and intrigue with openness and candor, frankly to declare ourselves enemies to the double-hearted and the double-tongued, and warm admirers of honesty, thus making them sensible how much they would lose in our esteem, if ever we should surprise them in crooked paths.

Again, this excess of sincerity occasionally leads brethren to make each other their father-confessors. In their open-minded converse, one tells of his hair-breadth escapes from temptation; another confesses his ruling passion, another tells us how profligate, intemperate, or vain he was in the days of his impenitency, and tells stories illustrative of his former character. Some gratify their vanity by discoursing on their peculiar notions and whims; their weaknesses and idiosyncracies; their likes and dislikes; they cannot dissemble, they say; they must tell us all. Others lament their backslidings, wanderings and captivities. Now, these persons would be very sorry that we should think their overwrought accounts exactly true. Were they to suspect that we would take them at their own valuation, they would no longer speak in terms of self-depreciation. And were we to hint to them, with all gentleness, the importance of correcting the very faults they so willingly accuse themselves of, we should provoke their resentment.

Though we are commanded to confess our faults one to another, we ought to consider that the injunction is limited by circumstances. If our sin does not wrong our neighbor or bring reproach on the church, we are not bound to confess it. When it harms another, or he lays it to our charge, then it is time enough to show our sincerity by acknowledging it, without apology or palliation. When we are at variance with our brother, then it will be noble to censure ourselves, to make concessions or to admit the justness of the charges that are preferred against us, to confess our faults to the aggrieved party, and to entreat his forgiveness. Also when we are asking advice of our pastor or of some other person, we may confess the faults and habits which we would have him direct us how to overcome. Again, when we are exhorting, reproving or counselling another, we may confess to him sins which we were tempted to commit, by taking the course from which we would dissuade him. But he who is ever confessing to others sins which neither they nor the church have a right to hear or can be edified by hearing, seems to take a secret satisfaction in his own misdeeds, and to have so little sense of guilt and shame as to be vain of his very wickedness.

We should not indulge the habit of discoursing to our brethren of our bereavements, losses and ills. They will indeed think it due to the confidence of brotherly affection that we unbosom to them our sorrows and allow them to condole with us. And if we do it to obtain their counsels or their consolations, they will listen to us with pleasure, but it becomes quite another affair when they perceive that we take pleasure in descanting on our woes—that we complain not to obtain relief, but to amuse ourselves.

Do not, in general, complain to your friends of the injustice and ingratitude of men. "When I murmured against persecution," says Count de Bussy, "and so enhanced my misfortune by impatience, I would have died in prison, had I not a month before I came out, resolved to submit myself to whatever it should please God to do with me." This behavior touched the heart of Louis XIV., who at length recalled him from banishment. Especially do not complain of calumnies. Men claim the privilege of finding fault with you. It is nothing that you are perfection itself; they will then think you deserving of blame for having nothing blamable in you. If you convince the world that you are forsaken by your old friends, discontented with your condition, and want the strength of soul necessary to bear up against adversity, it will desert you almost to a man, and seek more powerful allies elsewhere. Yet, do not fly to the other extreme, and show a blustering pertinacity, but rather a bland resolution. "Resolved," says President Edwards, "to follow the example of Mr. R., who, though he meets with great difficulties, yet undertakes them with a smiling countenance as though they were little, and speaks of them as if they were very small."

We should keep clear of an ambition to set off our own piety to the best advantage by boasting of our spiritual conquests or deeds of beneficence; and, on the other hand, of a false humility, that while it is ever depreciating what we are and what we have done, is covertly seeking to impress others with an admiration for our lowliness.

But of all the abuses which attend the needful intercourse of spiritual minds, perhaps the most common is self-righteousness. The faculty of conversing on religious subjects, is liable, with some, to be confounded with religion itself; and, with others, to be substituted for it. A disposition to frequent discourse on spiritual topics is one mark of genuine piety; but though such a disposition is indispensable to true piety, yet it may exist in an unregenerated heart. One of the deceptions which our hearts not unfrequently practise upon us, is to magnify the slightest evidences of our personal interest in the Redeemer into meritorious and self-sufficient virtues.

One of the most profitable themes for discourse among brethren is that of religious experience—a theme which is less frequently treated now than it was some years ago; chiefly, perhaps, by reason of its perversion by fanatics and hypocrites. Another cause is found in the modern mistake of making all religion to consist *merely* in hearing sermons and responding to the calls of benevolent institutions, to the neglect of the religion of the heart, the closet, and the family: consequently there is less hope and fear, joy and sorrow, fight and flight, conquest and defeat. There are, we rejoice to say, many, very many illustrious exceptions to this rule; still it is a matter deserving serious inquiry whether the churches are not backsliding down this declivity. Some, no doubt, are backsliding in an opposite direction. They talk of their feelings as if they thought them to be the sum of religion. They never inquire about the advancement of the truth in their own family, or country, or in the distant regions of the earth. According to our Lord's commission to the apostles, they were directed to *begin* at Jerusalem; they were not to dwell there permanently. We ought first to inquire whether our own graces are thriving, but we shall find they are not, unless we make provision for their exercise. Our experiences and graces are not the field; "the field is the world," and in this field we should allow all the virtues to range. Nothing can be more instructive than a judicious disclosure of our temptations and conflicts. By these the young disciple is warned, and the aged confirmed in patience and hope. If we have experienced sustaining grace in affliction, trust in darkness, direction in perplexity, answers to prayer, illumination in studying and obeying the Scriptures, help in a pious undertaking, joy in self-denials, let us not withhold these things from our brethren. That our conversations on this subject may be in the highest degree useful, we should not introduce them too often, nor allow them to grow trite; neither should we lightly mingle pious remarks among the hurried negotiations of business; or, like Bunyan's Talkative and Foot's Mother Cole, dodge by turns from sacred to profane and profane to sacred. In relating our religious experiences, we should state facts in the most simple and unadorned language, and shun all affectation and cant.

Some enthusiastic professors have their darling doctrines, to which they allude on all occasions, and on which they incessantly argue, ever repeating the same propositions, and ever quoting the same Scriptures to establish them. You run a great hazard by making the slightest allusion to their favorite theme; they will, in all likelihood, hold your button an hour for your pains. When two or more persons are known to hold opposite opinions on a subject, and are used to dispute concerning it, we do well not to refer to the vexed question in their hearing. To start that topic were as wanton a cruelty as it would be to set two pugnacious dogs by the ears. These orthodox brethren, as it generally happens, give some attention to one truth to the neglect of other truths intimately related to it, on a right understanding of which the settlement of the question depends. A doctrine may be true as being of a piece with others, but not true as broken off from them by the force of controversy. Scripture truth is true only in its connection. It is another error of this class of men to suppose they understand a doctrine because they are familiar with it. They have long believed it, long talked about it, yet most likely they have never sat down for an hour patiently to examine its evidences, and to consider its intricacies and mysteries. Could the doctrines speak, they might very properly ask many a babbler of this class the question our Lord asked one of his disciples, "Have I been so long time with you, and yet hast thou not known me, Philip?"

"We do well," says Baron Knigge, "to distinguish between religion and theology."[5] Observation teaches us that multitudes who are wholly wanting in vital piety, can talk fluently and confidently on the controverted points of our faith. A large class of these champions of dogmatism imagine they are giving the best possible proof of their piety when they are contesting some speculative notion, whereas the spirit in which they handle the question, and their utter neglect of practical truths, declare that their piety is little else than rodomontade. It denotes an unspiritual mind to like to dwell on mere *speculative questions* and *unsearchable mysteries.* We *may* and *ought to* search for the points where mysteries begin, and to examine the proofs on which they claim our belief; but this is different from an attempt to discover what *Infinite Wisdom was pleased not to reveal to mortals.* Were some of the mysteries of our religion cleared up to the satisfaction of some presumptuous inquirers, who shall say that the explanation of them would not be destructive of all piety? What virtue is there in admitting the truth of a mathematical demonstration? Left as they are, they aid our growth, not only in faith, but in docility and humility. Every attempt to explain them only makes them the more obscure, while it renders unintelligible what was simple before.

Let us not be misunderstood. We are not of the opinion of those spiritual non-resistants, who dream that they repose under the vine and fig-tree of true

[5] Uber den Umgang mit Menschen, p. 307. Hanover, 1844.

faith, while, in fact, they sleep under the upas of deadly heresy. We have been speaking of the barrenness of mere speculation about the unsealed mysteries of the gospel. We do by no means undervalue the importance of right views concerning all *revealed* truth, and of that sort of controversy which throws any light on the pages of revelation. Holiness is the outgrowth of a knowledge of gospel truths, and hence spring freedom and faith. It is a holding the Head that brings life; and whilst faith without works is dead, a rationalism that believes man and not God, is more than dead. It is death rampant and gory.

Pious as many of these controversialists are, few of them are remarkably attentive to the decencies of speech. It is said of Sir James Mackintosh, that he had a way of advancing things so mildly and interrogatively, that he always procured the readiest reception for his opinions, and that he had two valuable habits, which are rarely met with in great reasoners—he never broke in upon his opponent, and always avoided strong and vehement assertions. But the persons in question are so captious and belligerent, that they are tolerated by none but their brethren, "the meek of the earth." Perhaps reputed great in one thing, they are content to be contemptible in all besides. They presume on the weight of their dogmatic assertions, and express themselves roundly on all questions, no matter how critical or profound. They should never be allowed to commence debating unless they will choose seconds as duelists do. They make shouts of victory stand them instead of arguments, and give their opponents no quarter, because they know that they are too strong for them. "Will leviathan speak soft words unto thee?" Vain the hope; he is in his element, or rather fancies he is, and must be allowed to imagine that he "makes the deep to boil like a pot, and makes a path to shine after him," though often the "*shining*" is only that of the upturned ooze his lashing and contortions have raised to discolor and scent the waves.

Nevertheless, a perfect agreement of opinion among the members of the same circle is by no means desirable. It is a shrewd observation of La Bruyere, that the mutual pleasure of conversation is greatest among friends who agree in matters of taste and morals, and differ in opinion concerning the sciences; for so each one is either confirmed in his principles, or is disciplined and improved by disputation. Now Christian society is of this kind. The moral tastes and feelings of the brethren accord in the main, while they differ more or less respecting other subjects. And if they are not at all times benefited by their discussions, the general principle still holds good. It is impolitic to discourage discussion. It gives life and vigor to conversation. What can be more somnorific than the usage of some coteries, where each one withholds his opinion for fear of giving offence; or, if any one ventures to put forth an assertion, it meets with an immediate assent—and a long silence succeeds. Were the doctrines of our religion like the principles of the exact sciences, a few words would serve to despatch them; but inasmuch as they are matters of moral probability, any person of common sense is able to say something by way of qualification, confirmation, or denial. It is a remark of Chevreau's, that there are two classes of people whose conversation is equally disagreeable; those who always dispute what you say, and those who agree with you so constantly and humbly, that you feel to cry out with the enraged orator to his antagonist, "Do contradict me to prove that we are two persons." He who ever replies with a ready affirmation, seems to say you are only repeating commonplaces and truisms. Hence the wisdom of seldom broaching current truths, cardinal articles of faith, undisputed facts, and the fixed principles of art and science. Paradoxes, far-fetched opinions, singular facts, unaccountable events, the hypotheses and hasty deductions of the immature arts and sciences; these are the starting points of the most spirited and improving discussions. The man that is careful to be always in the right, and to advance none but indisputable opinions, must needs impose silence on all around him; people perceiving his anxiety to be thought infallible and irrefutable, do not like to oppose him. And since he must weigh all his thoughts before he offers them to our consideration, and choose the plainest and least ambiguous terms wherein to convey them, he must have long pauses to deliberate, frequent digressions to define, or qualify, or explain. If he would betimes speak at a venture, and put forth a proposition that lay open to reply, and give an opportunity to correct his negligent remarks, the rest of the circle would be much beholden to him for helping them unseal their lips. But his very silence is as great a bar to conversation as his strongly-guarded discourse. If others dare to open their minds at all, it is under the restraint which is laid upon them by his wise and critical ear. They cannot prevail upon him to commit himself till all have spoken, when he is prepared to expose their folly, and to establish his own wisdom. The statement of a proposition which is contrary to received opinion, or seemingly absurd, but really true, like the touch of Ithuriel's spear—gives sudden expansion to the minds of the company, and causes each one to spring up and appear in his real character. A man had better play the Jack Cade, challenging every body to deny assertions which he knows to be absurd, than to be an automaton courtier, that makes a bow at every pull of the wire. The advocate of a visionary theory or an erroneous principle ought, before the subject is dismissed, to declare his real opinions concerning it, unless he has at the outset intimated, as in most cases he easily can, that he does not receive what, for the sake of striking out truth, he sets himself to defend. Let him beware, however, of too great a readiness to argue for *victory* rather than *truth*, a fault into which the rash and the spirited frequently run. Johnson, who was a splendid and doughty talker, in his dying days felt and bewailed this arguing for victory as one of the sins to which he had been addicted.

One of the most liberal and beneficial kinds of conversation is what some call *building*. It consists in adding something to the remark of another; the interlocutors either fortifying each other's propositions, or saying something which the observations of another suggested. Instead of pulling down, they literally edify one another. Fellow disciples can conveniently adopt this method. They have a common fund of principles and sentiments which aids this reciprocation of thought. It is in this way that truth is best discovered and established. If this method had been more generally adopted in bygone ages, how much richer a patrimony of truth would have descended to the present generation. Then each one would not have thought himself bound to remove the foundations of his brother's intellectual edifice before he could proceed to build his own, but would contribute his own material and skill to mend the works of his predecessor, and, as far as possible, carry them up towards completion. Thus, by the joint aid of different minds, each contributing what no other could, the tabernacle of truth might rise and stand splendid, graceful, and complete in every part. The practice here recommended, is not that of some wise persons who never fail to improve upon every casual remark, ever getting the better of another, sure to have the last word, and letting slip no opportunity of showing that their intellect has still the mastery of ours.

Where members of the same church are accustomed to meet and talk on matters of common interest, they are liable to institute comparisons between their own church and some rival one, in the same city, village, or neighborhood. Its minister is contrasted with their own. Is a sister church thriving? They predict trouble from the accession of such numbers of spurious converts. Is it languishing? They had been long expecting it, and know all the causes of its adversity. Only set over against the emanations of such envious and jealous minds the noble and liberal language of Paul: "Some indeed preach Christ even of envy and strife, and some also of good will. The one preach Christ of contention, not sincerely, supposing to add affliction to my bonds; but the other of love, knowing that I am set for the defence of the Gospel. What then? Notwithstanding every way, whether in pretence or in truth, Christ is preached, and I therein do rejoice, yea and will rejoice."[6]

We should also beware of speaking contemptuously, or judging uncharitably of those who practice, or abstain from religious acts that are in themselves indifferent, or to which no scripture command can be brought to apply. "One man believeth that he may eat all things; another who is weak eateth herbs. Let not him that eateth despise him that eateth not; and let not him that eateth not, judge him that eateth. Who art thou that judgest another man's servant. To his own Master he standeth or falleth."

Such is the language of the inspired apostle, and yet it is notorious, that many a professor is the more censorious of his brethren, in proportion as they practice what he *himself believes*, that the letter and spirit of the scriptures neither condemn nor approve; but concerning which practice *they* believe, that the scriptures are positive. We are bound to endeavor to correct errorists by all gentle and charitable methods, but we should not satisfy ourselves with invective, to the utter neglect of argument, especially when the acknowledged silence of scripture rebukes our bitter loquacity.

It is well to keep clear of all denominational and sectarian topics when we are in the company of those who belong to different denominations. With a view to conciliate persons of another sect, some fall to praising that sect or some of its ornaments, and in return,

[6] Phil. i. 15—18.

expect to receive some golden opinions for their own denomination. It were more judicious to make an oblivion of such subjects altogether. There is, and it is a cause of devout gratitude that there is, so wide a range of common ground, that we are not compelled to turn aside into any very narrow enclosure. It is pleasant occasionally to mount to some serene summit where the artificial divisions of our common Canaan are lost in the distance beneath, and whence we may survey all the tribes praying, with their eyes turned toward one tabernacle, bringing their atoneing sacrifice to the same altar, and worshipping one Lord, even Christ.

Let us beware of being numbered among those whose church is their whole world, beyond which their conversation rarely strays. They must always be talking of pastor or rector, deacons or church-wardens, or sexton, or fellow members. To allow the church a large share of our thoughts, is a mark of laudable zeal and devotedness; but to limit our discourse to one congregation or denomination, savors of bigotry; at least, those who are of a different persuasion will think so, and the more bigoted they are themselves, the more displeased will they be to discover any indications of the same vice in ourselves. We must not indulge a habit of felicitating our brethren of like faith on the truth, superiority, and triumphs of our denominational doctrines, whenever we find ourselves in their company. For if haply, after a tirade against another denomination in the hearing of others, all of whom we supposed to be of our opinions, we should learn that a person belonging to that denomination was present and heard all we said, it would give us unspeakable mortification. And when we laud our clergyman exclusively in the hearing of those who go to another church, they will be likely to construe our words as a depreciation of their favorite, even should it not, as it often is, be regarded as oblique self-praise. When our own sect, denomination, clergy or creed is eulogized by a person of a different faith, we must beware of adding aught to his commendations, inasmuch as he probably intended to bestow upon us all the praise we deserved, and it will be making him a shabby return to insinuate that, after all, he has overlooked half our merit.

We occasionally meet with an aged Christian who delights to dwell on the history of the church or denomination of which he is a member. The honor which is due to age requires us to listen to what helps him to beguile away the heavy-footed hours. Perhaps he enlarges on the piety, talents and habits of the saints whom he once knew. He says, "that the former days were better than these;" and that "there were giants in those days, mighty men and men of renown." Versed in the scriptures he knows not when to cease discoursing on their blessed truths. From the feebleness of his memory, he tells you what you have heard him repeat many times before. To oppose him would, in most cases, be equally irreverent and unavailing; and, however tiresome may be his prosing, if we will only listen to him patiently, we shall gain from him a great deal of information. His counsels are valuable, and if he is occasionally petulant towards his juniors, it is because he beholds them wantonly disregarding the lessons which it cost him long and painful experience to learn. When we meet him in the social circle, we should frequently address our remarks to him; and, when there is occasion for it, ask his opinion and advice.

In talking with pious persons of defective education, we must not vulgarize our ideas in the attempt to simplify and suit them to their capacities. Some persons are nettled at our stooping to a level with them in thought and language, which they look upon as an under-estimate of their capacities and culture, but account it a compliment to be addressed as if they were more knowing than they are. Besides, it excites them to self-improvement. It was Richard Baxter's practice in every sermon to say something which was above the capacity of his hearers, and which they had not known before, in order, as he declared, to keep them humble under a conviction of their own ignorance. Nevertheless an ostentation of learning is very offensive to the ignorant, and they like to burlesque those who are guilty of it.

Not all unlettered persons are ignorant; in their own estimation very few of them are so. They plume themselves upon the thought, that, however ignorant of some things, they are competent to teach the most knowing person many useful lessons. Everybody has heard of the cobbler who pointed out an omission in the painting of Apelles, which he had himself overlooked. The knowledge of the illiterate is dear bought, thoroughly practical, and for the most part accurate as far as it goes. "The wisdom of the ignorant," says Goldsmith, "somewhat resembles the instinct of animals; it is diffused in but a narrow sphere, but within that sphere it acts with vigor, uniformity, and success." In conversation, therefore, we must allow them to discourse in their own way. To put them upon talking logically, or to correct their verbal errors, were to confound and discourage them. When they express their thoughts inaccurately, we should not tell them what they mean, but answer them directly according to their meaning. We must take care that we do not misunderstand them. They will sooner forgive our superiority to them in knowledge than for owning our inability to understand what seems very intelligible to their own minds; for they are apt to suspect that, by such an avowal, we would insinuate that they do not understand themselves, or, what is more commonly inferred, that we only betray our own obtuseness.

The profoundest student of the Bible may gain no small aid, in his researches, from the pious discourse of unlearned believers. He will find the views of the common people on scriptural truth more simple and experimental than his own. Their piety is more primitive: by primitive we do not mean that their piety is as intelligent as was that of believers in apostolic times; for it can hardly be expected that the greatest modern scholar could, by the studies of a long life, acquire as accurate a knowledge of the Christian religion as the bulk of primitive Christians possessed. We mean that their piety sheds a purer and more direct light. It is not blended with classical, philosophical, and mystical notions. Erroneous as may be their views on some points, their interpretations are, in the main, what all interpretations should be—practical. It is in the school of obedience that they have acquired their knowledge of the scriptures, and if they cannot illustrate them by their learning, they can exemplify them in their lives. Whoever deigns to hold intercourse with the pious in humble life, can study our religion in its primeval and most secure repositories, and "extract honey out of the rock, and oil out of the flinty rock."

We cannot dismiss this subject without alluding to a trespass which sociable brethren are prone to commit against one another: we refer to trespass on time. When we are weary of solitude, and flee to the society of a brother, we do not enough reflect that he may not have leisure for talk, and that if he stays to exchange thoughts with us, he is neglecting important engagements. We feel, perhaps, that as he is our brother, he ought to have sufficient patience to listen to us. The patience he may have, but may lack the hardihood of conscience; nay, he may have the desire, while duty is calling him to serious business. Or perhaps he has leisure for talking on some useful subject, but none to amuse those who wish him to help them kill time. Many think it no sin to spend hours in unprofitable parlance, who would recoil from the thought of wasting the same period in silent supineness. "Let no man," says St. Bernard, "think it a light matter that he spends his precious time in idle words."[7]

[7] Sermo de Triplici Custodia.

CHAPTER IV.

SUNDAY CONVERSATION.

The notes of a voluntary from the organ had just died away, and the coach was beginning to roll, when Miss Rose Restless, glancing through the pane, and seeing a shawled shoulder, the side of a bonnet, and the end of a nose, whispered to her cousin, Flora Galaday,

"Did you ever? See! Mrs. Gaudyage is dressed like a peacock, and yet she is turned of sixty!"

"Yes, I see; what depravity of taste! The old coquette!" returns Flora.

"Grandmother, who is very plain, you know, was walking with her the other day, past Babel Hotel, when Will Bottle, who is always drunk, staggered out, blurting, 'They toil not, neither do they spin, yet Solomon, in all his glory, was not arrayed like *one* of these!'"

"Well, Rose, you see what you will come to if you proceed at this rate. They say she was very dressy when she was young."

"Indeed, Flora! and you could not have looked in a mirror lately. But to be serious now, did you mark Helen Everton's bonnet. It was silk, with a frilling of tulle at the edge, without feathers and artificials."

"Not exactly, Rose. Helen is more obedient to tne will of Paris, than to put on such a bonnet. She wore a bonnet of lisse crape, with tulle puffed, and feathers and roses."

"You must be mistaken, Flora; I saw neither feathers nor roses, and I inspected the thing particularly."

"So did *I* inspect the thing *very* particularly. The brim inside was trimmed on the one hand with a tuft of roses; on the other, it had a feather placed outside, turning over the edge, and coming inside near the cheek."

"Oh my! How could your eyes deceive you so, Flora;—on which side were the feathers?"

"On the side towards where I sat. Besides, when she turned round to go out, I saw her full in the face, and there were roses inside. When she came near me in the aisle, I saw they were mixed with narrow white blonds."

"That accounts for our differences. You sat on one side of her and I on the other. When she turned round my eyes were on something else—on a scene that attracted all eyes—the young married couple, Mr. and Mrs. Honeymoon. Mrs. Honeymoon had on a paletot of crimson velvet, trimmed entirely round with a silk gimp. The crimson with the green lining of her bonnet, made her pale face look insipid and sickly. Such a flourish as they *did* make! You saw them, coz?"

"No, I am too near-sighted. It takes you to see what is far off, and me to see what is near—but don't you think the fashions favor me? I am *embonpoint*, you know, so that full skirts are just the thing for me. Don't you think so, Rose?"

"Yes, Flora, Paris takes pity on you this season; and don't you think white gauze bonnet strings become me?"

The opening of the coach door before No. — Incog. Place, prevented any reply to this important question. Entering the parlor, they find their mothers, Mesdames Restless and Galaday, who have just returned from the morning service at St. Picture's. It is enough to know that they are opera-goers, and consider themselves very exemplary Christians as the times go.

"Well, aunt, how did you like the *prima donna*, to-day? Did she sing as well as when we heard her at the opera last night?" asked Rose.

"Better, if anything. If she can sing at the opera she can sing at church, of course. A prime *cantatrice* like her can sing anywhere."

"Doubtless," replies Mrs. Restless; "and yet don't you think Signora Squallia has a certain trick of voice, as if she were aiming at artistic effect?"

"A *soprano* of her powers should not choke herself down to the notes like ordinary choir-singers. She is expected to show off her voice."

"Did you observe, sister, the gradual growth and *sostenuto* of her tones, especially in the upper and middle registers?"

"Yes, she has few equals there; but what did you think of the *mezza voce* shake in the hymn—I forget the words? It showed either a flaw in the voice or a slip in the execution."

"It was a slip in the execution, no doubt. Her voice is perfection itself."

"Don't you think, aunt," asks Flora, "that most celebrated *sopranos* render church music too operatically—too—you know what I mean?"

"Why no, Flora, not more operatically than your *barytones*, your *tenores*, and your *contraltos*."

"We can never have too much *virtuosita* in our church singing, so the art be only concealed by a little *abandon* and occasional *fioriture*," adds Mrs. Galaday.

Mrs. Restless was saying that she "particularly admired two or three of Signora Squallia's ornamental variations from the literal text which she had observed in the last hymn," when Mr. Galaday came in. He had been to hear Dr. Action, to "whose church" he always goes when he spends a Sunday in town. Looking at Mrs. Restless with an eye of wonder, he sportively asks,

"Then you have been to St. Picture's, have you? How *dare* you go to church on purpose to hear a fine singer—an opera *artiste*, too; leaving out of the question the deadly heresy taught at St. Picture's?"

"For my part, I can say," replies Mrs. Restless, "and I think I can speak for my sister also, that I have no scruples about going to hear an opera singer at church, and at an apostate church if you please. As to the heresy taught at St. Picture's, I do not approve that. Indeed, I never listen to what a preacher says; I always make up my mind to sleep during that part of the service. If I went to hear the sermon that would alter the case, but I

> "To church repair,
> Not for the doctrine; but the music there."

"Some go to church to see architecture, others to

look at pictures, and others to hear *eloquent speaking*. I have as good a right to indulge my taste as other people."

Mr. Galaday felt the force of this argument, especially of the emphasis which Mrs. Restless laid on the words *eloquent speaking*, as she at the same time tipped Mrs. Galaday the wink.

After a short pause, during which Mr. Galaday composed himself by caning the dust out of his gaiters, he rallied himself and said:

"But you ought to have heard Dr. Action this morning. Such smoothness and softness of voice! and then what graceful gestures!"

"What was Mr. Action's text?" asks Mrs. Restless.

"I don't recollect."

"You can give us the subject perhaps, or at least one of the heads of the sermon?" asks Mrs. Galaday, wishing to help her husband out of his difficulties.

"No ma'am, I can give neither text, nor subject, nor division. Thank God, I seldom pay any attention to those small matters; but his gestures were graceful beyond description. When quoting those words of—St. Matthew? yes, if my memory serves me; 'from Jerusalem round about unto Illyricum,' he turned his back upon us, and then faced about with such a curvilinear swing of the arm, and such a delightful toss of the hand when he came to 'Illyricum,' *Il-lyr-i-cum! Il-lyr-i-cum!!*"—all which Mr. Galaday accompanied with manipulations that would not have disgraced Cicero himself.

Mr. Restless and Mr. Coupon, his partner in

stock-jobbing, now came in. Mr. Galaday observing that Mr. Restless had an anxious look, asked:

"Any panic in the money market, Mr. Restless? You seem a little nervous."

"No, sir, there is no panic either in the market or among my nerves. Only I cannot digest certain doctrines which a mad preacher has just been cramming down my throat. Mr. Coupon would have me go with him to hear Mr. Evangely, of whom he had heard so much said that he felt some curiosity to know who he is. We were seated among a great crowd, and I soon saw there was no chance for speculation there. The preacher stood up, and among other things gave us all to understand that we were sinners. Then how vulgar! I did not hear one big word, such as *permeation*, or *adumbration*, or *obfuscation*. Tell me I am a sinner will he?"

Here Mr. Coupon, who was also troubled with convictions which he wished to get rid of, gave another turn to the conversation.

"Whether you are a sinner or not, Mr. Restless, I will not take upon me to say. That you are a stockbroker I am certain. How do you think fancies will open to-morrow?"

"Why, yesterday being Christmas," replies Restless, "there was nothing doing; so that to-morrow fancies must open buoyant and active, to make up."

"But the bears will try to break down the market."

"Of course they will try, but they will find it uphill work, or to speak zoologically, down-hill work; for the bulls will not only toss up prices, but will set the bears going down hill with a continual somerset."

"Yet the two special fancies, Bristol and York, ran down on Friday very fast. The former closed at a decline of seven and a half per cent., and the latter at a decline of three per cent. Some other fancies are now largely inflated."

"For all that, I think the bulls may feel confident of a rise of some importance."

While Messrs. Restless and Coupon were thus enlarging upon the stock-market, and Mr. Galaday listening with the close attention of a novice on 'Change, Mrs. Restless was questioning her sister as to some doubtful points of country scandal.

"I have heard that Byron Rake is flirting with Cecilia Christian. What did report say when you left?"

"It said as you have said—so Mrs. Tattle told me; she said she had it from Mrs. Gabble, who had it from Miss Prattle, who had it from Miss Whisper, who had it from Miss Lovejoke; so it comes direct, and must be true."

"It does not surprise me," sagely remarks Mrs. Restless; "I never thought Cecilia Christian as good as she pretends to be."

"Say what they will, I think Byron Rake good enough for her—quite good enough."

At dinner, which was the most sumptuous one of the week, the conversation grew more earthly; the gossip of the town, anecdote, badinage, and punning being indulged in by old and young. In this way, and by the help of some piano-forte and harp music in the style of Rossini, they managed to kill God's time, though they were not able wholly to smother his groans, or to hide the traces of his blood.

In the evening the whole company went to an Oratorio, except Rose Restless, who was engaged at home by the attentions of Mr. Simpleton.

Much of the small-talk which passed in this family during the day my pen refuses to record, saying it was so small that it can see no use in taking note of it, unless to show that the interlocutors are not rational, and therefore not accountable beings—but, my pen, they are all accountable beings, and some of them went to church in the morning, and confessed they were "miserable sinners." Yet they have contrived to pass the day very comfortable sinners—comfortable in making an oblivion of the resurrection of the Redeemer—an event which they profess on this day to commemorate, by a resurrection of their souls from the sepulchre of worldly thoughts and pursuits—comfortable in talking of millinery and fashions, music and eloquence, lucre and amours, flirtations and what not, instead of talking of Him, whose guileless tongue dropped with wormwood and gall to atone for our sinful words.

The due observance of this holy day requires us to keep our tongues, no less than our hands, from the usual employments of the secular week. As the tongue shares in the toil and moil of the week, it, along with the other organs, needs respite, that it may return with renewed strength to engage in the commerce of mind. By employing a share of this sacred time in abstinence from spiritual discourse even, devoting it to serious meditation and secret prayer, we shall improve the moral purity and intellectual tone of our week-day talks. The stream of conversation should not be always dashing on like an

Alpine torrent. If its waters are to flow musically and clear, they must be allowed to subside here and there in deep and untroubled pools, where the sand and mire they picked up in their swifter currents may settle at the bottom, and whence may be given back, in melodious tones, the echoes of the babbling rapids.

Of the promise made to the sons of Jacob, that they should find delight in the Lord, ride upon the high places of the earth, and be fed with the heritage of their father, one of the conditions was *that they should not speak their own words on the sabbath.* There is, in the keeping of this condition the working out of such a glorious result from natural causes, and apart from Providential interposition. The way we spend fifty-two days in each year, or the seventh part of our mortal lifetime, must tell incalculably for good or evil upon the present and eternal character of our souls. If it is our wont on one day in the week to select, with jealous care, the themes of our talks, the habit will do much to bring the tongue into that entire subjection which is the inspired mark of "the perfect man." On the other hand the habitual profanation of the sabbath by secular conversation, sinks the soul by degrees into the deepest moral degradation. An Oriental legend tells us that while Solomon was once on his way to pay a visit to the Queen of Sheba, he came to a valley in which dwelt a peculiar tribe of monkeys. Upon inquiring into their history, he learned that they were the posterity of a colony of Jews, who, settling in that region many years before, had, by habitually profaning the sabbath, gradually degenerated into the brutes he found them. This story has more foundation in truth than in fact, though it does not illustrate the whole truth as to the effects of sabbath-breaking; for while, in this world, it sinks the human soul and body nearly to a level with brute life, in the world to come it sinks both in a perdition, where to take the lowest place in the lowest rank of brute being, and to be allowed the lowest gratifications of brute instinct, would be an honor and a happiness which the despairing spirit will be denied the pleasure of hoping to enjoy even in the latest futurity.

CHAPTER V.

CONVERSATION IN GENERAL SOCIETY.

None but topics of common interest can, with strict propriety, be admitted into promiscuous companies. But, as such topics are few, and as some freedom is generally preferred to the risk of reducing the circle to silence, this rule is often disregarded. The weather, health, business, news, politics, history, art, science, and general literature, are among the themes that are usually tolerated here. Unhappily, the Christian religion must be omitted in this enumeration. We say the Christian religion, for religion, as a general subject, embracing the Mahometan, Braminical, in short every faith but our own, is welcomed in these circles. The evangelical system is studiously excluded, not so much because it is not a matter of general interest as because it is one of deep-felt concern, and liable, consequently, to raise zeal, hatred, or disgust, according to the principles and tempers of the conversers. The cross is a stumbling block in all companies where the tone is earthly; and since it is so, and nothing but the general prevalence of vital piety can make it otherwise, it were better for the friends of the gospel to keep it out of such companies, lest, by being forced upon them, it be loaded with needless reproach. The endeavor to couple Christianity with worldliness, and to exhibit it out of place, has often made it an object of indignation to men of the world. When they behold the cross in strange fellowship with their idols, they lose that reverence for it which it commanded when it was viewed apart. They regard our religion with nearly the same feelings that the Japanese do, who hold a yearly festival for trampling on the crucifix.

People of the world do but obey their depraved antipathies when they keep aloof from the cross of Christ, whereas they do violence to their nature when they abstain from talking on religion in general. There is a religious sentiment common to man, such as some idea of God and of a future state; and this sentiment generally finds expression by seeking some substitute for the humiliating terms of the gospel. Many deem it a mark of reverence to the Supreme Being, and to pious persons, occasionally to allude to the general subject—a mark of reverence which will, as they suppose, serve to distinguish them from vulgar and godless sinners with whom they would otherwise be in danger of being confounded.

Such persons are, for the most part, willing to talk on the subject of morality so long as we discourse in the style of Aristotle, Epictetus, or Marcus Antoninus. They are careful to keep clear of all the distinctive features of evangelical morality. While, therefore, the Christian should concede to their philosophical ethics whatever of excellence it may possess, he must not forget to point them to a higher code. This resolution of President Edwards was a good one: "When I am conversing on morality, I will turn it over, by application, exemplification, or otherwise, to Christianity."

It is seldom advisable, as we just now intimated, to drag evangelical themes into the gay and festive concourse. Those who do it, lay themselves open to the charge of plotting against the object of the party, of being misled by fanaticism, and above all, of lowering the dignity of religion and profaning its sanctities. It is a law of poetical propriety not to introduce a god, except on an occasion worthy of a god. The principle is as applicable to manners as it is to poetry. Evangelical religion does not look well shouldering her way into a crowd of jolly and unthinking worldlings. We would by no means drive piety from all places except church edifices, cloisters, and death-beds. We simply caution the Christian against too freely discoursing on his religion among those who would blame him as irreverent, or mock him as ridiculous. However, when we happen to be conversing with an individual out of ear-range of others, it is sometimes proper to dwell on the subject.

But when evangelical conversation is introduced in mixed companies, as it sometimes ought to be, it will be cheerfully tolerated by every true lady and gentleman, and instead of being shocked at it, as some exquisite people affect to be, these will take part in it. Lord Chesterfield and Lord Bolingbroke, deists though they were, showed their gentility by a pleasant and liberal bearing towards the pious persons with whom they lived on terms of intimacy. A well-bred unbeliever will also so far respect the feelings of a Christian, as to discountenance all ribaldry, scoffing, and profane swearing in his presence.

Moralizing is, in general, ill-received in these companies. We should not speak against a vice which individuals of the party are known or suspected to be guilty of, or praise a virtue in which they are notoriously deficient. All moral reflections, proverbs, and precepts, are liable to be received as personal attacks on character. Neither is it prudent in such circles to expatiate on the virtues of the absent; for some hearer will think his own excellences vilified in proportion as we exalt those of others.

It devolves on us, however, to defend the absent when they are calumniated; only not too warmly, for it occasionally falls out that he who speaks disparagingly of another, means only to give information that was, as he supposed, reliable or well known. To disabuse such à one with bluntness, pertness, or an air of conceit, is not to act the part of a gentleman, much less of a Christian. Another thing, by a too fervent vindication of our friend, we may give cause to think that his character is not beyond suspicion, or that we have some ulterior purpose to serve by flying to his defence.

The same may be said of our treatment of those who ridicule the doctrines of the Gospel, or speak contemptuously of its professors in general. As the gauntlet is in such cases impliedly thrown, we are tempted to take it up too eagerly. When the remarks of the malignant are likely to be received with disfavor, silence is perhaps the most pointed and effectual reply. But when foolish and vain talkers are heard with applause, their mouths must be stopped. It now becomes the Christian, meekly and composedly, to put them to silence. And though bystanders could have wished that he had not put a period to their chuckling, and spoiled the joy of a fancied triumph; still, even they, in their more sober moments, may inwardly approve his conduct. If they should not, it will signify little, so long as his own conscience blesses itself for the deed, and angels kiss his lips for giving a right answer.

It has been thought that the best way to promote sociableness in promiscuous society, is for each one to lay aside every peculiarity of religious and political opinions, and all professional and local habits. This rule may be advantageously kept by friends and acquaintances, who have been long known to one another. In an assembly of people, many of whom have never seen or heard of one another before, we should take a different course. Here, nothing is so great an aid to conversation as an unreserved confession of our religious faith, political principles, profession, business, and such like things. Many Christians mistake here. Misled by the aforesaid regulation, or dreading the charge of Pharisaic ostentation, they conceal their religious profession and belief from people of the world. The consequence is, that the latter are at a loss for suitable topics when they are in the company of those whose character and faith have not been disclosed to them. Aware that an offence against religious scruples or sectarian prepossessions, is of a very serious nature, they remain silent, or speak with fear and restraint. It ought to be considered an act of true courtesy, for strangers to make known to one another—in a modest and graceful manner of course—those facts concerning themselves which must be known before they can treat one another with complaisance, or even with respect.

The same observation holds good as to a frank avowal of our sentiments on any subject, or the bold announcement of any principle that, for the time, we choose to maintain. Then each one knows whom he is to meet, and the opinions with which he is confronted. Freedom of speech, when it is once proclaimed, is a wonderful peace-maker among ill-sorted groups. Every one feels that he has a property in it, and when he enjoys it and sees all who are around him enjoying it, he is brought into fellowship with all; he feels that all are related to him, if not by agreement, yet by antagonism. His strayed thoughts now come trooping to him as if at the blast of a rallying trumpet, and his once enthralled tongue rouses and shakes off its irons as the inspiriting sound of liberty breaks upon his ear. Hitherto the tyranny and intolerance of fashion forced him to repress the mighty risings of truth, and gather about his person a cloak of secrecy and reserve. Others did the like, so that while it was the interest of none to discover, it was the business of all to conceal. Now he finds himself among children of the light, who in nobly laying open their principles, cause truth to descend from the skies in all her divine charms, and dwell among her votaries. It is scarce possible that any important principle should be discussed, illustrated, or established among people who meet as at masquerades, not to appear in their own, but in fictitious characters.

The foregoing remarks are to be received with some limitations. Great freedom of opinion is hazardous where many of the company are mere transient acquaintances, whom we see no more, and where as is often the case, certain persons refusing to join in the talk sit as reporters and spies upon those who do. For this reason professors should not, in mixed circles, speak on awkward and scandalous affairs connected with church discipline. We have known professors to make the faults and infirmities of their brethren matter of animadversion and derision in the hearing of those who inly rejoiced at the exposure of the dishonorable parts of the church. "I said," is the language of David, "I will keep my mouth with a bridle while the wicked is before me." It is not our duty, indeed, to go into society chilled with suspicion : only we should be careful not to drop one word, in the company of the irreligious, that they can pick up and bandy about to the hurt of the Lord's little ones.

It must be apparent to any one, that there are some impediments to a free interchange of thought between those who are of so opposite a character as the saint and the sinner. The Christian cannot converse familiarly with the man of the world unless he finds in the latter a congeniality of intellectual tastes and of secular pursuits. He feels an awkward restraint, arising partly from the fewness of the subjects that are entertaining to both, and partly from a fear that the world-wide difference that exists in their moral feelings will inadvertently show itself in distance of manner. Hence he is forced to talk on neutral subjects only, or if ever on contested ones, he must studiously shun arguments drawn from his religion. He must touch upon the most soul-stirring truths with an unoffending indifference. The rising ardor which is inflamed by divine realities being thus repeatedly checked, finally languishes and expires. Surely piety cannot thrive in places whence God is by law excluded, and where not a single spark of holy zeal can kindle but it must be extinguished the moment it begins to glow. Out of a misguided complaisance we use mollifying terms to express mildly, truths that are in their very nature severe; we speak of doctrines which we find to be disagreeable to others, as if they were of little concern to us; we hear offensive truths questioned without defending them, and so by insensible degrees glide into indifference, doubt and unbelief. By often consenting to dismiss serious thoughts, He whose name is Jealous, is provoked to retire from the soul. This is the natural result of conformity to the world.

Men of the world exact of the Christian a stricter obedience to the laws of society than they do of any one of themselves. It is no greater infringement of good breeding to declare his religious principles than for the man of the world to deliver diatribes on his politics, his estate, his horses, or his dogs, or to interlace his frivolities with profane scoffs or reckless blasphemy. If the worldling may bring in his hobbies, why may not the saint bring in his fiery chariot; if the former may curvet and amble by the hour, round the circle on his favorite themes, what great crime can it be for the latter to take the cross upon his shoulders and carry it for awhile? When all are taking sides in every earthly cause, and no one leaves it doubtful what are his opinions on the great political and scientific questions of the day, who shall forbid the Christian to insinuate that he is a worshipper of God rather than of mammon, and that he espouses the cause of the Prince of Peace. We are aware that as the world now goes, the Christian who feels justified in going into such company must submit to all that custom imposes. Nor can we advise any one to set himself to change the tone or spirit of a company, inasmuch as this grows out of the very dispositions, talents, acquirements and vocations of those who compose it. When this tone is decidedly secular, he must in some degree chime in with it. Still, in the most worldly company in which the Christian may lawfully appear, he should at least casually touch upon the subject of religion, and in some instances he may speak there more at large.

It is evidently the duty of the Christian in society to endeavor, by every prudent means, to elevate the standard of morals, and to give a right direction to talk when it is straying on dangerous ground. Here success will much depend on a talent for improving opportunities, and more on the grace which ever keeps the mind in a condition to watch for them. Says the son of Sirach, "Refrain not to speak when there is occasion to do good, and hide not thy wisdom in her beauty." The code of morals which is received by the generality of people is little better than an abstract of the criminal statutes. The Christian should, at convenient times, and in an agreeable way, show them its scantiness by contrasting it with the gospel morality. As many persons do not disrelish the subject of morals, they will join him in condemning a breach of them. And though he should carefully avoid fault-finding and a wanton opposition to the opinion of others, he must, on the other hand, take care that his views and theirs of religious subjects, do not seem exactly alike, when, in fact, they are very dissimilar. It is enough that he consent to meet them on any common ground, without endeavoring, for the sake of pleasing, to reconcile his God with their Baal, and his faith with their refuge of lies. He may occasionally draw some moral or spiritual reflection from secular topics already started, and oppose Divine truth to the mischievous principles that so widely prevail in the world.

The consistent believer will naturally, in these companies, recognize the hand of God in events which other people are apt to impute to the agency of man, or to chance. He will not refuse to discourse on second causes, but he will always refer them finally to the Great First Cause. He will talk with the naturalist of the laws of nature, but he will not, as the naturalist is prone to do, stop at those laws. He will talk with the politician on the connection which war, intrigue, policy, and political economy, have with the present posture of affairs. This he will cheerfully do, in order to show that it is not from ignorance, but from piety, that he ever keeps in mind the operations of Providence.

It is worthy of remark that it is not necessary to the adornment of our profession that we be always talking *about* religion. We shall best preserve a character for piety by talking in its *spirit*. Many whose lips are often made the channel of religious thought, show in their demeanor few of the marks of operative grace. They have a haughtiness of mien and a severity of tone which true charity wots not of. She suffereth long and is kind. Those sticklers of orthodoxy who torture every sentence that will not exactly answer to the Procrustes' bed of their creed, and cry out against every sentence that is not just as they would have it, prove that the faith they so zealously defend has not made them meek and gentle in life. Such as rebuke without mercy, every transgressor that comes in their way, or such as set up for religious instructors, or always fly to the defence of religion before it has been attacked, do less to recommend their doctrines than those who, if they do not often allude to the letter of the Gospel, show, in a thousand nameless ways, that their hearts feel its power. To handle sacred things with due reverence, to manifest a spiritual mind in the selection and treatment of themes, to diffuse a heavenly savor over all one's communications, to speak of the faults of others with charity and compassion, to have a tender concern for the feelings of others, to bear submissively arrogance and rudeness, to abide affliction and wrong with cheerfulness, these and many other actions like these do more to convince the world of the reality of the Christian faith, than the aptest quotations, weightiest arguments, and the strongest protestations on its behalf. "Let your speech," says Paul, "be always with grace, seasoned with salt." He would have divine grace send out its holy and pleasant influences in all our discourse, and the salt of sacred truth—not in the crude mass, but in solution and diffusion, preserve all our sentiments from moral taint, and season even the most common and secular subjects. We hear plenty of people talk of this clergyman or the other, of the singing of choirs, of the people they saw at church, of the architecture of a church edifice—when shall we stop? Ah, we fear this enumeration of themes must end where the marks of heartfelt devotion begin. It is not enough that we ply our tongues about the forms and appendages of religion, all our words and actions should declare its effects. The whiteness of the galaxy, when viewed through a large telescope, is resolved into millions of stars, whose interwoven rays form the zone that girds the spangled robe of night. Even thus should the Christian, in his intercourse with the world, display a character to the formation of which every divine influence has administered its share, and a conduct in which, if every grace does not always severally appear, yet a conduct which is the pure, and mild, and sublime result of them all.

Hence the importance of going into society with a thorough preparation of spirit. So manifold and powerful are the temptations that compass the Christian there, he cannot pray too fervently for Divine guidance and protection. Without previous self-examination, meditation, and prayer, and without always keeping up the watch while he is in company, he will be liable, by his misdoings, to excite the contempt, if not the derision, of earthlings. In a thoughtless hour he will resolve, perhaps, to lose himself in the mazes of the gay assembly, but he is not, let him be assured, lost sight of by those who may appear to take no notice of his behavior at the time, and very likely that for the time some may forget his profession. But in an after-hour of sober review, they will call it to mind, and its incongruity with his conduct will be an object of scandal and scorn. As the person who would not appear ridiculous, must not go into company with higher spirits than those of other people, so the Christian who would not be despised must not enter the circles of the world with any other feelings than such as they have reason to expect from his religious profession. He must take care to say nothing that cannot stand the test of those who appear there under "a cloak of maliciousness"—nothing which, when separated from the hilarity that gave it birth, and was then its apology, can bear a meaning which the speaker never thought of. Against such surprises, prayer, and the grace it obtains, are the best of safeguards. He who comes down into the world, direct from the audience-chamber of the King of kings, will bring with him the recollection of the petitions he there offered up, and the gravity and moderation which he observed in that august presence.

CHAPTER VI.

INTERVIEWS WITH THE UNBELIEVER RELATIVE TO HIS SPIRITUAL INTERESTS.

CONVERSATIONS with unrenewed individuals on the subject of personal religion, is a very important, though much-neglected duty. The preacher addressing, as he often must, large mixed assemblies, cannot easily bring each hearer to feel the glad tidings of salvation to be his personal concern. Men but too often regard the arrows of truth as they do those of death, as never aimed at themselves, though they know multitudes who, in their opinion, are fit and appointed marks. The pious converser does not encounter this difficulty. He comes to the sinner as Elijah did to Ahab, and as Nathan did to David. He turns away the sinner from hearing and judging of the sins of others, and leads him to exercise contrition before God, and faith in Christ.

The generality of sinners expect that those who have experienced a radical change of heart and life, who are actuated by the love of Christ and the hopes of the gospel, will recommend to their kindred, friends, and neighbors, the grace they have found, and warn them of the danger to which they believe them exposed. The sinner asks himself, "Shall the Christian, who professes to be an heir of a celestial inheritance, and believes that I may, if I will, gain one equally rich, shall he neglect to persuade me to secure a blissful provision for eternity? Does he declare himself my friend, and yet when he sees my soul hanging over the brink of the fiery lake, into which if I fall there can be no rescue, cannot tell me of my peril? Has his great physician healed him, and can he refrain from recommending Him to me, who am, as he says, dying of the disease of which he is cured? He is concerned for my secular affairs: he counsels, warns, persuades me, with respect to them, and can he be silent concerning the supreme and the infinite good? If he be sincere, and if he be my friend, he will speak to me on this subject; and though I wish he would not do it, he cares not for my soul and he is a hypocrite, if he does not." It is a good rule in this case, as it is in many others, to enquire what does the man of the world expect of me? Though some may affect surprise that we should address them on this subject, we may be assured that such surprise is dissembled. There is a very general expectation among unregenerate sinners, that Christians will press upon their hearts and consciences the claims of the Redeemer.

And let the Christian be encouraged to the task by the consideration that the conscience of the sinner is on his side. However wide-spread may be the moral desolation within him, there is yet a voice crying in the wilderness of his soul, "Repent!" and that voice will answer to every faithful appeal on the part of the Christian. His conscience will not, to be sure, always lessen his present resistance: for being attacked both from within and from without, he may be driven to desperation, and lay hold of ungentle weapons of defence. But though the benevolent offices of his pious friend should be ungratefully resisted at the time, let him hope that he has left the memorial of them graven on a tablet that will one day engage the sinner's serious attention, be a motive to penitence, and a theme of gratitude throughout the whole course of his being.

It is a common remark that Christians are more apt to recoil from the duty of serious conversation with their kindred and friends than with other persons. We will not stop to inquire into the causes of this aversion—causes which operate with too fatal regularity. Whatever they are, our chief concern must be to remove them. The untold influence which relations and friends mutually exert over one another, for good or for evil, should be employed to break the spell which the world casts over the soul, and conduct it up the steeps of Golgotha. It seems as if the Destroyer used his wisest arts to dissuade the saints from taking advantage of the natural affections, to allure souls to the cross, by availing themselves of which, they might do most to lessen the number of his victims.

What bitter lamentations has the omission of this duty occasioned—lamentations rendered all the more bitter by the reflection that the consequences of such delinquency could not be remedied by any future diligence. How many have thought with one who excused himself till too late from the duty of speaking to an acquaintance on the subject of his salvation. His language is, "Oh," thought I, "that I had listened to the voice of God's Spirit, and had done my duty. Perhaps I might have saved his soul from perdition; at least I might have cleared my own skirts and washed my hands in innocency. But now, alas! it is too late! forever too late! his doom is irrevocably sealed!" A Christian mother, who had deferred from time to time the duty of leading the heart of her son to Christ, after his sudden death was heard to chide her fatal delays in these words: "He has gone into eternity and left me distracted with anxiety concerning the salvation of his precious soul! Dilatory wretch! Had it not been for my own sin, I might now have been consoling myself with the satisfactory conviction of having discharged the duty of a Christian parent, and enjoying the delightful assurance of meeting my child before the throne of God and the Lamb. Oh the accursed sin of procrastination! Oh the ruinous delusion that lurks in the word *to-morrow!*".

How much good may one do in a lifetime by seizing every occasion of speaking for Christ. The writer once learned a lesson from a slave, which has been very beneficial to him. Some years ago, while paying a visit to Mount Vernon, he chanced to be strolling alone among the cabins of the negroes belonging to the estate, when he saw an aged negress sitting on a threshold smoking her pipe. He ventured to draw nigh and ask her if she had known Washington. Instead of a direct answer she asked, "Do you know God?" "I hope I know something of Him, ma'am." "How then may one know God, sir?" "We may learn something about his goodness and handiwork, from what we see in yonder garden, and in these beautiful trees." "You're right, Massa;

but is there no other way of knowing Him?" "Yes, ma'am, we may also learn something of Him from his dealings with the sons of men, the history of nations, and the lives of individuals." "Can we? But in no other way?" "From the Bible we gain more knowledge of God than from all the other sources put together." "Yes indeed, and is there no other way?" "By experience."—Laying her hand upon her heart, and lifting her bleared eyes to heaven, she exclaimed, "Ah, now you have it, Massa!" That countenance, though it bore the marks of nearly a hundred years of servitude, seemed to reflect the smile of an angel. After further pious discourse, she told me she had seen Washington but once, and that was when she was a cook in the camp of the army that fought under him. When the writer left the door of the humble cabin, he felt that there were other spots at Mount Vernon not less sacred than the tomb, the house, and the garden of Washington; he considered how many blessed impressions she had made on the minds of the gay children of this world who daily visited the spot. This was piety not to be doubted of. In a painting of the Last Judgment, by Orcagna, Solomon is represented rising from the dead, uncertain which way to turn, and those about him seem at a loss whither to direct him—such is the uncertainty felt by too many of the great ones of this world, and such is the uncertainty too many of their acquaintance must feel concerning their eternal destiny. But who could talk with this poor slave for five minutes, and entertain a single doubt as to her citizenship? While men of patient research are anxiously comparing notes, to make out the shadow of a hope as to the hereafter of some of our greatest statesmen, the name of Hannah Nugent—that was her name—must ever be synonymous with piety, in the minds of all who knew her. Many whose names are adopted into all languages, never to be obsolete in any coming generation, and are written on the stars, will envy her glory when they shall behold her name recorded in the Lamb's book of life. Oh Lord, how long shall a doubtful piety be thought necessary to gain a political popularity. But we are wandering from our subject; however, we may sometimes become better acquainted with a country we are travelling through, by losing our way than by keeping the beaten road.

The very important work we are considering, should not be undertaken without previous prayer. We need to be impressed with the conviction that success will not depend altogether upon our address or a happy combination of circumstances. The faltering word, the broken but heart-felt entreaty, or the honest but ill-worded warning has, when directed by the Divine spirit, often been known to reach the heart, and prepare a place for repentance. Prayer is an essential preliminary to this duty, both because it obtains the co-operation of the Holy Ghost, and because the very act brings the soul into that humble, confiding, and earnest posture, with which we should enter upon the performance of the duty.

The Christian who is accustomed to perform this duty, will occasionally find the prayers with which he prepared for the conference, immediately answered, the Holy Ghost gone before him, already in possession of the sinner's soul, and waiting to welcome his approach. He will find the work, to which he looked forward with so many anxieties, anticipated by the sinner himself, and be happily surprised to meet with a true Israelite dwelling in Meshech, or perhaps one whose heart is transfixed with the arrow of conviction, and implores his hand to disengage its barb; or one who has a timid hope that needs encouragement. With what joy does it repay the tears of him who goes forth to the spiritual harvest, to see the sheaves in a manner already bound on the wain, and coming forth to meet the husbandman.

Another chief qualification is a tender spirit. To be able to recollect our own former stubbornness, blindness, and insensibility, and to bear them in mind in our exhortations to the ungodly, to realize his true, not his fancied condition, to have compassion on his lost soul, to "warn with tears," and to receive his taunts and rebuffs with meekness; these carry with them an eloquence that can melt the heart of flint, and break the iron will. There is no virtue more peculiarly Christ-like than this tenderness, and those in whom it appears, give to the sinner the best evidence of the reality and power of the Christian faith.

This duty should also be performed in a sweet and unpretending manner. Those greatly mistake who put on sour and sanctimonious airs, and use a studied solemnity of speech in urging the sinner to duty. Seriousness and earnestness there must be, but what need is there of a severe and repulsive bearing? Let it be sufficient to press upon the conscience forbidding truths, without adding thereto the weight of an offensive address. Yet, we would not be understood to favor that light and negligent behavior, by which some endeavor to gain for their persuasives a ready lodgment in the heart. This extreme is, if possible, more ill-placed than the other.

It is the current practice in introducing pious conversation, to follow the course of common talk until an occasion offers of turning it in a spiritual direction. This is done with a view to conciliate the person addressed, without startling or affronting him by a blunt and dashing address. In pursuing this method we must not suffer the secular topic to be so long dwelt on as to excite a livelier interest than can be enlisted on the side of religion. If we give worldly matters the start, they are apt to keep foremost, unless we speedily overtake them. We should not talk on such subjects so as to raise them into undue consequence, but so as either to make them appear in their own comparative insignificance, or to make them a graceful introduction to higher themes. But in doing this we should not indulge a censorious spirit which snatches up every word that drops from another's lips, and applies to it the rule of morality and the gauge of orthodoxy. Some good people talk with a man of the world as if their religion were the only object in the universe that deserved the slightest attention of mortals. If one admires a work of art, they observe that it is a trifle to an immortal being, or it is nothing in comparison with the achievments of divine grace. They seem to suppose they cannot do justice to Christianity unless they do injustice to everything beside. That baubles do captivate the souls of multitudes is a most deplorable fact; but we shall hardly convince them of their folly on those occasions when they are the most highly delighted with these baubles, or when they are calling on us to share the pleasure they take in seeing and talking about them. We should close our hearts against that cynical spirit which says to every subject that is like to eclipse our favorite one: "Stand out of my light." We should aim to make religion the most important concern, without betraying too strong a contempt for what others deem equally important. The indirect mode of address of which we are speaking is, we fear, oftener resorted to than is warranted by the dignity and sacredness of the duty or the simplicity and earnestness which should ever attend its performance. Though it may sometimes be employed in talking with individuals of their spiritual interests, it is principally useful in raising the tone of conversation in mixed companies.

And these indirect approaches would be less demanded were we more careful to bring forward the subject with a pertinent introduction. Such introduction might take the shape of an apology, confession, interrogation, or explanation. We do not suggest these as the only allowable ways of commencing interviews of this kind. Occasions and circumstances are so various, that no specifications would be adapted to every case. If, as we have hinted, we engage in a long talk on a subject foreign to the one contemplated, before the latter is introduced, we are in danger of dissipating those serious feelings which are answerable to the nature of the duty. But if the Christian comes straightway from communion with God, his lips touched with a live coal off the altar of grace, and shedding around him fragrance from the censer of prayer, making some introductory remarks relating either to the moral relations of the parties or to the subject to be urged, his manner will be marked by a noble frankness and gentle courage which are every-way worthy of the child of God and of his benevolent purpose.

The course here suggested is different from that of him who ushers in the subject of religion as informally as he does a secular affair, pronounces sacred names as familiarly as he does profane, degrades the most awful subjects to a level with the trifles of a day, and appalls even the confirmed Christian with unlooked-for and misplaced homilies. Nevertheless, when the feelings of the man are right, and his defect is one of judgment only, a generous man of the world will pardon much in him. His sublime intent will throw a faulty manner into the shade.

To converse successfully with an impenitent person we must meet him alone. While he is surrounded with his associates, he is kept in countenance by them. The fear of incurring their scorn, or perhaps the encouragement he receives from their presence, keeps him from hearing us with candor and seriousness. He is tempted to disguise his real sentiments and to play a false part. If we can only separate him from his confederates, he will probably talk on the subject with little reserve, especially if we are almost or quite strangers to him. We should not, therefore, in ordinary cases, appeal to several at a time. If we may be allowed to illustrate a work of mercy by a work of atrocity, we would say that the Christian should in this case adopt the stratagem of

Horatius in killing the three Curiatii; he should contrive to divide them by wide intervals, and then overcome each one in single combat.

Not only should such interviews be private, but what is said in them should be strictly confidential. If I blazon abroad what passed between us, it is a betrayal of the trust which the sinner placed in me when he opened his heart to me. This is the general rule. Special circumstances may justify a departure from it, as where the sinner has misreported our remarks, or where a dying penitent would make us the bearer of some message of consolation or warning to his surviving friends.

Some sinners will make the application for themselves, of religious discourse in which they take no part, and which does not take the shape of expostulation. There are many cases on record of conversions which resulted from overhearing serious conversations.

A great many account themselves excused from dealing with the souls of their acquaintance on the plea that they are petulant, unreasonable, or outrageous. They tell us that they would reject their testimony and assault them. They quote, in self-justification, that proverbial direction of our Lord to his apostles: "Give not that which is holy unto the dogs, neither cast ye your pearls before swine, lest they trample them under their feet, and turn again and rend you.[8] The apostles, to whom this precept was especially addressed, understood by it that they should not persist in preaching the gospel to such as should contemptuously reject it, and abuse them.

[8] Matthew vii. 6.

But they were in no case to *take for granted* that any individual was unworthy to receive the divine message before making a trial of his disposition towards them. They were commanded to preach the Gospel to every human being; whoever heard the glad tidings only to scorn it, and to maltreat the heralds, were at once to be forsaken by them. That this is the import of the general injunction is shown by the more specific directions which were given relative to the same subject.[9] Whatever house or city would not receive them nor hear their teachings, they were to depart from it, shaking the dust off their feet as a testimony against their conduct. They are nowhere directed to pass by any individual, or family, or community, for fear of being ill-treated by it. Their Master had forewarned them that He sent them forth as sheep among wolves; and the usage they commonly met with but too literally verified his predictions. They had themselves strong presentiments of the persecutions that awaited them in the cities they were to enter. Nevertheless they considered it their duty to go into the very cities where, as the Holy Ghost had foretold, they were to be received with wanton and vindictive cruelty. In this view no one is warranted to abstain from religious conversation with a person from a suspicion that it will be repaid with neglect, or contempt, or effrontery. We must not prejudge others to be dogs or swine, but are to account them such only when their treatment of ourselves or of our communications, has proved them deserving of these appellations. It is nothing that they have already resented the well-meant attempts

[9] Matthew x. 14; Mark vi. 11; Luke x. 10, 11.

of others. This does not demonstrate that ours will be so received. Our duty is done only when their opposition *to us* has rendered our further endeavors vain.

The precept in question may refer not only to the characters to be addressed, but also to the subject-matter of our conversations with unbelievers in general. It is, in most cases, injudicious to talk with them of the joys of heaven, the pleasures of Christian hope and faith, the doctrines of election, perseverance, assurance, the Trinity, especially the mysteries in which some Scripture truths are involved. Nor should we talk with them on what is peculiar to our religious experience or belief. We should dilate on the general subject only, noticing those features in experience which are common to most, if not all, spiritual persons, excepting always cases where *they request us* to give them a circumstantial account of our conversion. We shall sometimes be able to arrest the attention of a person that is insensible to his moràl condition and wants, by talking in a strain like the following: "I was once in the same state that you are now, and though I then felt no concern for my soul, I am now convinced I had every reason to be alarmed, and that, had I always continued in such a condition, I must have been lost forever. I found this very insensibility to be most hateful and loathsome to God. I forsook the course of life which nurtured it, and, as I humbly hope, repented of my sins, and believed in Christ." To aid convictions of sin in a moralist or a self-righteous person, some such sentiments as the following will not be useless: "I did not believe myself to be guilty before God till I seriously reviewed my life in the light of the divine law which reaches the thoughts, desires, and purposes, and in the light of the cross, which revealed to me the enormity of my sins, when I saw it was by a sacrifice of untold cost that their pardon was made possible. I now learned that those actions, such as honesty, generosity, and temperance, upon which I secretly valued myself, were prompted by wrong motives. I discovered that all my boasted virtues were essentially defective in the motive that prompted them; for I did not love God—my heart was enmity against Him." When the man of the world respectfully asks us to relate our experience, we should do it with a mild and reverent spirit. Says the apostle Peter, "Be ready always to give an answer to every man that asketh you a reason of the hope that is in you, with meekness and fear." We should always make a clear, unadorned statement of our spiritual exercises, not glorying in our experience, but in its Author; not making it an apology for present delinquencies, but a rebuke for them; not a test by which to try the experience of others, nor an occasion of vain-glorious triumph over others; but to deepen the conviction of our own ingratitude and unworthiness.

It may here be remarked, that, though the precept just quoted requires us to be ready to give a *reason* for our hope, it does not require us to answer every *objection* that a caviller could raise against Christianity. Objections may be brought by any one, who is in a humor to raise them, against doctrines that can be established by undeniable and overwhelming proofs. Objections neither prove nor disprove anything.

There are those who think that every mention of personal piety in the hearing of unbelievers is to give the holy to dogs and to cast pearls before swine. They would confine so sacred a thing as religion to cloisters, grave-yards, dark and bolted cathedrals, chained Bibles, and clasped prayer-books. But let those who thus keep the Christian religion at a ceremonious distance say and do what they will, she never shines with a more celestial radiance than when she walks in the light of daily life. What if the pearl must not be cast before swine? Shall it then be always locked in the casket and never adorn beauty. Divine grace and truth are the most comely ornaments that man ever wore, nor do they lose aught of their brilliance by their contact with human nature and with secular vocations. The diamond is despoiled of none of its brilliance by being set in gold. The foil and the bezel which enchase it, though they are not to be compared with it in material, yet they add to its elegance and its price.

It is incumbent on us to seize every opportunity for arresting the course of sinners and leading them into the way of peace. In our daily intercourse with them, suitable occasions will offer when a pious mind can hardly avoid calling their thoughts to the subject. Some incident will naturally start our theme, and furnish matter for its illustration and enforcement. Sickness, accidents, losses, favors bestowed or received, and numerous other occasions, will suggest an admonition, an entreaty or an exhortation. When the Rev. Peter Mill was once travelling on foot in Yorkshire, he came to a large pit whose brink was covered with drifted snow; at that moment, a young woman coming up warned him of his danger. After expressing his gratitude for her great kindness, he exhorted her to flee from the wrath to come, and expressed an ardent desire that as a return for the service she had rendered him, he might be the means of saving her soul from a more awful pit than that from which she had been instrumental in saving his body. While he spoke with gratitude sparkling in his eyes, and his countenance expressing more than his tongue could declare, she began earnestly to cry; "what must I do to be saved?" She soon after obtained peace to her troubled conscience through faith in her Saviour. When Dr. Payson was taking leave of an old lady who had entertained him under her roof, he said to her; "Madam, you have treated me with much hospitality and kindness, for which I thank you sincerely; but allow me to ask how do you treat my Master? That is of infinitely greater consequence than how you treat me." He continued for a time in a strain of appropriate exhortation, and then proceeded on his journey. This visit was sanctified to the conversion of the lady and her household, whence the work of grace spread in the neighborhood, and in a short time a church was gathered, and the ordinances of religion established.[1] In improving such

[10] How different the influence of such men of God from that of many of those who are popularly called "good *pastors*," i. e. them that spend most of their time in going to dinner and tea-parties, and in free-and-easy gossipping with their parishoners, avowing no higher purpose than that of adding to the number of pew-holders; and never showing any solicitude for the eternal welfare of their flock, in their nominally pastoral visits. An amusing and truthful, though somewhat antique picture of one of this sort of men is seen in an old, anonymous

occasions we must beware of that perfunctory manner which seems to say that we would not have made a solemn remark had it not been forced upon us by the occurrence, or did not our Christian profession exact of us something of the kind. We should ever cherish an ardent compassion and solicitude which needs but the slightest incident to fan it into a flame. A word to be fitly spoken, must be spoken not only at a proper time but in a suitable spirit. The apple of gold should not be heedlessly tossed into the basket of silver. Still, after all, there are those who make it a pretext for the indefinite postponement of this duty that they cannot find a fit time, a desirable state of mind, or some happy conjuncture. They do well to consider that the sinner may find a thousand ways of ruining his soul while they are

poem, "The Triumph of Infidelity," dated 1788—by the highest literary authorities now attributed to President Dwight:

"Each week, he paid his visitation dues;
Coax'd, jested, laugh'd; rehears'd the private news;
Smok'd with each goody, thought her cheese excell'd;
Her pipe he lighted, and her baby held.
Or plac'd in some great town, with lacquer'd shoes,
Trim wig, and trimmer gown, and glistening hose,
He bow'd, talk'd politics, learn'd manners mild;
Most meekly questioned, and most smoothly smil'd;
At rich men's jests laughed loud, their stories prais'd;
Their wives' new patterns gaz'd, and gaz'd, and gaz'd;
Most daintily on pamper'd turkies din'd;
Nor shrank with fasting, nor with study pin'd:
Yet from their churches saw his brethren driven,
Who thunder'd truth, and spoke the voice of heaven,
Chill'd trembling guilt, in Satan's headlong path,
Charm'd the feet back, and rous'd the ear of death.
'Let fools," he cried, "starve on, while prudent I
Snug in my nest shall live, and snug shall die."

waiting for one opportunity to attempt his conversion.

Accost some sinners on the subject of personal religion in the gentlest and most conciliating manner, and they will accuse you of impertinence or officiousness. Thus do they regard a point of spurious politeness as of more consequence than the welfare of their souls, and prefer that we should consult their momentary ease at the forfeiture of their everlasting bliss. They most grievously undervalue the Christian's endeavors. Had they ever suffered that pain with which he beholds them insulting his Father and his Saviour; had they ever felt his disinterested solicitude which follows them day by day and wakes and weeps and prays for them at the midnight hour: had they been seized with his shudderings when he sees them climbing along the sides of the bottomless pit—had they ever experienced these things, they would soon transform a presumed impropriety into an act of the highest courtesy. When the palace of the king of Spain was on fire, a soldier knowing the king's sister was in her apartment, and in danger of perishing in the flames, at the risk of his life rushed in and brought her highness safe out in his arms; but the Spanish etiquette was here woefully broken into. The loyal soldier was brought to trial, and as it was impossible to deny that he had entered her apartment, the judges condemned him to die. The Spanish princess, however, condescended to pardon the soldier, and very benevolently saved his life! Now, it is just in this way that your pretenders to gentility requite those who would "save them with fear, pulling them out of the fire"—those who for the sake of their eternal welfare perform acts of self-devotement in the presence of which the noblest services of mere good breeding shrink into utter meanness. Let no Christian allow such a hollow-hearted delicacy ever to keep him from going to the rescue of a fellow immortal.[11]

In matters of life and death, in all other affairs of great and urgent concern, it becomes us to be so self-devoted, as if needs be to break through the cobwebs of ceremony, and forget the restraint of modish frigidity. When Esther went into the audience-chamber of the king to intercede in behalf of her endangered countrymen, her act, though it was a violation of court etiquette, was not merely proper, it was more than heroic. When Mrs. Ann H. Judson went unceremoniously to the court of Ava to implore relief for her imprisoned husband, her very fearlessness and neglect of forms were more eloquent than speech. And if these informal intercessions in behalf of mortal life call for our admiration, so do unseasonable entreaties to those whose immortal spirits are on the point of passing beyond the reach of mercy and hope. The redemption of the soul is so unspeakably desirable, that when proprieties stand in the way, they should be disregarded as of no account. Every reasonable being will pardon something to the faith which makes the greatest affairs of time as less than nothing, when set over against the interests of eternity, to the benevolence that chooses to save rather than to please, and to the fear of being arraigned before the judgment Throne, clad in robes

[11] See "Principles of Courtesy," Part III., Chap. xiii., p. 265.

that are discolored with the blood of murdered souls. The conscientious servant of Christ hears voices from every part of the universe, calling him to "be instant, in season, out of season, to reprove, rebuke, and exhort with all long-suffering and doctrine."

We often hear wise and good men say, "Why, sirs, if we believed there is a hell, and loved the souls of men as we ought, we would run out into the streets and cry, Flee hell fire!" And there can be little doubt that if we did believe God, and love man in due degree, we would contrive a hundred methods of warning the wicked, where we now devise one; yet direct and urgent measures are not always expedient. A fresco painter seeing his fellow-artist walking backwards, so absorbed in viewing his work as not to notice that there was but a step between him and the edge of the scaffold, instead of alarming the endangered artist, immediately dashed his own brush over the picture; whereupon he sprang forward in indignation, and so escaped the awful brink. Here is wisdom. Rather than tell some men they are in danger of endless misery, we should draw them away from the sides of the pit by dashing a false hope, by holding up some motive of encouragement, or by convincing them of their guiltiness; or what is best of all, by setting forth the love and sufferings of Jesus Christ—we say some men, for there are many men, and perhaps they are the majority of men who are principally moved by their fears, and must look down into perdition before they can look into themselves, or unto Jesus. We should suffer no false compassion to flatter us that we are wiser than the Holy Spirit who says in Jude, "Of some have compassion, making a difference, and others save with fear."

In discharging this duty, as far as can be, keep clear of controverted questions. Very many of the unconverted give no other attention to religion than what they bestow on some trifling, speculative, or mysterious point in theology. Rarely do we hear them inquiring into the nature and obligations of any Scripture precept. They have plenty of futile questions to propose and discuss till they see the danger that hangs over their souls; then their single inquiry is: "What must we do to be saved?" We should therefore shun what they themselves would shun, did they see their peril as clearly as we do. The tendency of this kind of discussion, when carried on with this class of persons, is generally anything but salutary. They too often either begin or end in a want of seriousness, humility, or kindness. The counsel of Paul is: "Foolish and unlearned questions avoid, knowing that they do gender strifes." Unless these controversies are managed with unusual skill, the man of the world most commonly comes out of them more opposed to the truth, or to its advocates, than when he entered them, and the Christian who enters these fields of controversy, even though it be in the company of the meek, is exposed to a fate which may be illustrated by that of the traveller who wanders over certain savannas of the west, where he finds no path or way-mark, and where he is exposed to dank vapors, which cause paleness, weakness, disease and death. When an essential doctrine is denied, the Christian may be expected to defend it, and when it is not understood, to explain it so far as explanation is possible; but he is not called upon to encourage, or to undertake to satisfy an idle curiosity, or to bring to light what Infinite Wisdom has left in the dark. He should take pattern from his Master, as to the way to dispose of unprofitable and impertinent questions. When one put to him the question, "Lord, are there few that be saved?" He answered: "Strive to enter in at the strait gate; for many, I say unto you, shall seek to enter in and shall not be able." Without directly replying to the inquiry, he makes it the occasion of exhorting all the bystanders to immediate and earnest effort to secure their own salvation. The Christian can, in this way, turn the thoughts of the careless into a higher channel, fasten conviction on their consciences, and bring them to feel the force of the truth—very often lost sight of—that the records of revelation were intended not to afford matter for speculation, but to teach rules of life; not to envelope our immortality in darkness, but to bring it to light, and to illuminate a path thereto. It is not advisable, however, to waive the discussion of every question however fair, else we shall give occasion for the false imputation that our faith does not consist with reason. If we altogether reject reasoning in matters of religion, we shall provoke the unbeliever to take the opposite ground, and admit nothing else. The dogmatist is always the parent of the rationalist.

In conducting an argument with sceptics and infidels, the Christian will derive more advantage from a thorough knowledge of the evidences of Christianity, than from that of the sacred books themselves. Without such knowledge, no Christian is qualified "to give an answer to those who ask him a reason for the hope that is in him." When unbelievers find the generality of professors ignorant of the evidences of their faith, it cannot be a matter of wonder that their discussions with such persons should serve only to confirm them in their unbelief. It is not enough that the Christian appeal to his inward experiences. Such an appeal, if it had any weight with the infidel, would, among other things, go to prove the reality of an extraordinary divine influence. It could not of itself establish the authenticity of the Scriptures. It will not do to put off the doubter with such reasons, though a regenerate man may be satisfied with them. We are permitted, indeed, to excuse ourselves from bringing to the test of mere reason some things which our sacred writings contain ; not because they are contrary to reason, but because they are above reason. But Christian evidences afford a fair field for the exercise of our argumentative powers, and the infidel has a right to challenge us to meet him on this field, armed with every logical weapon.

On the other hand we should never stake the truth of any *scripture doctrine* on the issue of its reasonableness, or consent to defend it on metaphysical grounds alone. We are allowed, to be sure, to meet unbelievers on their own ground in testing the reasonableness of a revealed truth, but it must always be done with the understanding that we do not consider it the proper ground. With those who do not admit the divine authority of the Scriptures, we must establish their authenticity from external and internal testimonies, and not, as many injudiciously do, abandon Scripture proofs when their divine origin is denied, and tamely submit to the terms of their adversaries. With those who admit the divine authority of the Bible, an appeal should always be made "to the law and to the testimony," and on them and on them alone join issue.

When the infidel whom we would persuade is a veteran in wickedness, and in many cases when he is outwardly respectable, we can make an appeal to his conscience, and with some hope of success; inasmuch as it is easier for him to disorder the reasoning faculty to such a degree as to make it discordant with the sacred oracles, than it is for him to corrupt the moral sense so as to make it contradict them. How closely soever the understanding may be in league with the powers of darkness, conscience, the vicegerent of God in the soul, may yet in some degree maintain his allegiance to his Master. A voice like that of the demoniacs of old is still heard amid the ravings of a deranged mind, crying: "Thou art Christ, the son of God." Few, very few, have been the sceptics and unbelievers who have been able entirely to silence this inward witness to revealed truth. It speaks at solemn intervals during the most dissolute life, and in the hour of death it cries out in despair and terror. When the plain practical duties of the gospel are enforced on the conscience of the infidel, he stands convinced both of his sinfulness and of the reality of the Christian system. These addresses are to be made in a kind and humble spirit, and not for the purpose of evading the force of an argument which we are unable to answer, nor with the design of silencing an opponent; but with the simple intention to lead him to a cordial reception of the gospel.

Let no professor think he has acquitted himself of all negligence on this score, when he has merely observed to the sinner that life is short, death certain; that he has occasion for gratitude to God for earthly blessings; or formally spoken of the vanity of temporal good, and the importance of providing for our eternal felicity; the loveliness of virtue, and the odiousness of vice. No—no—this is not enough. Let us bring him to feel his guiltiness and danger before God, and when he has come to realize that he is lost, keep him from every false trust, until he finds rest at the foot of the cross.

During revivals it not unfrequently happens that zealous laymen are too ready to give their advice to awakened sinners, taking upon themselves a task which their minister ought to know how to perform better than any other person. They often give counsel which confuses the mind of the enquirer, if they do not lead him fatally astray. It is as if several physicians were to prescribe for the same patient.

In seasons of religious apathy the opposite fault commonly prevails. Then professors are continually rolling the responsibility of the duty upon one another, so that it is allowed to rest upon none. They are so tenacious of points of precedence, that, while they are adjusting them, the soul to be saved has passed to its account. It is somewhere stated, that the fire-maker of the court of Philip the Third of Spain one day kindled so great a fire that the monarch, who was seated by the fireside, was nearly suffocated with heat. His dignity would not suffer him to rise from the chair; the domestics could not presume to enter the apartment, because it was against the etiquette. At length the Marquis de Pota appeared, and the king ordered him to damp the fires; but he excused himself, alleging that he was forbidden by the etiquette to perform such a function, for which the Duke d'Usseda ought to be called upon, as it was his business. The duke was gone out, the fire burned fiercer, and the king endured it rather than derogate from his dignity. It heated his blood to such a degree that an erysipelas of the head appeared the next day, which, succeeded by a violent fever, carried him off in the twenty-fourth year of his age. This conduct of the king's attendants finds a parallel in that of many a professor. Is he a parent and begins to question whether he has neglected the religious instruction and admonition of his son? He straightway decides that this is more properly the duty of his pastor, or his chaplain, or his wife, or the boy's tutor; while those to whom he tacitly resigns the office, as tacitly shift the responsibility upon one another. Is he a new convert, beginning to feel that he ought to warn his former companions? He soon lays his conscience to rest with the recollection that the individual has a pious parent, other relative, or pious companion, more intimate than himself, who, it is to be presumed, will faithfully execute the task. If we except procrastination, there is no habit that is accessory to the loss of so many souls as this kind of deference.

He who guides the anxious sinner must be careful not to forestall the work of the Holy Spirit, or, by officious kindness, transfer the sinner's reliance from the Spirit to the wisdom of man. When "the still small voice" is whispering to the inquiring soul, it becomes even a prophet to wrap his face in his mantle, and listen in reverential silence.

In endeavoring to find out a person's moral and religious state, let your questions be kind and respectful—not too familiar, yet not too formal. It is not necessary to know one's whole history at the outset: some facts will discover themselves as you go on. Ascertain what are his purposes with respect to religion. If he is undecided or dilatory, bring him, if possible, to form a resolution. If you cannot induce him to do this, you ought to show him that such a refusal forbids his cherishing any hope of salvation.

Urge him to forsake everything that is unfavorable to serious self-inquiry, or to the operations of grace and truth upon his heart. Find out what particular sin keeps him from repentance, and insist on his abandoning it immediately.

It is not enough that he convince you that he would *like* to be saved; he should satisfy you that he *chooses* to be saved, and to use the means of his rescue. If he refuses the offer of eternal life, in that very act he chooses to go on in sin, and God regards this to be his decision. Every new neglect of the Gospel invitation is set down in the records of eternity, as a fresh rejection of Christ. Wishes and hopes are of less account than purposes and actions.

When the awakened sinner complains of doubt, fear, and difficulty, he should understand that his troubles arise from resisting the Holy Spirit. Remind him that he is a free agent, and that his own obstinacy and aversion of will is the great obstacle in the way of his reconciliation.

When the sinner refuses to submit to the divine will on the plea of insensibility, you should bring him to look not at his *feelings*, but at his *moral condition* in the sight of God, and to perceive that his contentment or unconcern does not lessen his guilt and danger, nor his being on easy terms with himself cool God's anger towards him.

The inquirer should not at first occupy himself with the question whether he is a *child of God*, but whether he has a disposition to forsake everything in his heart or life which is opposed to the divine law, and he should also be exhorted rather to the immediate performance of duty than to direct efforts to obtain *an assurance of pardon*. Most sinners are looking for the joy and peace which are the results of submissions, before they submit. They desire an evidence that Christ has received them before they have given themselves to Him; at least they are unwilling to repent and believe, and then *wait for* tokens of their acceptance.

It is possible to speak to the sinner with such an air and tone as if you spoke by virtue of your own authority, and as if he had offended you rather than the Almighty. Yet, when the demands of God's law are pressed upon his conscience by another, and the sinner is troubled, we must not take sides with him by apologizing for his sins, or by opening to him the arms of a blind sympathy and fondness.

Do not burden the mind with too much talk, nor distract it with too great a variety at once. Direct and discriminating addresses are to be preferred to general and rambling remarks. Hence, as we before said, too many persons should not converse by turns with the same individual.

Take care that when a serious impression has been made, it be not marred or effaced by after-thoughts. Cast not about you for forcible and memorable last words. Rather look to the effect of what you are saying, and then you will easily decide when to have done.

Inquirers are prone to make a merit of prayer, repentance, reading the scriptures, going to church, and the like; or this one places undue reliance on man for guidance and relief, while that one in his distress cannot rest anywhere, but like the unclean spirit, wanders through dry places, seeking rest and finding none, at the same time, perhaps, presuming that God is pleased with his restlessness. Such should be convinced that the Saviour is the only refuge and hope. Another flatters himself that he is *in the way* of obtaining a reconciliation, so long as he is attentive to the means of grace. Perhaps his friends have advised him to "wait at the pool of the ordinances." Now, though the means of grace are not to be spoken against, those inquirers who use them contentedly, and trust in waiting and seeking, will never obtain what they are professedly in quest of; in fact, they are not much concerned whether they do or not. They have taken this method of amusing their souls, and soothing their convictions of sin, and excusing themselves from immediate repentance. The sacred scriptures warrant no preparatory delays. Their language is, "Behold now is the accepted time; behold now is the day of salvation."

Some injudicious advisers endeavor to administer comfort to the inquirer before he is prepared for it. They heal the hurt slightly by healing it too soon. It is dangerous to set ourselves to persuade him that it is well with him, and that he has reason to be of good cheer, before he has found the Redeemer. If we proceed with such an one as if he were already regenerated, we run the risk of leading him to mistake fleeting emotions for renewed affections. The Divine Spirit and the Oracles of God will, in sufficient time, work assurance and quietness. It is one thing, however, to establish him in a blind confidence of his renewal, and quite another to strengthen his trust and hope in the Lord Christ. We must, of course, repeat the promises to the desponding. And when a sinner complains that his moral probation is at an end, that the Holy Spirit has forsaken him, or that he has committed the unpardonable sin, then it is high time to convince him that he misinterprets his convictions; then he ought to know that if he were deserted by the Holy Spirit, or smitten with judicial blindness, he would in all likelihood be free from anxiety with respect to his salvation.

It is especially desirable that the awakened sinner be allowed time for secret communion with God and his own heart. We must not at this stage of his experience keep his mind so fully occupied with public and social worship, or with hearing counsels and exhortations, as to leave him no leisure for private devotion.

In religious interviews we often have to encounter,

at the outset, objections which betray bigotry, prejudice, or a superficial knowledge of religion. When we are met with absurd or malicious charges against some doctrine, practice, denomination, or ourselves, it will be wise, in general, to waive, in a respectful and good-humored manner, the consideration of all objections, or yield to whatever force they may have, and attempt no vindication of our character, or our particular opinions, but proceed at once with a direct application to the objector's conscience. Sinners often endeavor to keep clear of a searching exhortation, by tempting the exhorter to enter the lists with them on some speculative question. Perhaps they make their objections and difficulties an apology for a continuance in sin, or resort to them in self-defence, or to make a display of their intellect. When any one attacks a doctrine on the ground of its unreasonableness, at the same time admitting that it is taught by the sacred scriptures, we do well to show him that he mistakes the parties involved in the controversy; that he is impeaching divine wisdom and goodness. We may adopt the language of the Apostle: "Nay, but oh man, who art thou that repliest against God."

We should recommend to the inquiring sinner, not merely God the Father, but especially "God in Christ." The human mind, especially the unrenewed mind, can form no very intelligible or attractive view of the unembodied Jehovah; but it is more easily brought into sympathy with the Lord Jesus Christ—the incarnate God. When the Divine Being took upon himself human nature, he came nearer the sinner than he could otherwise have been brought by symbols and descriptions. Our blessed Master has anticipated a work which would have been too hard for any of his servants to perform. By appearing as Immanuel, in a two-fold nature, by becoming "God with us," he has, in some sense, returned from his banishment, and re-enthroning Himself among his revolted subjects, he offers a free and full pardon to all who choose to return to loyalty. We are required not to ascend into heaven to bring God down to earth, but now that he has already come among us, to bring sinners to his feet. Those who talk merely of one uncreated Being inhabiting eternity, cannot bring Him nearer the sinner than the third heaven. Whatever divinity they may bring him, in imagination, to enthrone *in heaven*, they leave him literally "without God *in the world*."

Nor should we fail to remind the sinner, that he lives in the dispensation of the Holy Spirit, and that he is resisting not only the calls of his own conscience, but the convictions wrought in his mind by this Divine Person. When he pleads inability to feel or act as he ought, let us tell him that the Holy Spirit is freely offered to them that ask His aid. "If ye, being evil, know how to give good gifts unto your children, how much more shall your heavenly Father give the Holy Spirit to them that ask him." From the evangelical doctrine of the Holy Spirit, may be drawn motives at once the most admonitory and the most encouraging—admonitory to him who grieves, or resists, or blasphemes the Spirit—encouraging to him who is convinced of his native weakness, and is yielding to doubt, fear, or despair. We should also speak of the connection of His offices with the work of atonement. To talk of the Saviour without making mention of the regenerating Spirit, were to leave the heavy-laden pilgrim in sight of the Cross, without the help of the invisible Hand which can unloose the burden from his shoulders.

CHAPTER VI.

RELIGIOUS CONVERSATIONS WITH PREJUDICED PERSONS.

It was a remarkable feature in the primitive churches, that their polity, forms of worship, and all their operations, were so simple as to create the fewest possible prejudices against them, and to overcome many that already existed. All observation teaches that the minds of men are more easily inflamed against some trifling peculiarities of an institution which is newly introduced,—peculiarities that are opposed to the existing order of things,—than against peculiarities of greater consequence, which common minds are less competent judges of, and which are not at war with their habits and customs. In this view we see the wisdom of the Divine Founder of the church, in instituting no other ministry, ordinances, and government, than were absolutely necessary to her existence and enlargement in the first and every succeeding age. The absence of rituals, liturgies, and all appendages of art, left her at liberty to adapt herself in non-essentials to the customs of the people among whom she should be introduced. Had all her externals been at first unalterably fixed, they could not have been admitted along with her into the various nations of the earth without the greatest opposition; or if not opposition, without a resort to artifice. And it deserves to be deeply graven on our minds, that all unalterable forms and ceremonials that are innovations on apostolic simplicity, are not only calculated to foster hypocrisy in those who practise them, but also double-dealing in those who would make proselytes to them.

But what connection have these remarks with the subject under consideration? Unless we are greatly mistaken, they show the importance of believing and practising, as essential parts of our religion, only what is taught by the Bible, in order to prevent or overcome those prejudices which would hinder the hearty reception of the gospel. He who is wedded to a particular ritual, impresses the commonalty with the notion that he believes these to be necessary parts of the Christian religion. Being first stumbled at these extraneous rites, they are prepared to stumble again at the all-important doctrines which are connected with, and consequently confounded with them. The same holds true of those who advocate strange, fanciful, or superstitious tenets respecting any of the mysteries of the gospel. The Christian, therefore, who is intent upon the salvation of sinners, should, in his conversations with them, keep aloof from his own peculiar views, his speculative questions in theology, and all his opinions respecting religion, that are not clearly warranted by the word of God. Such a course will keep him clear of a great deal of fruitless contention about inferior matters: it will also save him from incurring the guilt of allowing his own speculations to take the precedency of saving knowledge, and of amusing with trifles those who ought to be striving to secure the grace of immortality.

These precautions should be observed by those who would be well prepared to meet the hostile feelings that are arrayed against true religion. And our success in managing them will depend quite as much on our known character and creed, as on our wisdom and address. Some suppose that prejudices cannot be overcome by mere direct argument. Swift observes, "reasoning will never make a man correct an ill opinion, which by reasoning he never acquired." This opinion of Swift is not quite conclusive. Would it be fair to argue in what seems an equivalent fashion: "Medicine cannot expel a disease that was never contracted by the use of medicine"? Men may, and frequently do, relinquish prejudices, formed and cherished because they never reasoned, and relinquished them as soon as they began to do so. On the other hand, we are not to suppose, because a prejudice has been formed by education, habit, interest, or affection, and admitted without examination, that it is therefore erroneous or pernicious. It may safely be averred that the prejudices of the generality in Christian countries are on the side of the gospel; a circumstance which gives the advocates of evangelical principles a great advantage. But though the prepossessions of those with whom we converse are perhaps in favor of the Christian religion as a general system, they may nevertheless be opposed to the specific doctrine we wish to advance, if not to every distinguishing principle of our religion, when it is separately offered to their consideration. With a view to reconcile these and other prejudiced persons to evangelical doctrines and duties, it may be proper to adopt one or more of the following expedients:

It is in some cases advisable to leave undisturbed prejudices that are hurtful, for the purpose of more easily inculcating those truths which will eventually remove them. Our Lord and his apostles found the world strongly intrenched in errors and abuses, and instead of directly assaulting their muniments, they wisely drew them out of them, as the hosts of Israel by a retreat led the defenders of Gibeah without the walls, and then set the city on fire. When we meet with a person who belongs to a heretical sect, we should not stigmatize him with reproachful epithets, nor assail his whole creed, but, passing by his peculiar opinions, meet him as a Christian on common ground, and then bring him to admit that which, if admitted, will disarm, if not destroy, his prejudices. When our opponent venerates some great human authority, we should not, in all cases, stay to call it in question, but respectfully taking leave of characters and leaders, we should conduct him to the divine testimonies, and convince him that his positions are unsound: this done, his revered master will be forsaken of course. When the person expresses strong predilections for particular phrases or formulas, which we cannot prevail on him to disuse, we should endeavor to settle him in just notions of the doctrine which he misnames. We should choose to leave men in quiet possession of their party names and shibboleths, rather than expose them to the shipwreck of their best hopes, while they are driven from the truth in the obstinate defence of a word. The mass of mankind will sooner resign things than names; and some may be found in almost every sect or party, who, though they were long ago convinced of the heterodoxy of some part of its creed, choose still to cleave to its fellowship and its forms.

We may sometimes bring people to abandon a prejudice by engaging their thoughts with a virtue which is the antagonist of the vice which first warped the judgment, or by leading them from a trifling subject to one of importance, as from a speculative to a practical question: above all, from a question which genders strife to one which pacifies and liberalizes the mind. Once lured out of the sterile pass for which they are contending, up to some eminence whence they can behold broad and fruitful fields, they will blush for their folly in wasting their noble energies on mere futilities. An effort of the kind is the more laudable inasmuch as it aims at goodness of heart and devotedness of life, and not merely at soundness of faith.

A person can be led slowly, gently, and circuitously, to receive those truths which, if they were directly pressed upon his mind, he would sturdily stand out against. It were judicious, therefore, to unfold the truth to one strongly set against it by slow degrees, observing its effects upon him, dropping the subject before it begins to call out opposition, and adverting to the subject at intervals, when the person is in a calm and yielding mood.

When a person of winning wisdom perceives that the one to be conciliated dislikes every kind of opposition, and that his delusion proceeds more from ignorance than obstinacy, he will avoid open disputation, and set himself to *explain* and *recommend* the doctrines to which he would gain proselytes. He will attend to the counsel Paul gave to Timothy, when he directed him not to strive, but in meekness to *instruct* those that oppose themselves. By using the expository and didactic, rather than the controversial tone, he will prevent, or at least allay, irritated feelings—cause those who no longer see themselves attacked, to desist from opposition, and, by enlightening their minds, bring them to yield up what, for lack of knowledge, they before maintained. Yet he will not instruct in a dictatorial or upbraiding manner, but humbly and submissively, not pretending to superior abilities, but showing a deference for the judgment of others. In stating facts and quoting, he will presume not so much to inform his opponent as to remind him of things he is already supposed to know. He will pass over in silence, or touch lightly on the objections made to his own faith, and when forced to say anything on the *doctrines* of his opponent, he will not always formally confute his *arguments*, but will chiefly reason against the system those arguments were framed to support; for he knows that his opponent will allow him to attack his faith as a mass in preference to his method of defending it. In this way he will, perhaps, convince his erring friend without exposing him to the mortification of feeling himself to be confuted; and instead of laboring to show him how far he is from the truth, he will furnish him with the facts and arguments by the help of which he will be able to arrive at the truth for himself.

It is another useful rule, to avail ourselves of a prejudice or erroneous opinion of another, in order to convince him of a truth by reasoning with him on his own principles. It was in this method that Christ and his apostles argued with the Jews by citing their own sacred books, and that Paul especially, reasoned with the Greeks by quoting their own poet, and reminding them of their habitual worship of divinities. It is one of Lord Bacon's maxims that "Nature can be controlled only by submitting to her laws;"[12] and this is true, not only of the material world in general, but of human nature in particular. Accordingly, we may use for illustration popular opinions, which, though they are wholly or in part without foundation in reason, commend us to the hearing of common minds; Christ did so when he spoke of the unclean spirit going out of a man and wandering in dry places. We may also use their own venerated names to contradict them; and when they oppose us with quotations, silence them, if needs be, by quoting their own authorities more fully and fairly than they have done. We should not always make use of such arguments as are of most weight with ourselves, but such as will be most convincing to the persons we address, careful, however, ever to use those only which are sound.

When any one harbors a prejudice against our religion which comes of a dislike for the behavior of some of its professors, we shall best dislodge it by carefully avoiding the behavior of which he complains, and especially by studying to win his affection and respect by uniform kindness, and when

[12] "Naturæ non imperatur nisi parendo."—*Nov. Org.*

there is occasion for it, by acts of generosity and self-devotion; taking care to inspire him with a gratitude which is not chilled by a sense of dependence upon or of obligation to us. We do well to postpone all applications to his sense of duty, till we have gained his confidence and regard, when, perhaps, the warmth of friendship may have already melted his hardness not only towards the doctrines of the Gospel, but also towards its professors.

When a prejudice stands directly in the way of the furtherance of the truth, we must neither overlook nor humor it. There are prepossessions which defy all the milder arts of reasoning to manage them. By whatever avenue we approach them, they come forth to meet us. Prejudices of this class are chiefly those which have their source in the corruption and perversity of the heart, and are fostered by earthly interests. Nothing short of a powerful appeal to the understanding and the conscience can put them to flight. The biased person must be brought to distinguish between the suggestions of a corrupt heart and the dictates of conscience, the calls of present interest and the claims of moral obligation, the authority of human opinion and the command of God. And besides being brought to make a difference between these opposite principles, he should be persuaded to forswear the sway of the former and submit to the dominion of the latter. We must not, however, charge him with prejudice in plain terms. He will hardly be made to believe himself capable of a weakness that is so dishonorable to his mind; and if he were convinced of it he would be reluctant to confess it. He will not be likely to part with it the sooner for our having cast it in his teeth. Little is ever gained by making bare assertions, however true, that are not believed by the hearers, or of accusing a person of sins before his conscience is prepared to upbraid him with them.

And it is worth remarking upon this whole subject, that these prudential rules will be of little use to those who do not bring to the task a sweet and benignant temper. An exacting, dogmatical, or scornful carriage towards the erring, is apt to drive them only the more deeply into darkness and corruption; whereas the expression of a kind and complacent spirit, though it should not be directed by common prudence, will draw them out of the toils of Satan sooner than great prudence if it be not softened and cheered by such a spirit.[13]

[13] See "Principles of Courtesy,"—last Chapter.

CHAPTER VIII.

DISCUSSIONS.

Dr. Johnson being asked by a friend whether there had been any conversation at a party from which he had just come, replied, "No, sir; we had *talk* enough but no *conversation;* there was nothing *discussed.*" It was his opinion that the agitation of a subject with a view to elicit truth is alone worthy the name of conversation. Present usage, however, pays little deference to the great moralist and lexicographer, and throws the charitable mantle of the word over even the senseless gabble of triflers and dullards; nay, the most hideous monsters that ever human lips gave birth to. Still, it must be granted that discussion, in its strict sense, is one of the noblest and most useful parts of conversation. The utterances of this Grand Khan of literature, and, for thirty years colloquial dictator in the literary circles of London, as reported by his numerous friends, are mainly of this nature. And he would have set us a good pattern in this kind, had his reason always kept the ascendency of his prejudices; had he oftener taken the side of truth and piety; and had he habitually observed that gentleness of speech which he so well understood and knew how to prize in others.

There are many important questions which a sociable group might be well employed in debating. Yet the usual mode of conducting private discussions is not calculated to afford a great deal of improvement. And the fault lies less in the questions themselves than in the manner of treating them. The bulk of people fancy that instinct teaches them the best method of reasoning, and they enter the lists presuming that nature has armed them at all points, and given them skill sufficient to meet all comers. This delusion, which self-partiality seems to maintain, has kept not a few men from giving due attention to the art of reasoning in the *conversazione*. Trusting to the native merits of the questions discussed, they have not enough considered the best mode of managing them; or engrossing their attention with the unguarded points of the foe, they have overlooked their own. Many a controversy, both in public and private, has been needlessly prolonged by the faults of the disputants themselves. They would fain believe that to have truth on their side, and to support it by sound arguments, are enough to secure a speedy triumph. But they too often deceive themselves. The fact is, that truth is full as much beholden to the disposition and deportment of her advocates as to the soundness of their arguments. Those who go forth into the field of controversy invoking the aid of the furies, provoke their antagonists to call on the same goddesses, while the graces stand aloof to weep over the defeat of the cause to which they could have given the victory.

In colloquial discussions, and in all others indeed, our success or failure will depend not a little on our character and life. We cannot hope to convert to our principles those who inwardly despise our practice; on the contrary, a consistent Christian life will give a weight to our arguments which nothing else can.

Besides taking care to form a good general character, we should endeavor to enter the lists open to conviction. This will greatly aid us in the search after truth, and prepare our opponents to receive it when found. They will ever carry a shield as broad as our own; if we show by our tone and air that we do not expect to hear from them anything new, unanswerable, or convincing, we shall only raise the same spirit in them.

We should also conduct our part of the discussion with perfect candor and fairness. For though a resort to quibbles and tricks will now and then give us a momentary advantage, it generally results in a permanent injury to ourselves and to our cause. The world is slow to believe that truth can be at all related to mean artifice. We must likewise drive from our hearts bigotry and party spirit, being ever more zealous for gospel truth than for our articles of faith, or for our particular tenets. Whoever calmly watches the motions of his own spirit, will often be mortified to find that his earnestness in the defence of any point proceeds almost as much from a fondness for his own opinions as from a zeal for the truth. We never lose anything by conceding to our opponent the merit of sincerity and ability; at any rate we should argue with him on the supposition that he is not deficient in either. Nor should we be quick to discern any immaterial defects in our opponent or his argument. Since those who enter the lists with us are ever supposed to be our equals, if we succeed in lessening their reputation, we also, in an equal degree, diminish our own.

Let us not, at the same time, affect that large charity which overlooks essential defects in religious opinions, and discovers a peculiar excellence in each sect which throws its errors quite into the shade. For one, nothing could induce me to adore those pictures of the Virgin Mary which represent her sheltering beneath her enormous cloak, popes, harlots, monks, nuns, thieves, murderers, and what not. Nor could I ever highly value the favors of that liberality which can enclose the motley crowd in her large embrace, and whose eyes are so dim as to mistake all for her favorites. Such sentiments are commonly held by those who are equally indifferent to all religions. If our opponent is a man of sense, he must respect us for having a definite belief, and for a sincere and intelligent adherence to it. We shall forfeit his respect by excusing ourselves from the discussion of a subject which he considers important, on the plea that it is unessential or insignificant. He will be apt to understand such an excuse as an intimation that we can at once perceive the trivialness of the subject on which he is expending so much fruitless effort. To recoil from the question with affected disdain, is sure to make him suspect either our sincerity or our judgment.

We ought surely to cultivate the charity that thinketh no evil, but we should beware of boasting of our charity to our opponent in religious debate. Paul says that this virtue "vaunteth not itself." When our charity has been put to the test, then it will best appear to what degree we are swayed by its power. How often do we hear language like the following: "For my part I think all denominations should love one another, overlook one another's faults, and respect one another's conscientious differences. I love all Christians — but I cannot bear those who style their own denomination *the* church, and those who exclude from the Lord's Supper all who do not agree with them in faith and practice. Neither do I like those who are forever contending for their sectarian tenets. I hate those who claim for their own sect the most scriptural creed." These generous persons do not stay to think that there can be no pretension more extravagant than that of having reached the perfection of charity—that coy grace which the most advanced Christian confesses that he has not yet overtaken. They also fail to reflect that in holding up to detestation the uncharitableness of others, they do but the more proclaim their own. And if, as not often happens, these praisers of charity can be consistent with themselves while they are in company, they are sure, in private, to show that there is as much of the gall of bitterness in their composition, as there before appeared to be of the milk of human kindness. They advocate the cause of charity that they may be thought to be blessed with a large share of this virtue, when in truth they are in beggerly want of it, and their conduct calls for the protection of its cloak; but this is a delicate subject to handle, and we leave it, lest we betray this vice in the very attempt to describe it.

After inquiring whether we ourselves have proper

qualifications for the discussion of a question, we should consider the character of our opponent or respondent. We should not consent to enter into a debate with one who is ignorant of the question, or an unskilful reasoner, preoccupied or volatile—who is very inferior to us in ability or attainments; for as we must begin with the advantage, our victory might be thought to be owing more to the weakness of our adversary than the merits of our cause; and should we be worsted by such a person, it would be discreditable either to the truth or ourselves, perhaps to both—who is proud, overbearing, or frequently interrupts us, or tries to silence us by clamor or laughter—who usually begins by boasting of his familiarity with the whole question—who talks to show to bystanders his knowledge, his argumentative skill, or his volubility—who is positive, tenacious of his own opinions, or never retires before the most powerful onsets of argument—who has a hasty or an irritable temper, is easily insulted, or is accustomed to put wrong constructions on the remarks of another—who is accustomed to quibble, whiffle, or wander from the question—who uses sophistry when sound reasoning fails, and resorts to anything for self-defence—who aims to be witty, and deals in jibes, jokes, and puns—who betrays an irreverence for the sacred scriptures, allows little or no weight to their testimony, and garbles and wrests them—who, when silenced, conceals his defeat by accusing us of trifling with sacred things, shocking his moral sensibilities, at the same time shrugging his shoulders, crossing himself, and stopping his ears against what he calls blasphemies—who is unwilling to allow another to finish his remarks, but endeavors to engross the time himself, and listens with impatience to our arguments. Yet whenever we are unwittingly drawn into a debate with any one of the character just mentioned, we should retire from it in good humor, without airs of disdain, or words of reproach. "But," it will be said, "if I must not debate with persons of this description, I cannot debate with any; for where is the arguer who has not one or more of the faults you mention?" In reply, we admit that it is not in itself morally wrong to enter the lists with such people; often quite the contrary: remember, however, that if *you* betray any of these faults, you have no right to complain when your opponent faces about and leaves the field without asking quarter.

It is perhaps worth while here to inquire whether women may properly take part in conversational discussions. Some women uniformily excuse themselves from arguing, and some men studiously keep aloof from controversial topics in talking with them. It appears, however, that our Lord considered it becoming to discuss at least *religious* questions with them. His interviews with the woman of Syrophenecia and with the Samaritaness, recognize their right to take part in an argument. He would not, it is certain, encourage a contentious spirit in them any more than in man. The deference and subjection to their husbands which the apostles require of them, do not accord with a controversial tone. Nothing is more unseemly than the conduct of those women who enter the noisy arena of political and theological combat, presenting a spectacle not unlike that which was anciently witnessed in the Island of Mona, where women fought in defence of Druidical rites, by the side of the priests. Should Christianity number no more defenders than idolatry had on that occasion, it would be heroism for them to show an equal zeal in its behalf: but as our faith is likely to have many pugnacious defenders for a good while to come, it is their part to seek, by a calm and conciliatory behavior, to assauge polemical fierceness and tumult. This they may do, and often have done, by acting as mediators in angry debates, by kindly intimating the best manner of unravelling knotty questions, and by setting a pattern of the spirit in which a rude opponent ought to be treated. In moral gifts for argumentation they are manifestly superior to men. Their peculiar patience and delicate regard for the feelings of others, often greatly assist in the settlement of questions which take a strong hold on human passions and interests. They are, equally with men, obligated to cultivate the reasoning powers, and it is their duty occasionally to take part in discussions. Still they have a higher office in relation to the truth than that of mere debaters, incessantly harping on some vexed point, and regularly disputing every assertion that one happens to make. It is theirs to allow their greater kindness, their holier conscience, and their nicer intuition of the becoming, to speak in the ear of the misguided wrangler, and to aid in the disposal of questions in which these feelings are often more efficient than argument. It is theirs to utter divine oracles, which are meditated in the sequestered retreats of home, remote from the blinding passions and loud contentions of the outer world. It was when Belshazzar and his nobles, and his astrologers, and his soothsayers were all confounded and dismayed by the writing on the wall, that the queen came to the relief of their despair, and made honorable mention of Daniel as one who could interpret the appalling words. Even the dream of Pilate's wife, as she was slumbering in a retired apartment of the palace, dictated more of reason and more of justice than were to be found in the deliberations of Pilate, Annas, Caiaphas, the chief priests, Pharisees, lawyers, and the undistinguished mob.

The gentle sex do, and ought to, despise those men who disown their reasoning faculties, whenever they talk with them. Let not gentlemen think that ladies are soft in thought because they are soft in behavior and tone. It is no compliment to them to affect their effeminacy. Let gentlemen consider that the natural strength and roughness of their sex ought to appear in their thoughts, style, and voice. Your pretty fop is ever telling the ladies that he cannot differ from them; it will go hard but he will be of their opinion. If he ever dissents from an assertion, it is contrary to one to which he gave his assent a little while ago. He regrets that he cannot possibly contradict himself, otherwise he would never be so rude as to except in the slightest degree to madam's proposition. By-the-bye, he needs but to talk two minutes longer to retract his first opinion, and agree with madam most cordially and absolutely. He cringes and bows at every word she speaks; he would not be positive, not even about his personal identity, if any lady should deny it. Like Launce, he would say, "I am the dog—no, the dog is myself; and I am the dog —oh, the dog is me, and I am myself—ay, so, so."

With respect to the *subjects* of discussion, four important cautions are to be heeded:

1. Never discuss trivial and insignificant questions. It is, to be sure, not always easy to decide what are such, since many questions which, at first thought, appear paltry, are found upon a closer examination to be very important. We are permitted, in colloquy, to treat questions less grave than would become a public controversy.

2. Do not often make principal doctrines and precepts, and admitted duties, matters of dispute. The habit leads us first to question, and then to disbelieve the weightiest testimony, and to a systematic disobedience of known commandments. It brings on scepticism, if indeed it be not an indication that it has already gained some footing in the mind. "He that is too busy in the foundations of a house," says Sir Philip Sidney, "may pull down the whole building about his ears."

3. Avoid speculative questions, that is, such as if decided would serve no practical purpose. Disputes concerning the Millennium, and others of the kind, seldom administer to our improvement.

4. Let not incomprehensible and mysterious truths be made subjects of inquiry. There are some parts of divine revelation which, though evidently not contrary to reason, are out of its province. Controversies as to the mode of the Divine existence in the Trinity, and as to the reconciliation of the purposes

of God with the free agency of man, may be referred to this class.

By the agitation of such questions little has been or can be gained for our temper, our information, or for the furtherance of Christian truth. The most pernicious questions are those which belong to the first class and to the last—the first, because as the history of all controversies attests, contentions are bitter in proportion to their unimportance—the last, because it is impossible to tell where those controversies will end, which begin without proof, just as those wars are apt to be long which have no definite object; for it is altogether uncertain what will purchase a peace.

Discussers should begin by ascertaining whether they can agree on some fundamental principle, or on any conditions as to the kind of testimony to be admitted; as whether the sacred scriptures, or the writings of the fathers, or decrees of councils, or tradition, are to be allowed as proof.

When they have agreed to take some common ground, let them inquire how near they can approach each other. Let them lessen the distance between them by mutual concession, ascertaining the points of agreement rather than of difference. They should not suppose, because they differ on one point, they must needs differ upon all. Those who are ignorant of one another's opinions, generally suppose themselves to disagree far more widely than they do in reality.

As another preliminary, the meaning to be attached to the words and phrases used should be settled between the opponent and respondent. Doubtful or ambiguous words or terms should be defined or rejected. In many cases, where the meaning of the question is determined and understood, little, if anything, will remain to be done. Whereas those who hastily enter upon the discussion of a question which they do not understand, each perhaps inwardly blessing his own superior acumen, and emulous of victory, after having exhausted breath and argument conclude to go back to ascertain the meaning of the question, and find, to their inexpressible mortification, that they have been engaged in a mere logomachy—not a moral, but a verbal contest, that some ambiguous word, viewed from different points, was the sole cause of so much strife.

Besides settling the signification of words and phrases, the exact point of inquiry should be fixed. It should be mutually understood whether the question is to be discussed in a limited or a general sense; and when the question is qualified, there should be a strict and honorable adherence to it. A neglect to define positions occasions confusion and ill-will. Some who leave the original ground and retreat to a different question, resort to this method of showing their inability to defend their post and of begging a truce.

He who takes a side which he at length finds not to be tenable, should frankly confess his inability to maintain it. Let him not think it an exposure of his own weakness; it will be received as the indication both of his candor and of his discrimination. If he still persists in arguing a question which the company deem settled, he exposes himself to the imputation either of disingenuousness or of obtuseness. He who can cheerfully and unreservedly own himself confuted, has won a more glorious victory than his confuter.

There is nothing helps to confirm men in errors like the fear that the renunciation of them will be received with upbraidings by their own party, and with exultation by the opposite party. Were the erring kindly and respectfully welcomed back to truth, they would oftener return. Where there is a whole party ready to break out into a contemptuous laugh at one's recantation, he is strongly tempted to withhold it. We should conquer without seeming to do so, and account it enough that the opponent feels, without confessing, his defeat; but rather divert him from it by passing to another subject even though it should be less important. When Augustus, king of Poland, was brought into the tent of Charles XII., of Sweden, who had just deprived him of his crown, Charles turned the conversation wholly on his jack-boots, telling Augustus that he had not laid them aside for six years, except when he went to bed. Let this incident teach the victorious debater how to save his vanquished opponent from needless mortification.

Carneades is said to have resolved never to defend what he could not prove, nor attack what he could not overthrow—a wise resolution, but more applicable to public than private discussions. In a circle of friends where we ought to make it our aim to examine and correct our opinions, we are at liberty to put forth and defend a principle which we have but superficially examined, and on which we wish the views of others, that we may have their help in settling our minds in just conclusions.

Almost any other species of trifling is more allowable than that of discussing trite and useless questions. As we have already remarked, there is in conversation a strong inducement to commit this folly, inasmuch as it is understood that many subjects may be handled here which would not be dignified enough for other occasions, and that the mind may here abandon itself to its lighter movements. Nevertheless, a wise man will take care how he warmly espouses what it would be as ignominious to contend for as to lose. Grecian fable tells us that when Hercules went down into the lower world, the shade of Medusa confronted him; he was about to draw his sword upon her, when Mercury reminded him that she was a mere phantom; whereupon he returned his sword to its scabbard. Even Hercules had no strength to waste on a shadow.

But when a detrimental opinion, though absurd and trivial in itself, is likely to gain currency from the earnestness and pretension of its advocates, it then becomes our duty to set it in a proper light. The champion of infidelity and the vilifier of virtue may, when his own character is considered, be too contemptible to deserve notice; but when he is evidently corrupting the minds of the ignorant and unsuspecting, he ought to be withstood and rebuked. In silencing such persons we must proceed according to the lights and shades of circumstances. Solomon points out both the Scylla and the Charybdis of which he would have us steer clear. On the one hand we have, "Answer a fool according to his folly, lest he be wise in his own conceit:" on the other, "Answer not a fool according to his folly, lest thou be like unto him." The first direction is applicable to cases where the pride or vanity of an irreligious person calls aloud for rebuke. If he is impudent and rude, we are to treat him with severity; if positive, we must be equally positive, and not be tender of the feelings of one who is destitute of the sensibilities of the human kind. By a satirical imitation of his own language, we are to show him to himself as in a mirror; by copying his air, tone, or mode of reasoning, we are to make him ashamed for his corruption and shallowness. By the second direction we are to understand that it is not our duty to correct an ungodly or an immoral person in his own language when it is profane or obscene, or to reply at all when his speech or behavior is of a description to render him undeserving of the intercourse of his species, or when a reply would be a self-degradation or an infringement of Christian gravity. How far we may go in reply is shown in the well-known story which is told about the salutations that passed between Dr. Barrow and Lord Rochester.

To make this nice point more clear, we remark, that the two precepts are to be reconciled thus: within limits, meet a man on his own ground; beyond, stir not a foot to follow him. These limits are to be found—*first*, in the *topic*, and *secondly*, in the *tone* and *state of mind*. They may be illustrated by our Lord's dealing with cavillers of his own nation. He gave them the miracles they needed—miracles various, wondrous and numerous; but he refused the miracles, sneeringly and captiously asked. He had given them John the Baptist to mourn and had sent apostles to pipe. They heeded neither. He would not, therefore, fiddle to scepticism and profligacy, and hence he wrought no miracles when brought before Herod and Pilate.

There is in the world many a group of persons confidently contending about matters of which all are wofully ignorant, darkening counsel with words without knowledge, or speaking evil of things they understand not. The least-informed persons pronounce on the subject with "a frightful degree of certainty," as Fontenelle would phrase it, and each is talkative on great affairs in pretty exact proportion to his ignorance of them. Let a man of information enter the crowd, and his presence soon brings them to a pause. "I have heard," says Jeremy Taylor, "that all the noise and pratings of the pool, the croaking of frogs and toads, is hushed and appeased upon the instant of bringing upon them the light of a candle or torch." Jefferson says, that in the Provincial Congress neither Washington nor Franklin spoke until the debate was well-nigh ended; then but for ten minutes, and only on the main points. It was John Somers' brief speech at the trial of the seven bishops, that fixed his high character as a lawyer. Howbeit, these are better parliamentary than conversational examples. Whoever, in colloquial debates, is addicted to enlightening the ignorance of the talkers, or unasked, to taking upon himself to decide every question, instead of rising to eminence in esteem of the company, may some day find himself sprawling on the floor, and hear the bystanders whom he asks to call in the police, quoting to him:

"There are a sort of men whose visages
Do cream and mantle like a standing pond,
And do a willful stillness entertain,

With purpose to be dress'd in an opinion
Of wisdom, gravity, profound conceit;
As who would say, 'I am Sir Oracle,
And when I ope my lips, let no dog bark.'"

A man of prudence does not hastily determine the merits of a question, or speak on it in a dogmatic tone. By keeping close a half-formed opinion, he is at liberty, on further deliberation, to alter it before a final and avowed decision. He does not crave the responsibility of propagating immature notions, nor the honor of retracting them.

Let your debates be marked by good humor and calmness. If you do not allow your mind to be ruffled when you are overcome in a discussion, you will keep yourself from being in all respects a vanquished man. It is a too common practice for debaters to aim at throwing each other off their guard, by provoking their resentment. This is Cain-like. He who would give his arguments weight with his opponents, and bring them over to his own principles, will endeavor to conciliate their good-will, and preserve, as far as he can, the serenity of their minds; for he knows that if their anger is roused, they are incapable of weighing his arguments. To attain this end he should be their friend, and persuade them to embrace his views, not for his benefit but for their own. When will the generality of men learn that there is a difference between a moral and a martial combat—that in the former, men meet as friends, in the latter, as enemies—that the proper object of the one is to discover truth, and that of the other to redress wrongs. And when will they learn that the weapons that prevail in the one are powerless in the other?

Seldom allude to denominations, sects, and theological schools, and their founders, but confine your citations to doctrines and principles. Speak not of men but of opinions, not of names but of things. We are aware that to follow this rule is often difficult, and sometimes inexpedient. Could debaters, like the mythical nymph Echo, be changed into a mere voice, and dispute unseen, they might easily keep aloof from personalities. But as passion is often mistaken for reason, and the larger share of what pass for principles, are nothing other than prejudices, it is very often hard to keep characters and creeds apart. It should be our care not to use the phrases or the technical terms which characterize sects or denominations, and not to charge with heresy or impiety all who do not choose to employ the same phraseology. When we are driven to mention names, we do well to cite those of the individuals who first broached the doctrines in question. This will not often offend our opponents, for the generality of men are very ready to disown those to whom they are indebted for their creed. If we impugn a denomination, our opponent may appeal to its numbers, learning, or piety, and we shall provoke his brethren to come to his support, then the colloquy will become like a "faction fight" in an Irish fair, where all the men of the family name must take up the bludgeon.

The most of us are exceedingly tenacious of those opinions, agreeably to which we have long shaped our conduct. In taking ground against us, our opponents have need of great delicacy and prudence, for we consider every attempt to confute us but an attempt to prove that our conduct has been hurtful or unwise; in a word, we are apt to mistake an argument for a rebuke. Hence, in persuading us to change our views, they must not brand our former tenets with vice or folly. After they have won us over to their side, we shall be able to examine the tendency of our former doctrines more impartially.

When a person is supporting one article of a creed, we are to beware of accusing him of receiving all the other articles of it. Perhaps he prefers it in general to any other, and at the same time indignantly disclaims certain articles, or at least certain constructions of them. And when a person broaches a sceptical sentiment, we must not, without due cause, suspect we have before us a monster of the French or German schools of atheism, who cordially accepts all the blasphemies of those schools. Men should not be held responsible for the consequences of their tenets, when they disavow those consequences. But in reasoning, we have a right to show how one tenet hangs by and draws on another.

After our best endeavors to bring others over to our side, we must not wonder how they can differ from us still. We ought to reflect that our own views are as widely at variance with those we once held, as theirs now are with our present opinions, and that future years may greatly modify even these.

An over-earnest defence has harmed many a worthy cause. The common world has thought it must have been a weak point that called for the presence of so strong a guard. Those who are most solidly grounded in their own principles, may often quietly re-examine them, but they very seldom challenge a discussion of them; while those whose faith is not settled on a rock, are in the habit of calling out to every person to come and behold the solidity of their foundation. Still, however, it is one thing to be often called to defend our principles, and a very different thing to be continually challenging others to attack them.

The vital doctrines of the gospel afford the least matter for contention because they are simple and practical. Like air and water they are as transparent as they are useful. It is when the practical truths of revelation—and all are such—are turned into speculations, and treated metaphysically, that they become subjects of unending strife. Every body remembers Milton's description of the lost spirits engaged in theological disputation.

> "Others apart sat on a hill retir'd,
> In thoughts more elevate, and reasoned high
> Of providence, foreknowledge, will and fate,
> Fixed fate, free will, foreknowledge absolute,
> And found no end, in wandering mazes lost."

The poet thought, with great truth, that these questions, as the disobedient understand them, will never, even in the light of eternity, be satisfactorily settled. The truths of scripture were revealed to men not to metaphysicians. They are therein set forth not as they are abstractly, but as all fallen mortals can and ought to view them—practically. These truths have to do with their character, duties, hopes, fears, temporal and eternal welfare. Scarcely any mystery is so obscure that all the faithful, how widely soever they divide on their theoretical opinions respecting it, could not agree as to the lessons and duties it should suggest. When will outcast man believe that the tree of forbidden knowledge is kept by a guard of cherubim, and no longer blind his curious eyes by too near a view of their flashing weapons, but be content to catch distant glimpses of the inaccessible fruit, and to believe in Him, whose incarnation is a mystery which shall solve all others, and move the celestial guard to sheathe their swords, and open again the gates of Eden.

Paltry questions sometimes rise into importance in the eyes of the unthinking, from the earnestness with which they are opposed. The din of contention which was at first heard only among the learned few, at length reaches the ears of the unlettered many, who swell it into the voice of the stormy Atlantic. Either oppose unimportant questions with moderation, or pass them in silence.

In contesting a point about which your opponent shows great feeling, suppress your ardor, if you would enlist bystanders on your side. Your cool manner will command their feelings, and seeing you laboring to suppress your emotions, and giving a plain and unexaggerated view of the subject, they will render you double for all the feeling you have withheld, and fully supply in their own minds the deficiences of your representation.

Generously concede to your opponent all the virtues, talents, and attainments he can claim. Dr. Johnson was opposed to treating an opponent with respect, alleging that as the generality of men cannot judge of reasoning, if you allow your opponent a respectable character, they will think that though you differ from him, you may still be in the wrong. With great deference to so high an authority, and to the practice of multitudes, we must venture humbly to except against such a course. Besides being disingenuous, it is impolitic to traduce your antagonist, more especially when you would reclaim him to truth. When men thus begin to defame their opponents, it is clear they do not mean to make them proselytes ; for they cannot be proud to have such characters in their ranks, at least if they are as bad as they represent them. Our Lord granted to the Scribe that he was not far from the kingdom of God, and Paul admitted to the Athenians that they were very religious, and that they ignorantly worshipped the true God. By an unsparing onslaught you will only rally the friends of your opponent to the vindication of his character, and believing your charges to be unreasonable, they will be easily led to suspect the soundness of your arguments. Candid admissions will prepossess all minds in your favor, provided always that they are not extravagant; if they are, they will be received as satires rather than as compliments. Let not your lamentations over his errors be overwrought. An affectation of compassion will be resented as disguised contempt.

Where no important principle is involved in the name by which a sect styles itself, in talking with a member of it we should call him by that which is least offensive to himself: with a Catholic, say *Catholic* rather than Papist or Romanist; with a Churchman, say *Churchman* rather than Episcopalian; with a Baptist, say *Baptist* instead of Antipædo-Baptist or Anabaptist; with a Unitarian, *Unitarian* rather than Socinian; at the same time where fidelity to Gospel truth exacts it, we may add that we do so in compliance with general usage, though we cannot but think it an unwarrantable concession. Nevertheless *we* should allow others to call *us* or *our* sect by whatever name they please, however improper, unintelligible, or reproachful. We shall best conciliate them by meekly and cheerfully allowing them to choose their own epithets.

The expression of a mere *personal* preference, taste, or feeling, must seldom be contradicted. But *standards of taste* in the fine arts are legitimate matters of discussion, as Sir Joshua Reynolds, La Bruyere, and others maintain. La Bruyere says, "There is a certain point of perfection in art; he that perceives it and likes it, has a right taste; he that perceives it not, and likes what is on either side of it, has a vicious one: so that there is a good and a bad taste, and some reason for disputing about them." But matters of sentiment and taste cannot be discussed profitably, except by cultivated minds whose judgments concerning æsthetics and the fine arts have been formed by much study and reflection. Minds of this description can reason as logically on this as on any other moral question. With them the old maxim, *De gustibus non disputandum* does not hold. But those whose religious connections are the result of sentimentality, will still cleave to them when their reason is convinced of their error. He who attempts to reform them by setting forth the unreasonableness of their preferences, goes about to perform a great undertaking. A person that is charmed with the ceremonies and pageantries of the Church of Rome, and beholds in them all that is beautiful, grand, and awful, cannot be persuaded to embrace the doctrine and ordinances of the evangelical churches by discourses on the simplicity and dignity of their worship. His present choice, so different from that to which we would bring him, declares an incapacity to relish the qualities we commend. The taste that prefers the painted diamond or the essenced rose to these objects in their native purity, is too far gone in degeneracy to be restored without the help of Divine grace. The only way to reason with a person of this sort is to set aside the question of taste altogether, and bring him to discuss the comparative merits of the two systems as decided by the documents of inspiration. But we must not count too much upon argument; nothing short of the transformation of his soul by the Holy Spirit will wholly correct his taste.

The same course is to be pursued in the management of those who choose their church, their creed, and their preacher, just as they do their physician and their costume—because they are in fashion—because those whom they look up to as arbiters of elegance adopt and patronize them. The religion of too many is like that of M. de Grammont, a Marshal of France. Having gone, by order of the king, to visit the minister Morus, who was dangerously ill, the king asked him, on his return, how he found him. The marshal answered: "Sire, I saw him die like a good Huguenot. What I think most to be regretted is, that he died in a religion which is now as unfashionable as a peaked hat." Now any one must perceive how vain would have been an attempt to persuade this courtier to embrace the religion of the Huguenots on the ground that it was more worthy of royal patronage than any other, or on the ground that it deserved to be in good fashion.

Young infidels are not always to be argued with; there is danger of flattering their vanity and self-importance by answering them with grave and labored arguments. If they are our own children or wards, we had better disabuse them of their pestilent doctrines by the use of the rod; for as infidelity is a vice in itself and the parent of many more, seasonable chastisement will teach them in what light they ought to view it. A young man who had dipped into many authors of an infidel turn, and had acquired just enough knowledge to make him a conceited atheist, began to make proselytes in his father's family. His father, who had borne with his dangerous and schismatical opinions some time, heard him one day remark that Carlo, his setting-dog, was as immortal as any of the family, and that for his part he expected to die like a dog. With this the old man started up and cried out; "Then, sir, you shall live like one," and taking his cane in hand cudgelled him out of his system and brought him to more serious reading. Coleridge tells a good anecdote of himself very similar to the above. "I had," says he "one just flogging. When I was about thirteen I went to a shoemaker and begged him to take me as his apprentice. He being an honest man took me to Bowyer, who got into a great rage, knocked me down, and even pushed Crispin rudely out of the room. Bowyer asked me why I had made myself such a fool. To which I answered, that I had a great desire to be a shoemaker, and that I hated the thought of being a clergyman. 'Why so?' said he. 'Because, to tell you the truth, sir, I am an infidel!' For this, without more ado, Bowyer flogged me,—wisely as I think,—soundly as I know. Any whining or sermonizing would have gratified my vanity and confirmed me in my absurdity; as it was, I was laughed at, and got heartily ashamed of my folly." We do by no means recommend this method with adult infidels, nor with all young ones. We must answer every one that requires a *reason*, while we must treat with compassionate silence those who are incapable of receiving a rational answer. In general, men are sooner won by reasoning than by ridicule, and by gentleness than by severity. Man is like the herb basilique, which, as the Italians say, if you handle gently, it will yield a sweet smell; but if you rub and tread upon it, will engender serpents.

Much more freedom is allowable in a conversational than in a public or printed discussion. The former is to the latter what a tournament is to a mortal combat. The knights sally forth to break a lance as a trial of skill and strength. The object is not the triumph of a just cause, but the glory of those who enter the lists. Yet this remark holds good only when minor questions are handled. In discussing subjects that are really important, we should always aim at truth. He who lets off his arrows up into the air for mere self-display, will some day fall transfixed by them. If he will not find them a mark they will make him their mark. Let him not fancy they will, like those which Virgil sings of, take fire in the mid heavens and burn up. He who takes what he knows to be the wrong side of a *moral* or *religious* question, or talks sportingly or aimlessly on the right side, will at length suffer, if not perish, by the recoil of his own arguments.

An old man should not browbeat his juniors, as if it were impossible for a young man to be a sound reasoner. He should ask no concessions by virtue of his seniority; if he does, it is a virtual admission either of the weakness of his faculties or of his arguments. To take sides against gray hairs is not such unpardonable insolence, so we only treat them with due honor in our *manner of speech*.

We must not offer to pursue an argument which another started, unless he has fairly given it up, and given us leave to do so. Even then, we must not take his place with an air of superiority, as if we were the only persons in the world who are able to do the subject justice. Some like to anticipate our reasonings —bystanders, who make us their mouth-piece when it serves their turn, and when we have a remark on the end of our tongue they take it out of our mouths, saying, "That was just what I was going to say—you mean so-and-so." "Exactly what I would have said, had I your 'gift of the gab.'"

When another shows by his replies that he has mistaken your meaning, do not say to him, "You do not understand me;" but rather, "I do not make myself understood." When you fail to gain a clear perception of another's idea, do not tax him with obscurity, but by a question draw out an explanation, or modestly request him to assist your want of penetration by saying, "Pardon me, I did not understand."

Do not raise objections abruptly, or deny assertions with rudeness, but when you dissent from any view, say that some would raise such an objection to it. Why common civility should not be shown to an opponent we have always been at a loss to conceive. In conversational debates its observance is of the last importance. If the controversy is carried on through the press, the parties may be severe without detriment to their persons or to those about them. But a truce to your noisy altercations in the social circle, which begin by shaking the finger and end by shaking the fist, to the terror of a bevy of ladies.

When debaters are roiled and boisterous, it requires some address to pacify them aright. It is difficult to interpose directly, as intentional interruption is generally considered a rudeness. A little pleasantry addressed to bystanders will sometimes quell the strife. If we attempt to part persons that have fallen together by the ears, the danger is that they will leave each other and fly at ourselves, there being nothing more easy than to make anger, when once it is fairly roused, to fasten upon an unoffending object. We can occasionally put a period to contention by exciting laughter, or by making ourselves subjects of merriment. When Juno was once quarrelling with Jupiter, the crippled and awkward Vulcan, by turning cup-bearer, so greatly moved their mirth, that they forgot their strife, and passed the rest of the day in festivity.

When you are answering an argument, quote accurately the propositions you design to examine; give them their full force, and, if possible, strengthen them by additional reasons of your own. When you refute objections state them strongly, allow them more than their just weight, and mention other objections not alluded to by your opponent. So you will preserve a character for honesty at least, and for ability also, if after giving them the vantage-ground you briefly and effectively refute them.

Be not one of those who tremble at every objection raised against their opinions, and are unwilling to make any concessions to their opponents. Be rather of that easy temper which can perceive the force or originality of an objection, and can pleasantly suggest to another, objections of greater weight than any he has yet urged, and even help him defend himself against you, or vanquish you. Debate in the spirit of Socrates. In the Gorgias of Plato, he says, "I am one who would gladly be refuted if I should say anything not true, and would gladly refute another should he say anything not true; but would no less gladly be refuted than refute. For I deem it a greater advantage to be freed from the greatest of evils than to free another; and nothing, I conceive, is so great an evil, as a false opinion on matters of moral concernment."

When the proposition you wish to establish is likely to meet with a cool reception from the circle, or has strong passions to encounter, you do well to give your proof first, which will be examined with more candor if you withhold the conclusion till it is established. If you first shock the company with your naked opinion, they will not listen calmly to the reasons by which you support it.

Endeavor to retire with a good grace from a dispute which you do not wish to prolong. Do not break off with the remark that you think the question must be submitted to abler hands before it can be properly determined; or that much remains to be said on both sides. It would be better to say "I am hardly able to convince you, so let us agree to differ, and talk of something else;" or, "You and I have now ascertained upon what points of the question we differ, let us, if you please, inquire upon what points we can agree." George Fox, the founder of the Society of Friends, relates a very good remark Oliver Cromwell made to him, at the close of an interview he had with him at Whitehall. Cromwell caught him by the hand and, with tears in his eyes, said: "Come again to my house, for if thou and I were but an hour a day together, we should be nearer to each other."

Some of the foregoing maxims will, no doubt, be thought undeserving of regard by those who have not learned from repeated experiments, that even though the truth be supported by undeniable proofs, and recommended by the highest authority, it cannot often be fixed in the mind as the main-spring of action, unless it is assisted by the arts of persuasion. The Son of God came down from his heavenly abode invested with every amiable virtue, bringing the most joyful tidings, and teaching the most beneficent doctrines; yet he did not always make a direct appeal to the hearts of men, nor exhibit at once the whole scheme of salvation and the nature of his kingdom; but unfolded them by degrees, as the prejudices of his disciples, and their progress in knowledge and piety, would allow. Endowed, though he was, with Divine power, and though he had at his command all the angelic hosts, he did not compel assent to his teachings, but used prudence and dexterity to pacify and win over a rebellious world. And the Sun of Righteousness still continues to send abroad his light over the earth, like His fittest emblem, whose rays, astronomers tell us, come down through our atmosphere in curved lines.

CHAPTER IX.

REPROOF.

The timely rebuke seems to be regarded by the Mosaic law as an expression of brotherly love. The command is; "Thou shalt not hate thy brother in thine heart; thou shalt in any wise rebuke thy neighbor, and not suffer sin upon him." Were the performance of this office, made as it ought to be, a criterion of fraternal affection, few, it is to be feared, could abide the test. An intelligent charity would direct us to give a brother a momentary pain, which issues in spiritual healing, rather than to allow a culpable fear of offending to prevent his rescue from guilt, sorrow, and the verge of perdition. He must be hard-hearted enough who can knowingly leave his brother to be admonished of his sin, only by its deadly consequences—refusing to draw aside the curtain which shuts the light out of his soul, leaves it at last to glare in upon it through the ruins of his character.

For another reason may reproof be the dictate of brotherly kindness. We have, perhaps, suspected another of misdeeds which he has not committed, or have misinterpreted his motives, or have judged of his conduct on the testimony of perjured witnesses.

In such cases, our censure will give him an opportunity to remove misconceptions that are afloat in our minds. "Admonish a friend," says the son of Sirach, "it may be he hath not done it; and if he have done it, that he do it no more; admonish a friend for many times it is a slander, and believe not every tale." Were this precept faithfully kept, the tribe of whisperers that seek in a thousand dark and winding ways to destroy the confidence good men repose in one another, would be greatly thinned, if not exterminated.

He who discharges this obligation to his brother, should first institute a self-inquisition, lest the person rebuked be tempted to retaliate by saying, "Thou fool, pluck the beam out of thine own eye." David says, "Let the righteous reprove me;" and Paul advises that the spiritual be employed to restore a brother that has been overtaken in a fault. But as those who are "righteous," and "spiritual," are likely to be unconscious of their virtues, it is implied that such are to be selected by the church for the work of leading back wanderers. The occasions are more frequent, where one is called upon to admonish his brother in private, and for offences known to few or none except himself. In such a case, however unworthy he may deem himself to perform the service, such unworthiness, whether real or imaginary, cannot excuse him from its execution. In order to prepare the heart of his brother for the reprehension he is about to administer, it is in some cases expedient to begin by making a confession of his own faults. By this means he will secure himself beforehand, from any charge that might otherwise be brought against him, and at the same time provoke the person to be reproved to exercise the same frankness and humility in confessing his sins.

The rebuker should take care that not only his own life be without reproach, but that his relatives be not allowed to go unreproved for the very offences which he rebukes in his friends and acquaintances. A story is told of a venerable archdeacon, who, having heard of his clergyman's hunting propensities, sent for him to lecture him on the subject. Soundly did he administer his rebuke, long was he about it, while his poor victim spoke not a word in his own defence. Suddenly the archdeacon, perceiving a smile on the culprit's countenance, said: "Ah! I see my admonition has little effect upon you: alas! you too much resemble Gallio, who cared not for these things." Now was the climax, and the expected penitent, drawing himself up to his full height, and fixing a wickedly merry eye on his reverend elder, replied: "Mr. Archdeacon, I have heard you with patience: you may have rebuked me rightly, and I may be a Gallio; but this I have to say, that if I am a Gallio, your own son Richard is a Tally-ho; and so, Mr. Archdeacon, I wish you a very good morning." The son Richard was a noted clerical fox-hunter.

According to the Apostolic precept, the reprover should restore the faulty "in the spirit of meekness, considering himself lest he also be tempted." He who takes upon himself to reprehend another, seems to claim a superiority to the offender as to moral or intellectual qualities, assuming that he is himself free from the sin, or that he can discern a blemish which his brother was so careless as to overlook. In order accordingly, to prevent resentment, he must not reprove in a tone of accusation or reproach, but as sensible of his own infirmities and of his liability to commit the fault he would correct in another. And if the reproved person takes umbrage and casts forth abusive language or unguarded accusations against him, he ought to bear the ill-treatment with an uncomplaining spirit; and to avoid rousing stonger opposition, or fixing him in obstinacy, he should not attempt a self-vindication, but rather confess the charge, if just, or pass it over unnoticed. He may, if the case requires it, go further, and confess faults that had escaped the notice or memory of the accuser.

We must take care that another be not made worse by our attempts to make him better. When, instead of salving the sore, we only irritate it, inflaming his passions rather than soothing them, we are making him but the more a transgressor. We are tempting him to add to the sin in question, hatred, revenge, evil-speaking, and perhaps other sins besides. If the person is not at the time in a sober mood, or if his temper is habitually irritable, a mild and cautious course must be taken. There are many yielding moments, in the lives of the most stubborn natures, whose return it is wise to watch and improve. "The guilty," says Seneca, "are like one that has an ulcer which at first is hurt with every touch, and at last even with the suspicion of a touch."[16] Those who feel the force of a warning which they have resolved not to obey, are the more displeased the oftener it is

[16] Epistles, 97 and 105.

repeated. Nevertheless it is now and then incumbent upon us to expostulate with those who are keenly sensible of their guilt, and if upon every fresh rebuke, they manifest a growing sensitiveness, it shows that they are either advancing in the career of sin, or discovering in their hearts new depths of depravity.

It is in general less hazardous to accuse a man of a failing of the heart, than of a weakness of the intellect. Most men would rather be blamed for want of virtue than want of sense. Accordingly we should go no further than to convince them of their guilt. If we set ourselves to show them their folly also, they may be provoked to a denial of both. When the transgressor has shown shrewdness and sagacity in committing sin, we may express to him our regret that he should have prostituted his abilities by exerting them in acts of disobedience, and that the perversion of them should serve but to enhance his criminality. They err who set themselves to convince a man that pursues an unlawful but lucrative calling that he would realize greater pecuniary gains by a lawful employment. It is true, that, in many cases, he might reasonably expect this result, but he could have no warrant to expect it in every case. The New Testament nowhere holds out pelf as a reward of virtue; on the contrary, it exposes the error of those who suppose that godliness is favorable to the accumulation of earthly gain.[17] It declares that, for all the penitent forsakes, of temporal good, he is to receive a hundred fold in this life, of spiritual benefits. He who renounces sin does not thereby increase his

[17] 1 Timothy, vi. 5.

wealth, but he obtains what is infinitely better—what "with contentment is great gain." He does not, in that act, win more of human honor than he had before, but he does obtain the hope that in a little while he shall hear from the lips of his Great Taskmaster, the words, "Well done, good and faithful servant;"—he does not gain a release from sorrow and pain, yet he receives the grace that disarms them of their sting, and converts them into untold blessings. The attempt, then, to persuade the sinner that, by a life of piety, he will more rapidly amass earthly substance, to say nothing of perverting and degrading the Gospel, is but to reflect on, or at least to contradict, his own understanding, which has come to a different conclusion. We ought to help him to distinguish between what is lucrative and what is right, and between inferior and limited good and supreme and infinite good. Until he can perceive the difference between these ideas, he has not taken the first step towards virtue, and to hold out to him a temporal motive to the pursuit of it, is only to remove it further beyond his reach.

In rallying another in the way of gentle reproof, some are addicted to such frolicsome speeches as are received as flatteries rather than corrections. "But must I not preserve the character of a friend, and should not kindness prompt all my reprimands?" Without the shadow of a doubt. Yet your flashes of wit, like lightning in a dark night, should not reveal the fault for a moment only to conceal it in a deeper gloom. Also avoid sly and equivocal satire. Let your reproofs be open and manly. There is a great difference between rudeness and plainness. The erring forgive severity sooner than cowardice and meanness. They are of the opinion of the old philosopher, who said, "If I must suffer, I had rather it should be from the paw of a lion than the hoof of an ass."

Intimate acquaintance should not rebuke one another before company. It is as bad to throw out a mysterious hint as a plain accusation. Whether it be English or Arabic to the stranger, the impression it makes on his mind is the same.

A person may sometimes be most effectually called back into the way of duty without revealing to him our knowledge of his wanderings. A chief officer in the emperor Adrian's army, whom he knew to be a malcontent and a maligner of his glory, was going to run away in the midst of a battle. Adrian, seeing him turning his back on the foe, stopped him, and with a sweet and affable air, only said: "You are going wrong I perceive; this is your way." Whereupon the officer turned his horse, as if it had been a simple mistake of his, and not a meditated flight.

Aim to bring your admonitory remarks to a mild and soothing close, so that the feather of the arrow may heal the wound inflicted by its point. One of the kings of England was highly incensed by reading a keen satire against himself; and as he read on declared again and again that the author should suffer for his libel, but forgave him the moment he read the last two lines which were these;

> "Now, God preserve the king, the queen, the peers—
> And grant the author long may wear his ears."

We have known the severest rebukes to be kindly

received when they were brought to some such conclusion as the following: "Bad as you are I do not think you so bad as to be unwilling to be informed of your faults."

We ought to beware of reminding another of too many faults at a time. There are but few who can bear accusation upon accusation. It is wisest, first to suggest amendment in *one* particular, and then wait to see whether the hint is heeded; if not, we can hardly hope that further admonition will be. Queen Caroline pressed Bishop Rundle to tell her of her faults. "If it so please your majesty," said he, "I will tell you of one. It is to be lamented that you talk so much with the king during divine service." "Thank you, my lord bishop," said the queen, "now tell me another of my faults." "That I will do with great pleasure," said he, "when you have corrected the one I have just mentioned."

There are some persons whom it is inexpedient ever to take to task. "He that reproveth a scorner getteth to himself shame." The Christian is not required to give himself up to the tender mercies of sarcasm, ribaldry, or waggery, nor allow his soul to be harrowed by termagants and blusterers, and "sons of Belial, that a man cannot speak to." Our Lord has too tender an affection for his little ones to consent that they be sacrificed to the fury of his enemies, unless their martyrdom can help to lessen the number of his foes by making them His friends. A fable in a Hindoo collection, the Pancha Tantra of Bidpai, so beautifully illustrates this point and is so rarely met with in English, that we must be pardoned for repeating it. A number of monkeys who lived in a mountain, on a cold, windy and rainy night sought for a fire to warm themselves; at last they saw a glowworm, and thinking it was a spark of fire, they gathered some wood and threw it upon it; not far off there was a bird upon a tree, which, observing what they were doing, cried out to them and endeavored to convince them of their error. This scene attracted the attention of a man that was passing by who told the bird that it was wasting both time and patience, and that no one thought of proving a sword upon a stubborn, impenetrable stone, or of making a bow out of a piece of wood that would not bend. The bird, however, without attending to him, flew down to them to prove to them that the glowworm was not fire, but in recompense for his pains was seized by one of them, dashed upon the ground and killed.

It must be borne in mind that private offences are to be corrected in private. Whoever checks a private misdeed in public will be thought more desirous of dragging it to light than of preventing its repetition—of deepening the offender's mortification than of effecting his amendment. Nor is this all; the reprover becomes himself a public offender, meriting a public rebuke. When Socrates once reproved Plato at a feast, for some private offence, Plato replied that it had been better to tell him of his fault in private; for to mention it in public was an impropriety. Socrates answered, "And so it is for you publicly to condemn that impropriety." Socrates was, we humbly conceive, in the wrong here. It was admissible for Plato openly to reprimand him; for by holding up Plato's fault before the whole party, he had done him a public injustice, and had also wronged the guests by disturbing their peace. As to public offences they are to be reproved as publicly as the offence was committed, that is, in the presence of those who witnessed the obnoxious act, and at the time when, and in the place where, it was committed; with this salvo, however, that where it is impossible from the nature of the case to rebuke the act on the spot, and where the offence is of flagrant nature, and an injury to society at large.

It is, for the most part, needless to reprove those who are already self-rebuked. Sometimes we shall find that the transgressor's conscience has forestalled us; so that there will be no need of repeating the duty. To remind another of a sin of which he stands self-convicted, and to deepen remorse which is even now excruciating, is less likely to bring him back to rectitude than to drive him to despair.

In some cases the reprover will keep clear of provocation, by addressing the misdoer in the language of the Sacred Oracles. And where he may not think it wise to commence with quotations, he should at least prepare himself to fortify every charge with suitable texts. The citation of a scripture command, warning, entreaty, or exhortation, has two advantages; it carries with it instruction and conviction, no less than correction—and if the sinner should resent it, he can be easily convinced that he is resisting God Almighty, and not the reprover alone. He who performs this duty should be well furnished with Scripture instructions and promises relating to the case, in order that the rebuked, like Telephus, may be healed by the same spear that inflicted the wound.

Brotherly tenderness oftentimes requires us to allude to the offence in the mildest terms. The plain Saxon may need to be displaced by words more polite and euphemistic. Our object should be, not to conceal the idea to be conveyed, but only to cover its grossness. Many being more shocked to hear the names of certain vices than by committing the vices themselves, we must be careful not to offend their taste when we only purpose to make them loathe their sins. We do by no means direct any one to use, with all sorts of persons, those belittling words and phrases by which sins are hardly hinted at. They serve in too many cases to flatter the offender with the delusion, that his sin is no worse than the delicate name which the polite world consents to give it. But at the same time it is our duty, when dealing with persons that are habituated to this style, as far as can well be, to adopt it. And even where we are called upon to denominate sins by their proper terms, we should beware of doing it in a harsh tone. Gentle methods, by paying a due respect to the person dealt with, and by showing the good will and compassion of him that uses them, are armed with moral power of the highest kind; so true is that paradoxical proverb of Solomon, "A soft tongue breaketh the bone."

Some persons are so sensitive to blame, or so jealous of their reputation, that a censure seriously disturbs their peace. Even some have been taken to task in such a way, or in such circumstances, that they have never fairly recovered the stroke. It behooves us accordingly to consider the temper and nerves of the subject. And it is well if we can manage with such a good grace, as to leave the rebuked so pleased with the manner, as for a time to forget the matter, and as to merit the praise Adam is made to pay to the angel who brought to him the decree of banishment from Eden.

> "Gently hast thou told
> Thy message, which might else in telling wound,
> And in performing end us."

It is here that circumlocutions find an appropriate place. They are a sort of gossamer in which the seeds of censure are wrapped, borne slowly along, and made to light softly upon their destined place. "The mischief of concise sayings," remarks Lord Bacon, "is, that they are darts supposed to be shot from their secret intentions; while long discourses are flat, less noticed, and little remembered." Strong passion speaks with brevity and directness, and rouses a kindred passion in others. But as the reprehender is supposed to be swayed by no pique or prejudice, such language does not comport with the nature of the duty. The most of us never forget a reproof received, though we sometimes despise it, and we may count ourselves happy if we are not pestered with the recollection of some harsh word or short sentence, which seemed charged with something beyond the needful sense, and looked like a design to gratify secret malice.

Our Lord and the prophets betimes conveyed their reproofs in parables, with most admirable effect. We may take pattern from them in this particular, and occasionally set another right by the help of a real or supposed instance, either with or without the application, as the case may warrant.

The gift or recommendation of a tract, sermon, or treatise on the sin to be rebuked, will at times prove more serviceable than a personal address. One of the most delicate mediums of performing this duty is an epistle. The missive should in all cases bear the name of the writer. Such a course is dictated by Christian frankness, and prevents groundless suspicions.

Occasionally we can best check a vice by a general remark on some moral or religious subject, and without being directly personal, leave the transgressor to be admonished by a plain inference from our remark. John Howe excelled in this kind of reproof. Several anecdotes are related of him which prove him to have been an admirable pattern in this particular. We must venture to relate one. At the time the Conformity Bill was debated in Parliament, Mr. Howe passed a noble lord in a chair, who sent his footman to call him, desiring to speak with him on this subject. In conversation, speaking of the opponents of the dissenters, he said, "d——n these wretches, for they are mad." Mr. Howe, who was no stranger to the nobleman, expressed great satisfaction in the thought that there is a God who governs the world, who will finally make retribution to all according to their present character. "And he, my lord, has declared he will make a difference between him that sweareth and him that feareth an oath."[18] The nobleman was struck with the hint, and said, "I thank you, sir, for your freedom. I take your meaning,

18 "Oath" was here intended as an equivoque: The oath required by the Oxford, or Five-Mile Act, was at this time agitating the nation.

and shall endeavor to make good use of it." Mr. Howe replied, "My lord, I have more reason to thank your lordship for saving me the most difficult part of a discourse, which is the *application*." Oblique admonitions of this kind may be given with excellent effect. They are not likely to irritate, and if they do they afford a shield to the admonisher. Still those reproofs which spring from a propensity to deal in ambiguities, are more vexatious than useful, and when they proceed from a habit of moralizing on even the most trifling foibles of others, little or no good comes of them.

A good way to reform some people is to provoke them to laugh at their own faults. A sportive wipe, a little raillery, or a lively passing allusion, is often more effective than the most serious and formal rebuke. The Roman bondmen took advantage of the liberty granted them during the Saturnalia, to open before their masters the budget of their wrongs, and amidst mirth and festivity made bold to teach them how to rule with clemency. The merry-andrews which princes formerly kept at court, had a way of rallying the great which wrought all the effect of rebuke, with nothing of its asperity. To do this with success requires some discrimination. Persons naturally morose, or of slow parts, or of a suspicious disposition, can seldom be so dealt with. It answers best with those who are of a cheerful temper, and those who know how to relish wit and humor. Even to these the correction should be administered with an air of pleasantry which is not the least tinctured with sarcasm. One advantage of these jocund strokes is, that they clear the monitor of all suspicion of malice and censoriousness. They also give the corrected person an opportunity to pass on to another subject, as if inattentive or insensible to the chiding, and by keeping him in a good humor, prepare him to give it a dispassionate consideration. It is worth remarking, however, that peccadillos only are the proper subjects of raillery. Notorious vices and great transgressions must be treated with seriousness. To sport with these were to show insensibility to their heinousness, and prevent its being felt by the transgressor.

When the offender is our superior, our correction must not take the form of a rebuke. The direction of Paul to Timothy is: "Rebuke not an elder, but entreat him as a father, and the elder women as mothers." He means that we should reclaim such by a respectful and affectionate request, asking them whether the habit or action in question is in their opinion sanctioned by the Divine authority; whether they would not so far indulge our scruples as to adopt a certain course, taking care to express our submission to their better judgment, and our deference for their wisdom, experience, and years. We do not undertake to give any form of entreaty. Every one must be left to use such expressions as circumstances suggest. The proper performance of this duty depends not so much upon the words employed as upon the meek, tender, and reverential spirit, that should prompt and pervade them. Many persons excuse themselves from correcting their elders on the plea of their youth, but if they have a modesty answerable to their years, the merest hint from them is more powerful than the most methodical rebuke of older persons. Milton's Satan is never ashamed but once, and then it is at the reproof of a youthful angel:

> "So spake the cherub, and his grave rebuke
> Severe in youthful beauty, added grace
> Invincible; abashed the devil stood,
> And felt how awful goodness is, and saw
> Virtue in her own shape how lovely! saw and pin'd
> His loss."

In some instances a young person, or other inferior, ought not to correct a superior in any manner, but should prevail on some person of equal years or rank to perform the duty. This cannot be effected in cases of private injury, nor where the fault was previously unknown to the superior. The offender will not account it a kindness in us to divulge his misdeed to another, simply for the reason that he was a more proper person to reprehend it.

In reclaiming Christian brethren, the form of entreaty is to be used in preference to that of rebuke. In the connection of the above cited precept, the apostle adds: "*Entreat* the younger men as brethren, and the younger women as sisters." Paul exemplifies his own precept in his letter to Philemon, saying, "Though I might be much bold to *enjoin* thee that which is convenient, yet for love's sake I rather *beseech* thee." From these Scriptures we learn what is very generally overlooked, that no fellow disciple in good standing and of unimpeached character is to be in strict sense *rebuked*, but rather *entreated*, when he is in error or fault. The endearing ties which unite brethren provide them with milder means of reclaiming one another. The rebuke partakes more or less of the nature of a command or prohibition, and can properly be administered only by a church or its officers, to stupid, or obstinate, or gross sinners, who are subjects of discipline, and by those who correct secular men.

When those who have made the general request that whenever we find them erring, we admonish them, do not receive our admonitions as thankfully as we could have wished, we should not conclude that they were insincere when they asked us to do the duty. Possibly they took for granted that it was to be performed in a becoming manner, and that some allowance was to be made for human infirmity. We cannot expect them to patronize a fault-finding spirit that taxes every action that does not exactly tally with our ideas of rectitude. So long as absolute Perfection Himself appears to have blemishes when contemplated by the disordered minds of the wicked, it is no wonder that such fallible creatures as we are should discover some faults in one another. We should tenderly respect a mind that has its *scruples*, but when it comes to *grains*, that is quite another affair. Were we not to set some limits to reproof, the whole earth would resound with the clamor of accusation.

On the other hand, there is a species of reproof which lulls one into self-deception with respect to the drift of his conduct, or the mass of his character. It consists in reproving him for a trifle, while we are silent as to some deep-seated vice, leaving him to suppose that we know of nothing else that calls for reprehension, and tacitly flattering him that he is guilty of no other, or at least of no greater sin. "If my friend," he says to himself, "is so faithful as to notice so small a matter, certainly he would not leave me unwarned of a greater." Most of those who are addicted to this species of flattery do not intend to hoodwink and mislead others. Nothing is more foreign to their thoughts. But whether they purpose to deceive or to please, in either case the consequences are the same. The transgressor is left to commit the most glaring offences unchecked, and what is worse, is left fatally blind to his own guilt. This negligent way of dealing with souls is practised to an appalling extent. There are spiritual guides who are careful to set their followers right as to matters of mere opinion or ceremony, but pass by their covetousness, or prodigality, or sensuality, or some other vicious habit. With pharisaic niceness, exacting of them tithes of mint, and rue, and cummin, they allow them to live altogether remiss in weightier matters. They admonish them of a venial weakness, but it is only that they may cause them to fall a more easy prey to some giant passion.

It is incumbent upon us to mingle merited compliment with faithful reproof, that while we point out to others their vices, we shall not seem blind to their virtues. This is the more important, inasmuch as devoted and active Christians betray faults which others conceal in inaction and conformity to the world. He who dares to step in advance of his brethren, becomes a more conspicuous object than he who is lost in the multitude of formal professors or the throng of unbelievers; Peter is more blamed for following his Master a great way off, than the rest of the disciples for seeking safety in flight. A single blemish on a character generally fair, is more remarked than one on a character thickly set with them. The wise reprover will consider these things. He will also reflect that he who is known to be meek and deferential invites animadversions and receives them from such as have not the hardiness to deal with a person of a different description. Observing that he is not hurt and thanks them for their fidelity and kindness, they are encouraged to be lavish of their admonitions, and they withhold the emollient of praise in proportion as he seems not to suffer from the wound. But none the less justice is due to such a man because he does not exact it. "Those," says Pliny, "who bear censure most patiently, most deserve our praise."

It is meet that we express our gratitude for reproof and our determination to give heed to it. To none are our thanks more due than to those who seek the amendment of our morals. They exercise no small self-denial who call our attention to our faults, and they could not confer upon us a greater favor than to assist us in the pursuit of moral excellence. We ought to receive reproof as singular marks of affection and good will. Only let us never show our gratitude by making a return in kind. To do this is to declare that we intend to return injury for injury, by revealing to the reprover faults which we should never have made known at all, had not our resentment invited us to the duty.

It being the proper use of reproof to bring another back to duty, when this end can be better compassed by other means, they should be employed. In some, a vice is sooner subdued by implanting an opposite virtue, than by a direct endeavor to uproot it ; and there are numbers whose vices are of such a nature that it were better to avoid all mention of them, and aim to procure an entire renovation of their hearts.

Happy is he who has a brother that knows when, and where, and how, to perform this duty—that does not set himself up for a censor—blaming by rule, and ever on the watch for motes ; and happy is he, who is cordially thankful for the word of admonition, and gives diligent heed thereto. "As an ear-ring of gold and an ornament of fine gold, so is a wise reprover upon an obedient ear."

CHAPTER X.

FLATTERY AND PRAISE.

It may look like presumption in us to attempt to add anything to what has been written on the subject of flattery. Yet the vague and erroneous notions that are current in the world, nay and among Christians, upon this subject, and which some popular authors have helped not a little to advance, require one who professes to treat of the moralities of speech, to give this subject some consideration. There are authors in abundance who reduce flattery to a system, and recommend it without scruple. Chesterfield, La Bruyère, Duclos, and other kindred names approve it, while others are at a loss whether to condemn it or not. But we have a guide that does not leave us in the dark on this point. It says, "He that speaketh flattery to his friends, even the eyes of his children shall fail." Again, "The Lord will cut off all flattering lips;" and again, "Meddle not with him that flattereth with his lips." These words, and others like these, stand the Christian instead of a world of mere human documents, and with him set the matter forever at rest.

Flattery is the condolence of people of fashion, making amends for the decay of beauty, and for the loss of fortune, cast, and character. It raises them in their own esteem in proportion as they sink in real worth, and fills up with vanity every void that exists in the mind. It seasons the insipidities, and settles the disgusts of company, and by the soothing recollections it suggests, relieves the languor and restlessness of occasional solitude.

Many of them know a real friend from a flatterer, and yet they caress the flatterer, and dismiss the honest and faithful friend. They receive with secret satisfaction the most extravagant and impudent panegyrics, and tamely allow themselves to be deluded by declarations which they know to be untrue. Such an ambiguity is man. His vanity countenances those who overrate him, and brings him at length to act upon their words as though they were strictly true. And if he is one of those rare spirits that will not credit all the fine things that are said to him, he still perhaps takes pleasure in reflecting that others are so dependent on him, as to resort to this vile means of propitiating his smile, or of appeasing his frown. So that this implied acknowledgment of his power has the effect of the grossest flattery, and betrays him into the power of others.

Rife as this vice is in the unbelieving world, would that it were confined to it alone. It is with pain that we say it is not unknown among professors of religion. They do not, to be sure, flatter one another for the same qualities that the world do; but, what amounts to the same thing, for those which they most highly value. Since there is nothing the sons of glory so eagerly covet as humility, devotedness, benevolence, and the like virtues, they laud one another for eminence in these. Critobulus said to Socrates,

"You remember the song the syrens used to charm Ulysses with? It began thus:

'O stay, O pride of Greece, Ulysses, stay.'

Such was their language, Socrates—but did they not mean to detain others by their charms as well as Ulysses." Socrates replied, "Not at all, Critobulus, words like these were only designed to allure noble souls and lovers of virtue." It is in this way that the skilful flatterer always addresses the ruling passion. Not a few seem to suppose that the Christian is in no danger of overrating his virtues, and of priding himself on them, else that their flatteries are somehow sanctified by the holy qualities which they ascribe to one another. The truth is, however, that they are never so criminal and pernicious as when they circulate among brethren.

Among those who fall victims to this kind of adulation, we sometimes find the preacher. A man can hardly be raised above the heads of his fellows without giddiness, and it increases in proportion to his elevation. The clergyman can dispense with studied cajoleries; the high rank he holds in society, and the incomparable dignity of his office, keep him duly mindful of his own importance. The praisers of sermons are in general strictly honest in their eulogiums; when they hear a sermon which is seasonable and beneficial to them, they will naturally commend it. They may properly speak of its effect on their minds; but to pronounce wisely on the intrinsic merits of a sermon immediately after hearing it, is one of the last achievements of the most practiced critic. Hence much that is intended for praise is not received as such by a sensible preacher. Those who laud a preacher's style, arrangement, or delivery, do but proclaim his inefficiency. Demosthenes filled the minds of his audience with his subject, not his oratory. Nearly all the panegyrics on the preaching of Whitefield we have ever read, say less of his sermons than of their wonderful effects. When Lord Brougham was once taken by Sir James Mackintosh to hear Robert Hall, he requested after the sermon to be introduced to him, and proceeded to compliment him on the discourse till checked by Mr. Hall asking: "But what of the subject, sir? What think you of it, sir? Was it the truth of God, sir?" When congregations go home, thinking or talking of the theme of the preacher, and the duties he has been urging, they pay him as high a compliment as he ought to desire.

The pest of flattery is not confined to the clergy, it rages among the laity: they infect one another. Is one discovered to be gifted in prayer? Soon he learns that his brethren know how to admire his petitions. Is he an able exhorter? How ready are some to puff up his vanity. Is he a liberal giver? The anointed press publishes his name to all Christendom: so that he is taught to forget that the gospel exacts simplicity in acts of charity. These spoilt children of the Church never do good by stealth, and in meting out to them what we consider just praise for some instance of generosity that has attracted our notice, they straightway strike up a strain of self-commendation to which the most brazen-browed of their flatterers would be unequal; telling over their charities item by item, so that you can make an exact calculation of all they have ever consecrated to benevolent objects. Now, we do not lay open the faults of any of these noble characters because we take pleasure in such work. Nothing of the kind. Only we would have these faults cease to be. We would have men who are pillars in the churches—pillars, too, crowned with comely Corinthian capitals—who do more in amount and with a great deal less pretension and noise, for benevolent objects, than any other class of men; we would have them keep out of the thinnest shadow of unhallowed motives.

The pious economiast is understood to expect for his services a return in kind. By saying fine things of us, he lays us under a kind of obligation to repay him with something equally fine; he both deceives others, and hires them to dupe himself. Those who thus live on the admiration of others, neglect the virtues and remit the duties which might make them praiseworthy. Finding that they can obtain the applause of their friends at the cheap rate of flattery, they do not barter for it a more valuable commodity. There are circles that wholly give themselves up to this game of flattery, as if this were the sole design of their confederation, till they have crowned one another with garlands of poppies, when they lie down in spiritual sleep. Many a coterie has adulation changed into such a drowsy elysium.

We sometimes hear it plead in apology for flattery, that he must be a churl indeed who can refuse to make another happy when a few words only are required to do it. It is much as if, for the like reason, we gave money to aid the opium-eater, impoverished already by his vice to procure a few grains for the renewal of his deadly dissipation. If happiness, it is ruinous and demoralizing. We shall not pause to examine this apology further—which is such as none but a flatterer would have the face to offer—but go on to say that, if we would please others, we had better be indulgent and good-humored towards their faults than ascribe to them qualities they do not possess; for flattery is little else than an endeavor to hide the known defects of a character by attributing to it imaginary excellences. Sincere kindness is the best policy here, and he pleases aright who frankly tells another his failings, and at the same time convinces him that he does not cease to love or admire him on their account. To be able to speak the truth without giving offence, is proof of greater skill in the art of complaisance than to tell an untruth on purpose to please.

We meet with more than a few who are passionately fond of receiving compliments though they rarely return one, and when they do, it is paid grudgingly. We have somewhere read of a nobleman, who, though he exceedingly loved to be flattered himself, was so far from being guilty of this vice, that he was remarkably free to tell others their faults. A friend one day said to him, he wondered that he who loved to be flattered better than any other man living, did not return a little of it himself. He replied that he could never think of giving away what he so eagerly coveted. Some refuse to repay adulation, because they think that others do them no more than justice. Too few omit to return it from a wish to stop this commerce in lies. The reciprocation of just praise sometimes springs from the laudable desire of giving another to know that, notwithstanding his high opinion of us, we do not count ourselves his superiors.

Blessed be the times! flattery is now beginning to be placed among the antiques. Whoever is detected flattering is, to make the best of him, set down as belonging to the old school. A shopkeeper we have read of, was one day dealing out to a customer the grossest flattery, when the latter interrupted him—"Sir, you are mistaken in your chronology." "Mistaken in my chronology!" exclaimed the surprised glozer; "what has that to do with the matter?" "Only this, that so early as the year 1540, this kind of complimentary insult had become obsolete." The flatterer was struck dumb, of course.

If we would not have one suspect us of any evil design in our praise, we should *add our reasons* for it. If another merits our approbation, certainly there is some ground for the merit; and we are bound to mention it. Then, on the other hand, many never approve you, lest they should appear to have some designs upon you. They are incessantly saying; "There, you are in the wrong again." "You are to blame for *this* reason and for *that* reason, and for the *other* reason." Many of your coarse and curt-tongued people, who are so very honest—are base mongrels, generated between the knave and the fool.

Many people would have us praise those whom they praise, not because they desire to exalt others, but because they seek an indirect compliment for their own judgment. If we will only bow the knee beside them before their Rimmon, it is all as if we had made themselves our idol.

There be those who are as malignant in their praises as they are in their detractions. They will praise a man before his rival, that they may wound his pride or inflame his envy. Those who praise one person in the presence of another who is distinguished for the same excellence, are likely to excite the antipathy of the latter towards themselves; for unless his better feelings hold the ascendency, he will either despise the stupidity or hate the malice that overlooked his own virtues, and extolled another at his expense.

There are those who commend others with the intent to praise themselves. They so ardently admire certain virtues, and show such a nice discrimination in the treatment of them, and withal such indignation at the opposite vices, that they draw people insensibly to the notion that they are themselves eminent for the same. And perhaps they gain a reputation not only for the qualities they panegyrize, but also for candor and liberality in acknowledging the merits of those who are their equals or superiors. Some again there are who eulogize a friend with an eloquence that makes the hearers forget the subject in their admiration of the orator.

Those who intend really to praise another, should not speak of him in the language of hyperbole. They run the hazard of inflaming the envy or the jealousy of their hearers, who are tempted to run him down as far below the merited mark as he was raised above it. It is more judicious to set some bounds to our admiration, and mention some fault which may justly be imputed to him; so we shall set off his virtues to better advantage, by way of shading or of contrast, and hold out to others no temptation to attack his imperfections.

The Christian must avoid, in his compliments, the indiscriminate use of that exaggerated language which, though it may become those among whom custom has given it a fixed meaning, it is otherwise not compatible with the character of those who are expected to observe at all times a moderation of speech, and to keep far within the bounds of verity. Something it is true must be allowed for the import of certain words and phrases, which have come to convey a conventional, not a literal meaning. Such may be used without the slightest departure from truth. To lie is to convey a false idea, and this can be as readily done by words which come short of the fact, as by those that go beyond it. In this view, he who expresses a sincere compliment in the tumorous style of the fashionable world, no more tells an untruth, than he who conveys the same idea in the language of rigid exactness. He who tries to couch his compliments in moderate terms, labors under this difficulty; that those who have been accustomed to be addressed in a loftier style, will receive his words as purporting less than he intended. Still, however, for the purpose of keeping clear of the charge of insincerity from those who are not habituated to this style, and of preserving the language itself from corruption, we should, where necessary, be ready to sacrifice eloquence to precision. Montaigne, speaking of the manners of his age, says that there never was, at any other time, so abject and servile a prostitution of words in the conversation of people of fashion; the humblest tenders of life and soul, no professions of regard under those of adoration and devotion, writers constantly declaring themselves vassals and slaves; so that when true friendship or gratitude sought to give utterance to its genuine feelings, words were wanting to express them.

We should be the more scrupulous on this point, because flattery is the worst sort of falsehood. Other lies are generally detected, and the liar exposed and punished, but flattery is a kind of untruth which the person for whom it was intended does not desire to detect, and when others demonstrate to him its falsity he is slow to admit it, because he loves to believe it true. Other falsehoods may expose us to the loss of friends, fame, or wealth, but this nourishes into a monstrous growth the original pride of the fallen soul, and involves us more and more in guilt and self-ignorance, and consequently in ignorance of others.

When others are flattering us unwittingly, and magnifying us for qualities and actions that do not belong to us, we ought to think it worth while to disabuse them of the mistaken estimate they have formed of us. "Princes," says Machiavelli, "have no other way of expelling flatterers from their courts, than by showing that the truth will not offend." He who listens with manifest pleasure to laudatory discourses which he knows to be not true, patronizes falsehood; but he who is careful to know, and to have others know, his real character will not long be pestered with glozers. We ought not to suffer others to repeat, without correction, rumors or anecdotes that are reputable to us, though misrelated or utterly without foundation, or fine sayings which are falsely attributed to us. We should correct every misstatement of this nature, and reduce it to the exact measure of fact. No man is the better for a reputation that does not grow out of real worth; for his true character will be known one time or another. But he who takes proper occasion to remove the gilding his admirers may have laid upon his character, instead of hearing the praises of his deluded admirers with a self-complacent smile, will, if he do it modestly, gain the confidence, though he may lose the eulogiums, of his fellow-men. There could be no higher encomium on the piety of Richard Baxter than the fact recorded by his biographer, that he was desirous that no one should overrate his Christian attainments.

A wise man is as highly complimented by being informed of the disapprobation of the bad as he is of the approbation of the good. For the reproaches and detractions of a mean man, though despicable in themselves, serve as clouds to reflect the glory of an enviable fame. Obloquy and abuse were thought to be essential parts of a Roman triumph; they are quite as needful attendants of victorious virtue. There is a tribe whose admiration is always ill-bestowed, and

> "Of whom to be dispraised were no small praise."

On the contrary, to be eulogized by the bad is to run the risk of losing the esteem of the good. Few men are duly appreciated except by kindred spirits, and he who pretends to admire a particular character, has, in the opinion of a different class of people, brought that character down to his own level.

For this reason, as well as for others that might be named, we should not praise another, unless we are qualified to judge of his deservings. We cannot properly praise a work in art, science, or literature, unless we possess a tolerable knowledge of the subject. A person who is not competent to judge of a work, is permitted to say that a treatise, or sermon, or painting, or statue, pleases him, or tell how it strikes his mind, but for him to declare, in a decisive tone, his opinion of such a work, is to incur the contempt or the derision of adepts. Men of sense are not proud of laudations that do not come from equals or superiors.

In the consideration of this subject, the desire of just approbation must be kept quite apart from the desire of flattery: the former springs from humility, the latter from pride. The man that courts adulation would learn whether he is as excellent in the esteem of others as he is in his own. Whereas he who desires the praise of the wise and the good would know whether there is any redeeming feature in his character, or any usefulness in his endeavors, or whether, as he often suspects, he is too partial to his own powers, or is misapplying them. He wishes some relief from the monotony of self-accusation, and from the fear that he is a useless or unwelcome atom in the immensity of matter. Without the encouragement of others, humility sinks into dejection, and faculties that might otherwise have been rewarded by action, are wasted in despairing sloth.

Accordingly, those who love flattery receive it with calmness and self-complacency, and those who desire deserved approbation are apt to be confused and disconcerted by compliments; they are ashamed to think that their deeds are matter of discourse, or their self-hid powers are exposed by others. "Merit," says Duclos, "like chastity, is modest; he pronounces his own eulogy who cannot receive one without blushing and embarrassment."

When we bestow praise on one who has been beneficial to others, together with ourselves, it is courteous not only to express our individual opinion, but also to volunteer to speak for them when they do not speak for themselves, and when we are sure they will agree with us in expressing the same sentiment.

Praise occasionally proves a good vehicle for a precept, or warning, or exhortation. Not that we should bestow the praise for the sake of its appendages; but, when praising another, we may use the opportunity to make him more praiseworthy.

We may often as strongly express our appreciation of another's merits by actions as by words. Indeed there are occasions when verbal praise is valued as it is seconded by an act of justice or kindness.

Some people eulogize from beneath the mantle of prophecy. They confidently predict noble things of others with a view to extol their present capabilities. This prospective praise gives confidence to diffidence, strengthens feeble virtues, and revives languishing hopes. It is most suitably conferred upon youth. More direct commendation may be given to aged persons. They have learned to set a just value on human applause, and have grown too wise to suffer themselves to be intoxicated by it. The laurel wreath becomes a bald head.

Let the Christian beware of setting up a faulty standard of excellence, or of being carried away with a blind admiration of the great ones of this world. Let him soberly inquire into the nature of their renown, and whether they have won it by just and generous means. Even the ancient heathen had juster notions of greatness than many nominal Christians. They so inclosed the Temple of Honor that it could be entered only by passing through that of Virtue. Some religious professors so use the epithet "good" as if they accounted goodness a doubtful, or at least a negative virtue. They say, "He is a good man" with an emphasis, or in a connection which denotes that there are many things in the world more estimable than piety. If they can think thus of the godly, the humble, the prayerful, and the beneficent, what can be their criterion of human worth? We will not undertake to say: it is, no doubt, best known to themselves.

CHAPTER XI.

DETRACTION AND SCANDAL.

We have somewhere met with the remark, that if we were to pin together all the passionate speeches, all the imprudent actions of the best of men, all that he had said or done amiss in a whole life, and hang it upon him, so that it might all be seen at one view, at the same time concealing his wisdom and goodness, the man in this disguise would look like a fool, or a fury, or perhaps a mixture of the two. So strange are the transformations that are wrought by the sorceries of the detractor—sorceries so powerful that they are successful in a thousand cases where the arts of the mere slanderer could avail nothing. The slanderer's falsehood has nothing but itself to commend it to belief; but the detractor's falsehood connects itself with truths which gain for it a confidence as general and implicit as that which they inspire.

To tell what is strictly true to the injury of another, is frequently as criminal as to tell what is false to his injury. It may be the same both as to the motive that actuated it, and the results which eventually follow. It is oftener worse than better, in every respect. If one circulates what is wholly false, the chances are that the slander will soon be detected, and the person vilified emerge from the cloud with brighter honors than ever; whereas, if we tell of a real misdeed of another, he may never have the boldness to deny it, so that it will go on circulating and gaining belief all his days, and perhaps long after he is dead. It will exert a secret, yet blighting influence on his reputation, and move on before him like some unseen hand, closing in his face every door to usefulness. No matter that he has repented of his transgression, and has radically reformed, no matter that he is now entitled to the highest admiration of mankind, some detractor has whispered a word that can never be recalled—a word which, most likely, represented him to be what he is not now, if not worse than he ever was. Yet every body boldly and industriously circulates the report, because, as he says, it is true.

It is not to be overlooked, indeed, that there are higher considerations than those of reputation, which sometimes require us to set aside the general principle in question, and to expose the sin or crime of our neighbor. There are cases in which it would be a breach of our obligations to the church or to the state to conceal it, and by doing so, we would be accounted accessories. When others are likely to be injured by mistaking ones character, or by not knowing his deeds, it is a duty we owe to their safety to caution them against him. Yet where the offence does not concern the public, but individuals alone, we have no authority for making it known. If we hear others speaking of him in too high terms, we have no right to state facts which would lower him him in their esteem, so their opinion of him does not control their action in any important affair. Every man is justly entitled to all the celebrity he enjoys, if he did not gain it wrongfully, or does not use it to compass hurtful ends. Even though he attained the eminence he has reached by offences against *God*, still, if withal he has not wronged *man*, none may presume to disturb him in his place, or in his honors: nay, *we* may not do it even then, if, though he has been unjust to *others*, he has not done us a mischief, nor made it obligatory upon us to bear testimony in behalf of an injured party. If it were otherwise, we might, with equal equity, plot the destruction of whatever belongs to our neighbor, on the plea that he acquired it by unlawful traffic. One may even use an ill-acquired reputation to support his attacks on the Gospel, without his being justly exposed to assaults upon that reputation, any further than to express our opinion of such an attack, and to show its incongruity with the character which is generally attributed to him, and to expose all such false pretensions as are set up on purpose to further error or irreligion. We cannot turn aside to attack his general character, which gives only an indirect aid to a pernicious cause. There are several reasons that forbid us to do so, one of which is, that every one holds a property in the good will and confidence of his fellow men.

We are allowed to lay open the real character and actions of another when the exposure is necessary to the defence of our good name. No man can lawfully hide hostile weapons under the cloak of hypocrisy, and he has no reason to complain, if we strip the cloak off his shoulders. At the same time we are permitted to expose the vices of another only so far as they take hold on our interests. We are not, indeed, accountable for the exposure of other vices and crimes which may incidentally result from the disclosure of the offence which concerns us.

It is perhaps worth while here to say, that in none of the foregoing instances is it admissible for any one to feel hatred towards the person he is forced to expose. He needs a truly Christian spirit who would bear witness against another in a case in which he is himself involved, in such a way as to shut out the suspicion that his own interests have given some coloring to his testimony. He who undertakes a self-vindication in a matter which is unknown to disinterested persons, commonly pleads to little purpose. For how much soever of justice there may be on his side, he can never hope that justice will be done him by society, inasmuch as it is not a legal tribunal, and if it were, it would call for stronger evidence than he can bring. The greatest and most numerous wrongs are those which the strong commit against the weak, in circumstances where none but the parties are witnesses to the offence, and in cases in which, from the imperfections of human law, redress is not to be obtained. The wise suppress such griefs in their own hearts, considering that society takes no pleasure in hearing individual grievances. Though it is extremely difficult to hush injured justice, as she laments bitterly within us, we can seldom speak in our own defence except at the cost of dignity, or probity, or candor. The aggressor who does not trouble others with arguments in his own defence, is better received in society than the aggrieved who oppresses them with the story of his wrongs, by repeating which he is sure to suffer additional wrong from their reviews of the case: he becomes like a column which having once begun to settle upon its treacherous pedestal, is pressed still lower, by bringing down upon its capital a mass it did not before support. We had better bear in silence the wrongs we suffer, than by our groanings wake up a tribe of surmisers, who will, in all likelihood, take sides against us.

When, however, it becomes our duty, as it sometimes does, to declare what is discreditable to another, we must strictly limit ourselves to the fact, carefully keeping clear of all comments, inferences, and opinions. The witness may not assume the task of the advocate or of the judge.

Some have a way of publishing faults in a strain of lamentation. They sorely regret that such a one did so and so, going on to describe most graphically the action that costs them so many sighs. Their tones are those of charity, but their intentions—over them we throw the cloak of charity. Clemens testifies of the Corinthian disciples, that they bewailed the sins of a brother as if they esteemed his sins their own. But these persons neither pity the transgressor, nor regret the dishonor he has brought upon the Christian cause. The Christian is not, indeed, to be forbidden to deplore the sins of his fellow-disciple; but when he joins the office of herald to that of mourner, people are tempted to suspect that he uses the voice of wailing only the better to incline their ears to his calumnies. A true report concerning a professor of religion, and spread from the best of motives, does untold mischief, by enabling the despisers of piety to repeat it with the sneering parenthesis, "(to the honor of religion be it said.)" When Saul and Jonathan fell on the field of Gilboa, David lamented the event in numbers, by whose inspiration every Christian's tongue should be swayed. "Tell it not in Gath, publish it not in the streets of Askelon; lest the daughters of the Philistines rejoice, lest the daughters of the uncircumcised triumph."

The detractor, strictly so called, is the most common and successful destroyer of character. He begins, it may be, with a panegyric on the amiable and excellent attributes of his victim. He expatiates on his ardent piety, his disinterested benevolence or his deep humility, but adds that he thinks him not scrupulously honest.[19] Another has more virtues than he has time to name, but he has cause to suspect the motives of certain actions. The life of another is marked by uprightness, devotedness, and kindness, but there is one passage in his history he knows not how to explain; it may be a fact, it may be a fable. He hopes that such an awkward report concerning his dear brother is not true; for his part he has a higher opinion of him than to believe it. He asks our opinion as to the rumor. The persons that use this artful sort of depreciation, would have us suppose that they are very

[19] This sort of detraction is sometimes carried to a ludicrous pitch. "There is a passage in Bede," says Swift, in a letter to Pope, "highly commending the piety and learning of the Irish in that age: when, after abundance of praises, he overthrows them all by lamenting that alas! they kept Easter at a wrong time of the year. So our Doctor Arbuthnot has every quality and virtue that can make a man amiable or useful; *but alas! he hath a sort of slouch in his walk.*"

candid so to interlard their evil speeches with morsels of praise. They intend, by relieving their detraction with an occasional compliment, to gain for themselves a name for honesty and high-mindedness. But their colorable honor and fairness serve but to shield themselves, while they are levelling their arrows at others. And though their detractions may not always be prompted by a specific bad design, they are, to say the least of them, the communications of a heart corrupt by nature and habit.

There is a generation who, if they do not practise the artifice above mentioned, are careful to cover their malignity under the guise of defaming others in the ears of confidential friends only. They would on no account have the thing noised abroad, and must bind us to the strictest secresy. But ah, how few can hold as a sacred trust what is told them in private. The most of us seem to regard such a secret as a casket which, though it is committed to our keeping, we think we are at liberty to open and show its contents to our friends. But we no more desire to learn a secret merely to conceal it, than we would desire a casket for the mere pleasure of keeping it out of the hands of thieves. Some people act as if a secret were a deposit which nobody had a right to make, forfeited as to the owner by the very act of entrusting it, and which they may dispose of at their own option, like smuggled goods which, when found, are confiscated for the public good; others forget that secrecy was enjoined, or, if requested, they recollect that they did not bind themselves by an oath, and having stolen the narrator's confidence by their silence, now betray it by their volubility; others again suspect that the narrator does not wish it to be kept totally hid, and have, apparently, good grounds for the suspicion; for they have heard the same secret from one or two others to whom also he had intrusted it. If the original narrator may tell it to all his bosom friends, why not each of these to his own circle of intimates? As everybody has acquaintance who can practise an inviolable reserve, each whispers the story in the ears of these till it is known in every part of the community, and when, as it speedily does, it begins to be a matter of notoriety, those whose ears drank it, quickly lift up their voices like trumpets, to proclaim their distinction as original shareholders in the secret; and soon all men are bold to publish it aloud to all.

It is in secret that rumors obtain the easiest circulation. Those that carry along with them a very questionable evidence or none at all, gain through this medium all the force of truth. Many a story which, had it at first been openly asserted, would have been promptly denied and suppressed, has, by being studiously withheld from discussion, gained an extensive currency before it was in the least examined, and the person concerned could not detect it till it had sprung up suddenly from all quarters, when, by reason of the number of those who had heard it, disproof and denial were out of the question; every attempt at refutation was met by a quotation of the vulgar maxim, that "What everybody says must be true." Most confidential matters that are whispered in our ears ought to be heard with suspicion. It is probable that the narrator is circulating in secret what he dares not speak in public lest he be charged with falsehood, or with reporting a truth of such a nature that it ought not to have been divulged. Beneficent truth loves the day, and never goes abroad under cover of night, while malevolent truth always walks within the domains of darkness, and like certain parts of the ancient Pagan worship, is kept in great mystery because it is too impure to abide the light.

It is by the arts of derogation that the crafty are able to disparage the character of their enemies, and inflame jealousy and hatred among mutual friends. Pouring into their ears the venom of falsehood, and taking every precaution to keep each from openly accusing the other till it has poisoned every affection, they prepare them for deep and ceaseless enmity to each other. In this manner "a whisperer separateth chief friends," and, we may add, sets whole communities at variance with one another.

Calumny many times originates in raillery and extravaganza. Loose-tongued people say the worst things of the best men for the sake of raising a laugh at the incongruity; else they invent strange stories concerning some distinguished person, and tell them to the unsuspecting in order to amuse themselves with their credulity. These experiments often turn out more serious results than was at first anticipated. These sayings are believed and spread till they are generally received as true, or till the gay babblers who started them are convicted of libel. "As a madman who casteth firebrands, arrows, and death, so is the man that deceiveth his neighbor, and saith, 'Am not I in sport?' "

Some persons make their friends confidants only

so far as to give them vague hints at a fault, and intimate that they know something of another, which it would be improper or inexpedient to divulge. They sharpen the appetite of curiosity to such a degree that it is driven to seek food among the unreal creations of the imagination. In this way they set the person aspersed in a worse light than they would if they were to blurt out the whole story. A single circumstance concealed, or discovered only in part, excites a suspicion in the hearer that more than makes up the deficiency in the narrative. There is a sort of people who will leave one's mind to dark conjectures as to one's faults, to which they give him a slight clue on purpose to make him believe a lie, and yet escape the odium of falsehood. They sow suspicion and fear in such broken hints as these: "As well, well we know;—or we could an if we would; or if we list to speak; or there be an if they might."[20]

Not a word of malice or envy or hatred should be tolerated in society. When anything of the kind intrudes itself into the circle, it should be driven out with frowns: "The north wind driveth away rain; so doth an angry countenance a backbiting tongue." To answer a detractor with the least show of approbation, is to encourage him to chill all hearts and to put a period to all genial discourse. There are passes in the Alps where the guides tell you to move on with speed and say nothing, lest the agitation of the air caused by your voice loosen the snows above and bring them down upon you. Even thus one approving word given to a defamer sometimes sets in mo-

[20] Hamlet, Act 1, Sc. v.

tion the whole side of some alp which overwhelms the company beneath the smothering masses of ill-will.

There is a spirit of fault-finding which it should be our care to avoid. Some professors impelled, as they feel, by a deep concern for the prosperity of the Church, deal out aspersions on their delinquent brethren with an unsparing tongue. If the group consists of the most zealous members of the church, it joins in running down the lukewarm; if of the self-denying and the benevolent, it speaks against the ease-seeking and the covetous. Saadi, the Persian fabulist, gives us an incident in his own history, which, though it was intended for the admonition of Mahometans, will, perhaps, prove instructive to some Christians. "I remember," says he, "that in my childhood I was very religious; I rose in the night, was abstinent, and was punctual in the performance of my devotions. One night I was sitting in the presence of my father with the holy Koran in my embrace, not having closed my eyes during the whole time, though numbers around me were asleep. I said to my father, 'Not one of these lifteth up his head to perform his genuflexions; but they are all so fast asleep you would say they are dead.' He replied; 'Life of your father, it were better that you also were asleep than to be searching out the faults of your neighbors.'" These complainers would, some of them, be excusable were they actuated by a compassionate spirit, but so habituated are they to talk of the failings of their fellow-saints, that they do it without the slightest touch of pity. Their tongues have grown hackneyed on such themes, and their hearts beat with their wonted regularity through the longest tirade against the children of the kingdom. Paul felt great sensibility when he called to mind the worldliness of certain of his brethren. He always spoke of it with increasing regret—"of whom I have told you often, and now tell you even weeping."

There are numbers who though they think it wrong to speak slightly of their equals or inferiors, do not scruple to defame their superiors, as clergymen, rulers, and candidates for office. One would think they had a dispensation to say all manner of evil against persons of this description. They pillory officers in the church or state, as though they were out of the protection of all law, and as though it were a sin to be nice in the choice of the epithets with which to brand them, or to fail in their treatment of them to outrage all decency and all mercy. How promptly and nobly did Paul apologize for having used reproachful language in addressing an abusive high priest. One of the charges that Peter and Jude bring against the dissolute heathen is, that they "speak evil of dignities," a deed which, as they declare, the angels themselves dare not do even of no better dignitary than Satan. The royal preacher goes so far as to forbid us to harbor secret enmity against our superiors: "Curse not the king; no not in thy thought: and curse not the rich in thy bedchamber; for a bird of the air shall carry the voice, and that which hath wings shall tell the matter."

All detractors do not begin with hating the person they lessen in the estimation of others. They wish, it may be, to warn their friends from leading the same life, by pointing out its dangers, or to clear themselves of a charge, by showing where the blame ought to lie; but what begins with gold often ends with clay. It is an inclination of the human heart to hate those whom it has injured. This maxim, which modern poets and historians have claimed as their own, was, in substance at least, first taught by the Holy Spirit. Solomon says, "A lying tongue hateth those that are afflicted by it." Even when any one reports what is true, if he knows he has done it imprudently as to manner, or uncharitably as to motive, or, at any rate, to the unnecessary injury of another, he can hardly help regarding the injured person with unhappy feelings. Self-accusation follows every recollection of the person concerning whom he has so spoken, and he no longer finds pleasure in the company of one, the very sight of whom brings to mind the wrong he has done him.

Hitherto we have been mainly attending to the subject of detraction. It will not be amiss to add a few remarks concerning scandal, which frequently originates in detraction, or rather, is but detraction circulated abroad.

The vice of scandal appears to have its source, partly in the love of falsehood, which is natural to man, and partly in a vain desire of being esteemed all-knowing, which leads him to pretend to information he does not possess. This original proneness to defamation is helped forward by a regulation of society, which, at first sight, appears as if it would check it. We allude to the tacit agreement that whatever passes between friends in the *conversazione*, is not to be repeated elsewhere. This rule is of ancient origin. Lycurgus ordered that when the Spartans sat down at their public tables, the oldest man present pointing to the door should say, "Not one word spoken here goes out there." The Romans of the better class adopted this usage, with some modifications. Horace, in inviting Torquatus to sup with him, assures him that it shall be his care, that among the trusty friends invited, there may be no one who will turn their words out of doors.[21] Whether, however, as is commonly supposed, the mutual understanding is, that such conversations are to be *sub rosa*, prevents scandal, may well be doubted. He who expects that what he says is to be confidential, gives a loose to his tongue, and allows it to range on forbidden ground, since he has no fears of being brought to answer for words he has there spoken amiss. If, on the contrary, he knows that which he says in secret will be proclaimed upon the house-tops, he will take good heed to keep clear of misrepresentation. When such confidence is clearly understood to be reposed, or secresy is expressly enjoined, the odium that attends a betrayal of it generally serves to tempt people to circulate calumnies all the more widely in a private way, and so prevent the arrest and exposure of the calumniator. But this usage is not, and never has been sacredly observed by all who frequent the best companies, and if it were, it would be far from preventing scandal within the limits of those companies; so that our wisdom is, never to say anything in the hearing of our nearest friend that can be tortured into scandal, or if so tor-

[21] - - - - ne fidos inter amicos
Sit qui foras eliminet. Epis. 5, lib. 1.

tured, can injure any one's reputation, or do any other possible damage.

Were such a rule strictly practicable, it would, it must be owned, effect one desirable end. It would hinder the spread of facts that are prejudicial to the character of another. If we tell a plain and strict verity that is derogatory to any one, the hearer is exceedingly apt, in attempting to repeat it, to make an untruth of it, either from carelessness, forgetfulness, ill-will, or a lying spirit. Unfavorable personal accounts are almost always exaggerated for the worse, while favorable ones are very seldom exaggerated for the better. We have heard many a good deed rumored, without acquiring additional lustre, but have known murders, as foul and cold-blooded as they well could be, made more so by common fame. Were an account to reach my ears reflecting on the character of Antichrist himself, if it had no better authority than hearsay, I would not believe it.

Having said thus much of *evil speaking*, let us now touch upon that greatly-neglected subject, *evil hearing*. We should refuse not only to repeat a fault that is discreditable to our neighbor, but even to hear another relate it. He who willingly listens to evil speaking must be, and commonly is, set down as accessory. The Psalmist David regards it as one qualification of the man who would abide in the tabernacle of the Lord, that he should not receive a reproach against his neighbor; and he expostulates with Saul for a similar offence: "Saul, wherefore hearest thou men's words, saying; 'Behold he seeketh thy hurt.'" A statute of Valentinian and of Valens made it death, not only to write a libel, but not to tear and burn one that might be found. At the judgment, he that heareth and he that maketh a lie will stand on the same footing. Not only before God, but also before the victim of scandal, are the narrator and the approving hearer of it arraigned for the same crime. When the injured party learns that he listened to the calumny without showing any signs of displeasure, even though he should not noise it abroad, he cannot look upon such behavior as prompted by a principle of kindness. By listening to evil speaking one not only injures another's character, but demoralizes his own mind. The habit of lending the ear to it, nurtures a malevolent disposition. Sir Peter Lely made it a rule never to look at a bad picture, having found by experience that whenever he did so, his pencil took a tint from it. If we allow ourselves to look at every caricature of a human creature that a malignant hand draws and passes round the circles of society, we must have tempers singularly happy if our own accounts of others do not borrow some of the deformities which have been exhibited to us.

When, however, we are forced to hear scandal—and hear it we sometimes must—let us conceal the information obtruded upon us. When asked whether we have heard what is reported concerning Mr., Mrs., or Miss Such-a-one, let us abruptly change the subject of conversation, or call to mind another engagement, and take leave. If we cannot honestly make good our escape in this direction, let us reply, as the case may be, that we must be excused from carrying the rumor any further, that we regret having heard a word about the affair, and with their leave would prefer to say nothing on the subject; or, that since we have not all the facts of the case, we can offer no opinion as to it. Some similar answers would in substance be dictated by that charity which "rejoiceth not in iniquity, but rejoiceth in the truth." There are those who listen to each latest false report with demonstrations of joy, put on knowing airs, are positive that they have an authentic account of the matter, and straightway set off with the speed of an Ahimaaz, to carry it to their acquaintance.

When we are compelled, not only to hear, but to believe a report disreputable to another, it is a good rule to ascribe the misdeed to a good motive, until it is found to proceed from a bad one,—dwelling on the extenuating side, suggesting that we have grounds for humble gratitude to Almighty God for keeping us from committing the same sin—that but for Divine grace we might be as criminal as others, or that we should look upon it as a warning against the like temptation; or that he who knows his own heart will not severely censure, though he must condemn such conduct. Bad as the human heart is, some offences may be actuated more by a habit of evil doing than from a long-meditated purpose. Defective notions of right, ignorance, and even mistaken kindness, sometimes give a milder hue to sin than they could otherwise take. Many who are thought to wear a cloak of hypocrisy, have only a veil upon their hearts; they do not intend to deceive others, but are only deceiving themselves. We would not be understood to offer an apology for sin of any name or degree; we only commend charitableness in making up our minds as to actions the motives of which we cannot fully discern. It is likewise the part of every right-minded man to volunteer his services, not only as the apologist, but also as the advocate, on behalf of an absent person who is spoken against. It is but common justice that the criminal should be allowed some one to plead his cause, especially when he is neither present nor informed of his trial. One of the prohibitions of the moral law is, "Thou shalt not curse the deaf;" to which we may add, When thou hearest the deaf defamed, ears be thou to him.

The professed scandal-bearer is never seen except as an apparition. Most defamers suppose themselves the furthest possible from such a character. They are in the common mistake of thinking that a person must maliciously and industriously report falsehoods among all their acquaintance, in order to be deservedly branded with the name; not considering that every individual who with no evil design tells a true but injurious account to only one of his friends, is a tale-bearer of the common class. Let each one carry a report but a single remove further from its originator than it was before, and enough has been done to send it all abroad. Yet because he is but a single link in the chain of scandal, he absolves himself of all the blame of its transmission from one end of the chain to the other.

Neither does he consider that scandal continually gathers new matter as it rolls. The originator only suspects Mr. Such-a-one has done the deed, or hopes he did it not; the second person believes it, or thinks it would be in keeping with his known character to do it; a third has no doubt about it; a fourth offers to make oath that he is worse than at first suspected. Thus does it go on increasing both in enormity and credibility. The apostle James exclaims, "Behold how great a matter a little fire kindleth! The tongue is a fire, and setteth on fire the whole course of nature, and is set on fire of hell." He would seem to liken the moral operations of scandal to stars on fire tossing flames to their fellows, till the whole universe is wrapped in a conflagration; and that, too, kindled by no extinguishable fire, but by the unquenchable fire of hell. A report may be only a spark and soon go out, being proved false or having answered the design of the originator. But before the spark expires, it kindles a fire of demoralizing influence, which will spread in all coming time, and a fire of guilt in multitudes of immortal spirits, where it will rage unchecked through an endless future.

The shafts of the calumniator often miss their mark, and are shot back on the assailant with deadly effect. He may expect some returns in kind—in kind do I say? not always, for he secretly shoots his arrows at the innocent, whereas those whom he wounds are able to draw their arrows from the quiver of truth, and send them to his guilty heart, flashing along their course through the light of day. Every real failing of the calumniator—and the calumniator must have many—is proclaimed in triumph. No one feels it a duty to give any quarter to so pestilent a creature. All set themselves to detect in him the sins he lays to the charge of others, and cannot but observe how fitly the epithets he applies to others apply to himself. He never so much as suspects that, while he is taking a wicked pleasure in dissecting his victim, the attention of some in the listening circle is fixed upon his own depravity. For my part I must own that of all the vituperative talkers I have ever heard, who did their best to make their victims appear odious to me, I have never met with one who was able, with all his volubility, to prove others to be half so bad as himself.

How graphic is that declaration of the Psalmist concerning wicked talkers: "Their throat is an open sepulchre." When an oriental sepulchre is opened, it pours forth an intolerable odor; and if it is neglected, it becomes at length the common shelter of every beggar, demoniac, beast, or reptile, that chances that way.

Evil speaking is the occupation of the ignorant, who, having nothing else to talk about, bring forward the imperfections of their fellow worms; and of idlers also, who, as they are commonly great talkers, and of course soon exhausting every lawful theme, must feed their loquacity with the reputations of their neighbors. When a conscientious man has cast about him for an innocent or profitable topic in vain, he holds his peace. Like the diluvian dove, after having flown abroad over the shoreless waters, and found nothing but carcasses whereon to perch, he stretches his wings towards the ark. He had rather be thought taciturn and haughty, than prey upon the vices of mankind. The common opinion that women are more addicted to this vice than men, is not without some foundation; the Romans set up in the forum the statue of a lioness without a tongue, in memory of a woman who had been distinguished for reserve. From the epistles of Paul it appears that the unmarried women of his times were given to idleness and gossiping. "They learn," says he, "to be idle, wandering about from house to house; and not only idle, but busy-bodies, speaking things which they ought not." He would have pious young widows return to the perils and cares of the marriage condition to prevent their becoming mischief-makers, and that, too, in a persecuting age when married disciples were especially exposed to domestic affliction. The apostle's admonition was not intended for his own age alone; it was meant for our age as well. The curse of multitudes of modern women in every class of society is idleness, which, coupled as it ever must be with ignorance, brings them into frequent conference, in which they retail personal news, and offer their speculations upon it. But as we cannot hope that many females of this character will take the trouble to read these pages, we drop the subject; only adding, by way of counsel to any gossip whose vacant eye chances to fall on these words: *Find some profitable occupation for your mind.* We do not offer this advice as the best that can be given, but merely as the best she is at present prepared to receive.

It is sometimes best to silence a detractor by turning his own weapons against him, pleasantly observing that we shall expect him to keep himself innocent of the fault he so much dislikes in another, or something of this sort. When a lad once addressed Pope Eugenio IV. a speech which, for gravity and wisdom, much exceeded his years, Cardinal Angelotto, who was very fond of taking something from every merit, hearing the audience praise the oration, said: "It is common for young persons who are endowed with premature talents to fall into early decay of parts." "Then, my lord Cardinal," replied the lad, "you must have had very extraordinary talents when you were young."

A pure imagination is a faculty in which detractors are wanting, most prodigiously wanting. This faculty is as important to the conversationist as it is to the historian. When a person quotes a remark of another, or speaks of his conduct, the hearer who would judge impartially, must have the power to transport himself to the spot where the report originated. A foul imagination is barren of everything but the criminating idea, while a well-purged imagination delights in beautifying every event with its circumstances, and thus tells more truth than the half-facts of your flat-headed maligners.

Ridicule may amount to detraction, and often does. Its wont is to skip over the virtues and abilities of a man, and pounce upon his imperfections and infirmities. Nay, but is it not the end of ridicule to laugh us out of vice or folly? Would it always were. We are afraid it has laughed a good many out of virtue and wisdom—not merely out of reputation for these qualities, but out of the qualities themselves.

We have somewhere met the remark, that the most *rigid* code of morality might be compiled from what *we* expect others to say and do regarding ourselves; and, on the other hand, the most lax of all possible laws of virtue would be supplied by putting into a system the palliations and excuses which we make for our own deficiences in speech and conduct towards others.

Thrice and nine times happy they who always feel such an inward good-will to their kind, as makes it needless to set a watch upon their lips. These are they whose goodness of heart renders circumspection a sheer superfluity—a very standing army in time of peace. If some people forbear evil speaking, it seems to be more from prudence and caution than from any compassion for the person spared. The sepulchre is locked, because a carcass is within. This sort of gentry have an excellent ear for scandal, and are the sole abettors of those who, in this way, break the peace of society. It is a wonder, that of the great cloud of preachers that have made their moan over the sin of evil speaking, so few have lamented the sin of evil hearing. It is time we had all made up our minds not to listen to a story that is not to the advantage of the person of whom it is related.

CHAPTER XII.

INTERROGATIONS.

THE questioner, like the rack, serves for the destruction of an innocent person who has a feeble constitution, and for the deliverance of a criminal who is naturally robust. Some people put one to the torture by their searching queries; if he has a brazen face and supple address, possibly they may not prevent his keeping his own matters to himself; but if he is ingenuous, or has a babbling countenance, they will rummage all his personal affairs, and leave him with scarce a thought he can call his own. If he attempts to conceal his mind by closing his lips, they discover it through the eye, the blush, or the mien. And the more meek he is, the more must he suffer; for as he does not complain of the cruelties of the inquisition, his tormentors are not softened by any touches of compassion.

Forasmuch as practical Christians are sometimes accused of impertinence, they should aim to keep clear of just grounds for the imputation by a moderate use of interrogations, in their expostulations with unbelievers. There are, to be sure, multitudes who are not nettled by inquiries as to their moral and religious principles, and verily, men of the world ought to account such questionings as the strongest possible expressions of good will. They are not displeased with those who inquire after their temporal prosperity; why then should they be so with those who express a kind concern for their eternal well-being? Most of those who put on airs of surprise when they are thus interrogated, are the votaries of fashion and pleasure, and persons of superlative effeminacy. Without questioning such, we may take for granted that they are of this or that character, and address them accordingly. If we mistake their principles, they will generally set us right.

To question us, is the privilege of a superior or equal, rather than of an inferior; though the latter may oftentimes beg the liberty to do so. It is proper for a king to interrogate his subjects, but etiquette forbids them to question him. The child or the pupil is allowed to question his parent or his instructor, when the question indicates a laudable desire for information. Members of the learned professions may be as inquisitive as they please, so they do not go beyond their vocation. It is so much their business to interrogate, that they are peculiarly liable to form a habit of pumping every body on all subjects indiscriminately. A question that springs from contempt or superciliousness, is improper, come from whom it may.

The Abbé Delille is of the opinion that a friend alone has a right to interrogate.[22] Though we cannot agree with this high authority in holding that

[22] Questionne toujours, et rarement écoute
Oubliant que ce ton léger
Dans un estranger est blàmable
Et que l'amitie seule a droit d'interroger.

this is the exclusive privilege of friendship, we must admit that fast friends and intimate acquaintance may question another more freely than others; but at the same time it should be considered that even friends and familiars are capable of being impatient under oft-repeated and irrelevant queries.

It is not proper to ask strangers questions about themselves or their affairs. Inasmuch as we must, after all, be very ignorant of their history, if we once begin there is no telling where we shall end. It is expected that a stranger will, without solicitation, tell us all that is proper for us to know concerning himself. Should he chance to be a person whose fame ought to have reached us beforehand, our questions would be most inopportune. There are enlightened people who might learn something on this point from the savages of the West. When a stranger visits their villages no one asks his business, and he is allowed his own time to tell the object of his mission. We should never ask a stranger what is his vocation, or that of any of his relatives and friends.

The tribe of indiscreet and careless questioners is a very numerous one. Many bolt out the first query that happens to be uppermost, without considering whether it is suitable to the person, time or place. The behavior of others may excite our curiosity or surprise when it would be intrusive to inquire about it, as for instance to ask people where they are going, or what they hold in their hands. When Æsop replied to one who asked him what he was doing with a lighted candle by day, "I seek a man," some have supposed that he intended to signify that men are scarce in the world. Phædrus, the fabulist, says he meant to intimate to the inquirer that it is unmanly to ask impertinent questions. Dr. Johnson once handled such a querist in his usual gruff manner. A gentleman asked him; "Have you been abroad to-day?" "Don't talk so childishly, sir," he replied, "you may as well ask if I had hanged myself."

Others betake themselves to interrogations as a kind of apology for their indolence. Unwilling to think or to consult books, they ask your opinion of a subject or beg of you a little item of information, like mendicants gathering their daily meals from the crumbs given at their neighbor's doors. Else, perhaps, they are persons of sluggish minds or little knowledge, and desire to be amused, and try to start you off upon an entertaining theme by spurring you with a thousand questions in slow succession.

Others again ask questions from vanity. By an artful construction of their questions they would have us know that they are men of genius, or wisdom, or learning, or they would convict us of folly, or ignorance, or stupidity. It is hardly in the power of poor human nature to receive such questions with thankfulness. We cannot wonder that the Athenians should have contracted a mortal animosity towards Socrates, when we consider that the philosopher went about among them to convince them of their ignorance and of his knowledge of his own ignorance. A modest question is betimes a good vehicle for conveying information or our opinion to those who would be offended with a dogmatical assertion. It may also be aptly used to assist the memory of others.

Those who ask questions on purpose to make a show of their talents or knowledge, are not to be numbered among those who honestly ask for information. Querists of this description deserve to be, and generally are, answered with respect. A great many live and die in the grossest ignorance for no other reason than that they deem it beneath their dignity to ask for information. When some one asked John Locke how he had contrived to acquire his multifarious knowledge, he replied: "By condescending to ask questions." It is a mark of affability to solicit instruction from those who have less general learning and culture, but a better practical knowledge of some matters than we. Yet it were unwise uniformly to suggest to people their business as matter of discourse. If we do, they suspect that we think them ignorant of everything else. When we wish information from a professional man, artisan, or man of business, we should go to his office; at any rate, seek some private interview. But in parties, men are to be talked with as if they had always lived as idle as the lilies of the field, or at least as those who have for the time, laid aside the habits and thoughts which are peculiar to their calling. By dragging back their thoughts to the round of daily toil we run the risk of beclouding their cheerfulness, and if we mention their vocation within ear-shot of strangers, we may expose them to mortification, or make them more conspicuous than their modesty approves. Still, however, many persons of limited knowledge wisely prefer to talk on subjects with which they are thoroughly acquainted; and if their ideas cluster around their daily duties—which is no great crime surely—they ought to be allowed to contribute something to their own entertainment. If they do as much as this, they will not fall below the average, who talk more for their individual amusement than for any other purpose.

Some absent-minded people have a habit of asking questions without staying for an answer; or if they do stay, their inattention shows that they make no account of it. Others edge in questions so trivial as not to admit of a serious reply, or so remote from the matter in hand as to indicate how far the mind of the questioner has been wandering during our remarks. Few are adepts in the art of bringing in a respectful and relevant question. An interrogation may sometimes be a happy substitute for an expression of assent, or show that we take a lively interest in the conversation.

Ingenuous people are never too inquisitive with their eyes and ears; they do not glance, and ogle, and leer with nice and crafty sagacity; they are not akin to those persons who retire a little from the talkative circle with seeming bashfulness, that their ears may stealthily take in, and lay up every untimely word. Their vicinity oppresses and embarrasses one. We are, to be sure, counselled to be swift to hear, and slow to speak, but must we then go into company in the quality of eave-droppers and spies? The sharp-sighted and the quick-eared do not acquaint themselves with characters quite so readily as they imagine; being ever suspected, they discover next to nothing. Common patience and attention will put us in possession of all that is worth knowing of human nature. Most people, if we but give them time, will, unasked, tell us everything that is creditable to themselves: they do not need to be incited to speak in their own praise, and questions are not likely to wring from them a confession of their faults. Their vices may not concern us; if they do, we shall learn them by inclining our ear a little while to their self-laudations: those who can praise themselves are not too nice to boast of their vices.

Uncourteous as it is to ask many unnecessary questions, it is more uncourteous to take umbrage at them. It is unworthy of a man to fly into a passion because a stranger, who has lost his way, is forced to ask several questions in order to learn his whereabouts and whither he should turn his steps, or because some one has mind enough to wish a little definite knowledge of a subject which others are vaguely talking about. There are plenty of people who discourse with wonderful confidence on almost all questions, and yet think the man very shallow who asks them to explain a point which he confesses he does not understand, and which in fact they do not themselves understand, but have not sagacity enough to discover their own ignorance of it. It would take a great many questions, and them very uncivilly asked, to fluster a true Christian gentleman, or to leave such an impression on his memory as to move him afterwards to complain daintily of the impertinences he has suffered. It is a rudeness, all the world over, to snarl at the rudeness of others. The real man of honor will treat effrontery with magnanimous indifference, as the Emperor Theodosius did those who cursed him. "If," said he, "it be uttered in levity, it is to be despised; if in madness, to be pitied; if in malice, to be forgiven."

CHAPTER XIII.

EGOTISM AND BOASTING.

A MODERN popular writer, describing the attributes of a gentleman, goes out of his way to say that self-illustration distinguishes modern professors of religion, and seems all but inseparably connected with the Christian character. This assertion has been quoted with admiration by other writers, and has been extensively read. It is too contemptuous to be quoted literally, and too glaringly untrue to need a labored refutation.

Every evangelized man must be less proud and vain than he was in the days of his impenitence. Whoever has witnessed the encounters of grace and truth with original pride, could not have failed to observe how strongly it is intrenched in the soul, and what lowliness follows its subjugation. The Christian enters the Church, forswearing allegiance to the prince of this world—confessing that his loyalty to him was the result of his own corruption and folly—performing an act of humiliation in his baptism, avowing that henceforth his soul and body, and all his possessions and services belong to Another. He forsakes his own wisdom, and gives himself up to a Divine Director; he laments the imperfection that yet remains in his heart in spite of renewing and sanctifying grace. If he talks often and earnestly of religious subjects, it is to magnify the Power that saves him, and to ascribe all his virtues to His unmerited gifts. If he is better than his neighbor, it is because his earthly nature has partaken of the Divine nature. "One day," says Saadi, the Persian fabulist, "a friend of mine put into my hand a piece of scented clay. I took it, and said to it, 'Art thou musk or ambergris? for I am charmed with thy perfume.' It answered, 'I was once a despicable piece of clay; but I was some time in the company of the rose, and the quality of my sweet companion was communicated to me; otherwise I should only be a bit of clay as I appear to be.'"[23] Of this spirit is always and everywhere the confession of the Christian. The virtues others ascribe to him, he traces, not to his own nature, not to his own exertions, but to the companionship of the Holy Ghost. In the words of Paul, he says, "By the grace of God I am what I am." If this be self-praise, let not a single human being be guiltless of it—no, not one.

That there is no vanity to be found among Christians, they are themselves ever ready to deny; that there is less of it among them than among people of the world must be, if they are at all actuated by the humbling principles that are peculiar to their religion. Even where they manifest any disposition to self-glozing, the things on which they value themselves are intrinsically excellent, and are superior to the qualities which the world is accustomed to make its boast. There is more of virtue in this fault of the Christian, than in the best qualities of

[23] Gulistan or Rose Garden, by Saadi.

the man of the world. "The gleaning of the grapes of Ephraim, is better than the vintage of Abiezer."

We cannot with strict propriety speak of ourselves, except when we relate simple matters of fact, without exaggeration or ostentation. When the fact stated reflects credit upon ourselves, neither our motive nor our manner can entirely save us from being suspected of vanity. "The accuser of the brethren" will never lack a pretext for plying the scourge of the tongue. The Christian is sometimes accused of egotism in describing what he has done instrumentally for the enlargement of the church, and the evangelization of the world. When duty calls on us to speak of the achievements of grace in connection with our own labors or charities, we cannot speak with too much modesty of the part we bore in the work. And in relating our religious experience we are to exercise especial caution. "Be ready," says Peter, "always to give an answer to every one who asketh you a reason of the hope that is in you, with meekness and fear." It is worth remarking, that the sacred writer directs us to give an answer to those who *ask* us concerning our hope. It is not wise to obtrude our frames upon the attention of unconverted men. We should not lay open our holy experiences to those who manifest no serious interest in such matters. And, as we remarked in a former chapter, we are to do this duty in a spirit of meekness and reverence—not in a pragmatical way—not citing our own experience as an undeniable fact in support of our assertions—not with an air of superiority or triumph over the unconverted enquirer. We are also counselled to handle the subject with reverence. Some professors are sadly remiss in this particular. They prattle of the Divine Spirit, regeneration, faith, and hope, in a bold or familiar tone, without awe, or humility, or contrition, or any feeling of the kind. Many are driven to this extreme in the attempt to show the error of those who stand at such a reverent distance from Christianity as to lose sight of her altogether, and regard the Lord Jesus in much the same light as Epicurus did the gods of the heathen—as deserving our reverence, indeed, but as quite above having anything to do with the affairs of mortals. True veneration is so far from concealing its object, that by a sort of self-annihilation, it makes it sublimely conspicuous. As subjects pay the lowliest homage to their king when they are in the royal presence, so those reverence God most profoundly who habitually feel the conviction of His presence; and they never do more to bring the thoughts of God into his own world, than when they speak of and worship Him with holy and humble awe.

But it is more to the present purpose to remark that there is a case where in speaking of ourselves it is allowable to go beyond strict narration and employ argument; it is in self-vindication. If we are known never to speak in our own defence but when we are driven to it, we shall not be suspected of vanity. When Paul is maligned by false teachers at Corinth, who have drawn after them some of his converts, he comes reluctantly to his own defence, and by way of apology for doing so, says, "I am become a fool in glorying; ye have compelled me: for I ought to have been commended of you." We should see to it that we do not defend ourselves with too much spirit. People suspect that he must have a vulnerable part, who makes too vigorous a resistance. It were better to make a calm and unconcerned statement of our claim to the confidence of others, with a very brief denial of the charges of our adversary.

We should not seek a reputation for humility by always daintily avoiding the pronoun *I*. The writers of Port Royal were so disgusted with the common practice among authors of speaking in the first person, that they uniformly shunned it as savoring of self conceit. But it may be questioned whether here as elsewhere, those excellent men did not somewhat overstrain the law of Christian lowliness. Pascal, the greatest of them, in some of his sublimest records of his own contrite experience and Christian hope, and heroic independence of the Vatican, uses, in forgetfulness of the maxim, the obnoxious I; and yet the word neither betrays pride nor assumption. The substitution of another and circuitous and impersonal phrase would destroy the verisimilitude, dignity, and point of the remarks. It is to his fragmentary "*Thoughts*" that we refer. It is not, then, the use of this part of speech which makes a man an egotist, but the feeling which prompts its utterance, as indicated by the connection and the tone. It is not impossible to covet the name of humility at the expense of almost every virtue. One may have such a horror of pride as to make him omit many duties, and to make him remiss in many more. A false humility, or in the world's parlance a false modesty, is as criminal and offensive as pride: for it is but pride in disguise. Pride need not prompt the frequent use of this pronoun: on the other hand, egotism in the first degree is often perpetrated where there is a careful avoidance of it; and in general, he who makes a show of great pains to keep aloof from a fault, does thereby declare that he knows himself to be addicted to it. Some of the vainest of mortals are often heard to say, "without boasting,"—"I do not like to praise myself,"—"Pardon me for speaking of myself." Again, there are very humble characters, who never use this kind of apologetical phrases. Let us beware of words; nothing is more common than to be misled by them.

Egotism consists in needlessly and voluntarily obtruding one's self or affairs on the attention of others. Nothing is more difficult than to determine whether a person is an egotist on the whole, for he may be very egotistical as to one thing and very humble as to another. The egotist does not always eulogize himself directly. He may make you his father-confessor, and acknowledge to you a fault or habit that is exceedingly dishonorable to him—"he cannot help it; it is his way." Perhaps he has resolved at all hazards to take a prominent part in conversation; even though it be at the expense of his character and the comfort of the company. Else he talks of his faults in order to demonstrate his sincerity or some other virtue. "He is none of your dissemblers: he must tell you all." Another confesses his crimes on purpose to show us his shrewdness, tact or courage in committing them, in escaping detection or punishment; or the generosity or high-mindedness with which he made amends for them; thus does he glory in his shame. Vainglory is to be expected from the ignorant, who rarely allow their minds to be transported beyond themselves. If we forbid them to descant on that all-absorbing theme—themselves, we seal their lips; but there is less apology for those whose intelligence ought to have taught them, at least, the appearance of humility, and who have matter for unpersonal discourse. On a subject in which others cannot bear a part, our words should be few—one's self is a subject of this description. Yet there are multitudes who talk incessantly about themselves whether anybody gives ear or not, and keep up as much of a soliloquy as if they were in solitude—nay more of one; for solitude might give back an echo, but their company returns none. We can say a great deal about ourselves if we once fairly set out, yet it is a topic on which it would be difficult for another to speak, even did we give him a chance. Our talk must therefore necessarily degenerate into monologue, and when it has come to this, we may as well bid our listeners good night, for they must needs have grown sleepy. It might be said of the subject of self what the epicure said of the haunch of venison, "It is too much for one, yet not enough for two."

Almost every circle is blessed with the egotist, who exercises a kind of dictatorship over it. Are you in a mistake as to a matter of fact? He cannot suffer you to proceed till you are corrected. Have you a word on the end of your tongue? He at once comes to your relief. Do you talk bad grammar? He quotes rules and gives examples like a pedagogue. Does he discover that there is a link wanting in the chain of your argument? He bids you stay till he has supplied it. Do you drop a word to which he has devoted much research? He asks you whether you know its primitive signification, and straightway inflicts on the circle a long philological disquisition. When you relate an incident which you suppose new and affecting, your friend listens without emotion. When you have done, he observes that he heard the same, long ago, and adds a very material circumstance which you omitted. He is never taken by surprise, and it is impossible to give him any information. And yet he never takes the lead in conversation, nor advances an original thought. It is his business to come after and pick up the words which others let slip in a running talk, or to check their impetuosity that he may point out to them their missteps. Had he lived in the days of Solomon, he would have flattered the royal sage with the intimation that some of his proverbs were but plagiarisms; or, had he been a contemporary of Solomon's father, would have felt himself bound to give the slayer of Goliath some lessons on the use of the sling, and hinted to the Sweet Singer of Israel his private opinion, that the shepherd bard did not perfectly understand the use of the harp.

It is egotistical to be perpetually talking about one's relatives, or friends, or associates. The common run of fathers and mothers have an abundance of stories to tell of the exploits and speeches of their dear children, which, entertaining as they may be to themselves, must necessarily be tedious to every body else, or redolent of the nursery, and savoring strongly of pinafores.

Others speak largely of their former youthful acquaintance with literature and science, now drifted away into oblivion so entirely as to have left no traces on their style of thinking or talking; and which remind one of the gentleman who boasted before Johnson of the knowledge he once had of Greek, though now lost. "Lost," said the stern moralist, "in the same year, probably, when I lost my great estates in Gloucestershire."

Others talk of their relatives in a strain of lamentation, or of deprecation. There is a great deal of sly satire in the conduct of that prince of travellers, Capt. Lemuel Gulliver, on his return from Bobdingnag, the land of giants. He now thought the sailors of his own country the most contemptible creatures he ever beheld. He looked upwards, and spoke to his own family in a very high tone, and regarded them as mere pigmies. It would be well for every traveller to read Swift's book immediately on his return home, or at least before he sends the journal of his adventures to his publisher. We could here, if we so pleased, be more than usually tedious in enumerating the many advantages which he might count upon deriving from such perusal. But he must pardon us if we relieve his patience by cutting the matter short; only adding, that some men are formed to become by travel like telescopes. They are pulled out to the most extraordinary proportions; and it takes the rest, it may be, of their lives, for their old neighbors to succeed in shutting up the elongated worthy into his narrow and natural dimensions.[24]

[24] The conversation of the intelligent, observing, and well-bred traveller is delightful. He harbors no narrow prejudices in favor of his

There are two sorts of egotists, who are fond of impressing you with the high rank they hold in society. The one tells you that the distinguished Mr. Eminence is his old friend, and that he is of such a set. This is the magniloquence of footmen. The other takes care to inform you that he don't know the obscure Mr. Lowly, and never has anything to do with that class of people. Now we must not only "be courteous," but the Apostle adds, "pitiful"—willing to hold familiar and sympathizing communion with the obscure and forgotten part of our species—willing to forget one's great self in bringing courage, hope, and joy to the stricken spirit, and the broken heart. The maxim of associating only with one's superiors or equals, is one of the most foolish and hurtful of vulgar errors: it contradicts every precept of the Gospel, and every feeling of humanity. Of what possible use to society are impudence and contempt, and the behavior they prompt? We have a great

own or a foreign land. He neither nourishes in his own countrymen a blind and conceited fondness for their own institutions, nor by indiscriminate praise of everything foreign, stirs up their patriotism. His judgment of the persons and places he has seen, is not formed on his own observations alone; he modestly quotes the opinions of other travellers, and gives his reasons for agreeing with, or differing from them. He does not pronounce hastily or confidently upon anything that he has merely glanced at in passing. Neither does he mix foreign phrases with his talk, nor give foreign proper names the foreign pronunciation, preferring the vernacular idiom of any other animal to the brayings of the travelled hybrid. He is careful to keep clear of imported manners, airs, and habits. The young traveller is prone to suppose that good breeding is only to be cultivated abroad, and wholly neglects his manners till he begins to travel, when it has come to be too late to acquire them anywhere. After a flying tour through Europe, he returns, imagining he is bringing all its elegance along with him.

liking for the motto used by Charles Brandon, on the occasion of his marriage with the queen at a tournament; the trappings of his horse being half cloth of gold and half frize.

> "Cloth of gold do not despise,
> Though thou art matched with cloth of frize;
> Cloth of frize be not too bold,
> Though thou art matched with cloth of gold.'

Egotism has sometimes been attributed to those who speak their own names in the same breath with those of the great. Shakspeare makes Cardinal Wolsey say, "I and my king." This is not historically true. In the record of the State Trials, the charge is, that he joined himself with the king in speaking and writing of state affairs; as "the king and I give you our hearty thanks." This is not quite so bad, though it is egotistical enough, and should warn us against mentioning our own actions along with those of our betters.

There is an extreme of modesty which the great alone can manifest with propriety, or rather in whom alone it is a virtue. For an obscure person to forget his fame, is to forget just nothing at all; whereas, for a man of renown to forget his renown is held to be a sort of prodigy and a sure mark of greatness. The man of low rank, who was elected chief magistrate of Aberdeen, and who, while receiving the congratulations of his friends, laid his hands upon his breast, and very emphatically declared that *after all he was but a mortal man*, showed pride and ignorance enough to sink any city in Christendom.

Nobody so completely puts himself into the power

of flatterers as the egotist; for, by proclaiming his master passion at once, he informs them how they may best manage him. This is especially the case when it consists in pride of wisdom, which is, of all mental diseases, the most difficult to cure, inasmuch as the disease lays hold of the remedy itself.

A man must have a reputation for singular veracity, who is believed to mean what he says when he runs down himself. Pride is so rife in the world, that a man cannot appear to be really humble without being suspected of being a hypocrite. Seeing one will be alike thought proud whether he speaks for or against himself, his only safety is silently to turn his back upon himself, and this he may do without the slightest incivility.

We have been speaking of general society. Among one's intimate friends, it is allowable to speak of what concerns ourselves, so it interests them also. Nay, even in public we may speak of such of our good qualities and advantages as the world notoriously attributes to us.

They commit a like impropriety who talk much of subjects pertaining to their profession, or business, or amusements. It savors of selfishness, if not of vanity, to be ever harping upon one's daily employments, and to allow such themes to swallow up those that are of general interest. A magistate once gave Dr. Johnson a long, tedious account of his exercising his criminal jurisdiction, the result of which was his having sentenced four convicts to transportation. The doctor, in an agony of impatience to get rid of such a companion, exclaimed: "I heartily wish, sir, that I were a fifth." The writer, at this moment, recollects having one evening called at the residence of a lawyer who entertained him till a late hour with a very circumstantial account of a petty case soon to come on, which the writer had never heard of before. Who was finally cast in the suit he has never since taken the trouble to inquire.

Authors of poems, orations, and other literary productions, should very seldom consent to read them in company. Now and then one of those who beg them to do so may really wish to hear their productions read; but authors should consider that such readings will, in all likelihood, be tiresome to those present who are unlettered; and to those of the lettered, who are not wont to go into company in quest of what they have already in their libraries. They should also consider whether the request is not made merely as a compliment to them. An emphatic caution is needful on this point, for the temptations to these readings are multiform and strong. We know an instance of a poet who recited his numbers before a company who heard with unmeasured applause till the genius had retired, when they expressed their mutual surprise that he should be so mad as to imagine that to be poetry. Cases of this kind are by no means rare. Even the Abbé Delille, who has obliged all coming generations with a charming poem on conversation, is known to have been overtaken in this fault, though he rebukes it in his verse. When the Abbé and Robert Hall were one day dining at Sir James Mackintosh's, one who was present says that the Abbé took up all the time in repeating his verses, and that Mr. Hall did not even speak. Sir James put in a word of approbation now and then, and the day was marred; but the Abbé was gratified, and Sir James and Mr. Hall were pleased for that reason. I detail this incident because it occurs to me as an admonitory example under this head, and not as an instance of unpardonable inconsistency; he must be the teacher of a scanty morality who acts up to his own instructions in every particular.

Men of letters must be warned against talking exclusively on literature in mixed companies. Even if they confine themselves strictly to their mother tongue, it is not to be borne with. Many an excellent woman has listened to the jargon of *literati*, thinking, in the words of Mrs. Teresa Panza, "Though I cannot read a jot, I can spin." Not a few men think that a knowledge of books is far from comprising all the useful information in the world—men, too, who can think and talk well on themes entertaining to all, and who have been so annoyed by bibliomaniacs, that they could almost wish that another Omar might rise and burn all the books in Germany.

Nor should scholars expose to the company the ignorance of persons they are talking with, except when it is likely to lead to some bad consequences. Neither should they boast of vanquishing in argument a person of shallow intellect or scanty knowledge. We should not draw our sword on the weak; if we do, let us, above all things, be ashamed to plume ourselves on having worsted them.

It is not advisable to praise very highly brethren of our own persuasion. Were others to know that our panegyrics were prompted by fraternal affection and an admiration of eminent virtues, they might hear them gladly, but a malicious world is ever ready to surmise that they are dictated by vanity or bigotry. When duty calls upon us, as it sometimes does, to speak of the piety of a brother, it is beautiful to attribute it to a Divine origin. Paul, speaking of the liberality of his converts, wrote to the church of Corinth in these words: "Brethren, we make known to you the grace of God bestowed on the churches of Macedonia." And Peter speaks of Paul as writing "according to the wisdom given unto him." We hear an abundance of eulogiums on distinguished Christians, with no mention of the fact that God made them all they were or could have been. It is taking nothing from the merits of the most illustrious mortal, to acknowledge that he is the creature of the King of kings.

Genuine humility is a scarce virtue, and is to be discovered only by the most diligent search. The most of us meet with it so rarely, that when we do, we know not what to call it. But all of us can, and often do, detect pride in our neighbors, and never so easily as when it clashes with our own. In proportion as they exalt themselves they wound our pride by denying our pretensions, or inflaming our jealousy. If they conceal their small excellences they excite our curiosity, and lead us to set a high value on what it costs us so much to gain a sight of, but if they force them on our eyes we naturally close them. He who does his duty well and says nothing about it, will win the good-will of his fellow-men, and this is worth a great deal more than their applause.

Self-praise occasionally succeeds with ignorant and credulous persons: very seldom with those who have much knowledge of the world. He who can make a discerning mind think more highly of him for what he says of himself, must, without doubt, be a person of unusual ability and address. He must deserve all the praise he bestows on himself: for successful self-praise is the last triumph of genius.

CHAPTER XIV.

ANECDOTES AND STORIES.

The charms and benefits of conversation somewhat depend on the proper use of anecdotes. The best conversers know how well they serve to enliven, illustrate and prove their remarks—and they not often fail to recall one pertinent to their purpose. Still it requires an exact perception of character and a cultivated taste to relate anecdotes with the best effect; and useful as hints on this subject may prove, they cannot supply the lack of a quick discovery of analogies, and a ready attention to circumstances of person, time and place.

Our first care should be to relate no anecdote which has a bad tendency, or is in the most remote degree associated with immodesty, blasphemy, or a derision of religion. Instances are not wanting, of professors who have in unguarded moments told anecdotes illustrative of wicked character, which, though designed to dissuade from vice, have served but to hang new pictures in the galleries of depraved imaginations; those who heard them cannot forget them if they would: each attempt to erase them from the memory has only fixed them more deeply there. When some one offered to teach Themistocles the art of remembering, he replied that he preferred to learn the art of forgetting. In one application of that art we are all proficients; in another none are; we find no difficulty in making an oblivion of the good, but we find it well-nigh impossible to forget the evil.

Again, there are anecdotes and stories which, though not exceptionable in themselves, become so when told in certain companies, and within earshot of certain individuals. It is not permissible to tell an anecdote reflecting on a denomination when members of it are present; or illustrative of the bad manners, morals, or condition of a country, when a native of it is one of the company; in a word, it is always unsafe, when we are thrown among strangers, to speak to the prejudice of any nation, sect, or person. It is a Spanish proverb, often, though not too often quoted, "that we should not talk of halters in the house of a man whose father was hanged." Accordingly, we should not describe a death-bed scene to one who is sick or bereaved, nor talk of bankrupts with those who have failed, nor of family quarrels with those who are not happy in their domestic connections. Full many a story that is told in society is pointed with a moral which secretly pierces some heart which has already bled too freely. We know Solomon has said, "The words of the wise are as nails and as goads"—they have point; but at the same time the wise are wary, lest their words wound where they were designed only to excite.

Long stories are of singular efficacy in hastening business, and especially in inducing sleep. Two ambassadors of Perugia went to Rome, and, on being admitted to the Pope, who was sick abed, one of them went through with a long, tedious narration, of which the Pope showed signs of dislike. Then the second said, "Most Holy Father, our commission directs that if your Beatitude will not suddenly despatch us with satisfaction, my colleague should recommence his speech, and pronounce it again more leisurely." The Pope was so much pleased with this remark, that he gave order they should be presently despatched. Sir William Temple says there used to be tale-tellers in Scotland, whose business it was to lull restless travellers to sleep at the inns with their humdrum stories about giants and dwarfs. Even short stories, told and told again, are equally soporific. Doddington one day falling asleep in the company of Sir Richard Temple, Lord Cobham, and several others, one of the party reproached him with his drowsiness. He replied that he could repeat all Lord Cobham had been saying. Cobham challenged him to do so. Doddington repeated a story, and Cobham owned he had been telling it. "Well," said Doddington, "and yet I did not hear a word of it; I went to sleep because I knew that about this time of day you would tell that story."

The best anecdotes come short of their intended effect when those to whom they are told are preoccupied, or are in circumstances unfavorable to attention. In most large companies, they are out of place. The variety of objects which engage the mind in such places expose one to frequent interruptions: here the talk must necessarily be of a rambling kind. If an anecdote is ever introduced, only the gist or moral is to be given, taking for granted that listeners either know or can supply particulars.

Neither should we undertake to tell long stories while we are travelling among attractive scenery, especially at the setting out.

We ought never to relate an anecdote with a view to eclipse one just related, or to show we can tell the most laughable or marvellous one. If we follow the anecdote of another with a story of our own, it should be purely for the purpose of establishing its truth or adding to its force.

When a person is illustrating a principle by an anecdote, and purposes to make additional remarks on the same principle, it is not proper to break in upon him by saying, "that reminds me of another anecdote"—one perhaps that has little bearing on the subject, and, when related, reminds another person of an anecdote still more alien to the matter in hand, and so leading off till the original point is lost sight of altogether.

It is not worth while to correct an inaccuracy in a statement, not material to the point in question, or, when the narrator has done, to give the circle an amended and improved edition of it, at the same time citing testimony, and observing that we have it from *reliable* sources. Nicely to discriminate between fancy and fact may do very well for historians, but we must not treat a teller of anecdotes as we would a mouldy manuscript, which has no sense of honor, and cannot revenge itself when we give it the loud lie. We should not then interrupt the relater for the purpose of correcting him. It is to be taken for granted that he who sets about telling an anecdote, relates what is unknown to the rest of the circle, or at any rate what he knows better than they. To interrupt him with a view to set him right, disconcerts him, and makes him go on stumbling to the end; even if it does not provoke him to stop short and insist on the corrector's proceeding, or, to crown the affair, to deny the justice of the correction.

When we are interrupted, and the listeners are suddenly diverted to something else, we should be diverted also. We should not, as some do, when they are deserted by their listeners, seem surprised, and wait in moody taciturnity for some one to bid us take up the thread of our story. If others are moved to mirth by something else, we should be as serene as if we had succeeded to admiration. When their thoughts take another direction we should immediately join them in the chase: nor should we go on with our story till particularly requested to do so.

It is not complimentary to the narrator when he has told his story to stare him in the face as if we did not perceive its point or moral, or to beg him to repeat, as we were not at the moment giving attention. "He that telleth a tale to a fool," observes the son of Sirach, "speaketh to one in slumber; when he hath told the tale, he will say; what is the matter?" It is also mortifying to the narrator to say that we do not perceive the bearing of his story on the subject, or that we do not think him as witty as usual. Intimates sometimes use such language in talking with each other, but it is in no case very respectful. Few can bear to be told, even by their best friends, that they talk commonplace or nonsense; while nothing is a greater encouragement to a talker than appreciation; a dull talker who is heard and applauded will outdo himself.

We should, in general, tell only such anecdotes as are novel. By this we do not mean that the actions and incidents they describe should be of recent occurrence, but merely unknown to the person to whom we relate them. When we tell an anecdote that is not new, as in rare cases we may, it is best to begin by owning that it is rather trite. In quoting a *saying*, we should take care to refer it to its rightful author, or else to no one in particular. If we would avoid untoward blunders, we should make no surmises on this score, as for instance, "I am of the opinion of that eminent jurist, Nimrod, who fought at the battle of Bunker Hill." Nor should we quote "That excellent work the Pilgrim's Progress, attributed to Thomas à Kempis, and published in England by Richard Baxter, shortly before he was beheaded by Charles I., in company with Lady Jane Grey."

When we quote a *witticism* from some book of *ana*, or *facetiæ*, we should notify listeners of the fact, lest they think we design to impose it upon them as original. It is pardonable to quote *anecdotes* that may be found in collections made ready to hand; for the work of compiling anecdotes is now-a-days carried to such lengths, that it is beforehand with the man of the most deep and various reading, who is not to be presumed to quote *from* these compilations, because he quotes what is to be found *in* them. An anecdote will rarely bear repeating, and if we have not an inexhaustible fund of wit, we had better not contract the habit of saying fine things, or telling anecdotes. Unless we have a good memory, we shall compel our friends to hear the same thing once and again, which is tiresome enough—not to say that the practice shows that we are so overrun with vanity as to plume ourselves upon these trifles.

When another tells an anecdote or story with which you are already familiar, do not intimate that you have heard it before, unless the question is asked you, and in confessing that you have, signify your wish to hear it again, that others present may not be deprived of the pleasure of hearing it for the first time.

Entertainers, and persons of consideration, whose duty it often is rather to encourage others to talk, than talk themselves, may call out the diffident, or the learned, by requesting them to relate the particulars of some anecdote or incident which has been alluded to in the course of the talk. Always when our *opinion* is requested, it is a graceful mark of deference to refer the asker to some individual present, who has more knowledge of the point in question, or is older or more experienced than ourselves.

We should not relate anecdotes for their own sake, or for the purpose of mere talk and display. Let them grow naturally out of the subject, explain some fact, or illustrate some principle. The converser must take heed lest he become a confirmed and incorrigible story-teller. Such a one may for a while keep a circle in good humor, but he cannot long be held in esteem. After hearing a retailer of anecdotes frequently, we discover that his stock of wit is mainly, if not wholly, borrowed, and of course soon disposed of; when, it is ten to one, he will become the most prosaic of talkers: we have known old story-tellers of treacherous memory, to make themselves more despicable than their stories were amusing. A story-telling professor of religion loses the respect of the worldly, and by causing his person and name to be associated with ridiculous ideas, he puts it out of his power to make any serious impression on their minds. So far do some carry their facetiousness, that they are known only in the character of merry-makers, and cannot open their mouth on the most common subject without making the circle titter in anticipation of hearing a witticism.

It is a remark of the eminent Vinet, that ornament of the Swiss and French churches, in his posthumous work on Pastoral Theology, that the Christian ministry are as a class liable to this error; and that clerical gossip has in some countries past into a proverb. He quotes, in allusion to the same topic, the saying of the distinguished German preacher, Harms, that no profession furnishes so many narrators of anecdotes, and of no class in society are more anecdotes told.[25]

These professional story-tellers are not often welcome in companies where there are several good conversers; they monopolize the attention of the circle, by simply making drafts upon their memories. Original thinkers do not like to be silenced by mere reciters; they are moved to envy them their memories, or to hate them for throwing their own talents into the shade. He is always well received in society, who is not only entertaining himself, but assists other people to be the same—who can justly apply to himself the words of Falstaff; "I am not only witty myself, but the cause that wit is in other men."

[25] Vinet, Theologie Pastorale. Paris, 1850, p. 158.

Most sedulously must we aim to tell anecdotes in strict agreement with the fact. We may indeed omit immaterial circumstances, but we are very seldom allowed to add aught thereto. Let us take heed how we attach to them ornaments or comments of our own for the sake of effect; for, however justifiable they may be in solitary instances, still, in too many cases, they amount to detraction, or if not, at least to a suspicion of an attempt at exaggeration or fabrication. Add to this that brevity and simplicity in relating an incident make way for its descent into the heart. These cautions are especially applicable to anecdotes that illustrate Christian experience and the doctrine of Providence. Many of these are of the nature of Christian evidence; so that to misstate them becomes detrimental to our religion, by giving to the world erroneous notions of the Divine government and the operations of the Holy Spirit. In relating *tales* and *stories*, however, we are not required to clip the wings of fancy; we may embellish and finish them with our best skill. To improve these in the relating, is a laudable aim.

Whether we are relating anecdotes or stories, we may omit those circumstances which, if left out, take nothing from their sense or effect. Minute particulars, preliminary remarks, explanatory clauses, parentheses, and digressions, there should be few or none at all, especially in telling anecdotes. Some begin by saying, "The man I am going to speak of was a physician about forty years old, tall, of dark complexion, the son of Mr. Strangeways, who used to live in Bond street. He married the only daughter of Alderman Immense, who died either of obesity or apoplexy—I forget which; at all events, his death drove his wife into insanity," etc., etc.; or, "before I proceed to my story allow me to mention one very important circumstance." People like to hasten to the catastrophe. To defer the conclusion tantalizes curiosity and expectation. Another annoying habit is to commence by asking such questions as the following: "Do you know Mr. Huge? Do not! Well, he is the son of Capt. Huge. You have heard of him, havn't you, sir? You must know him if you know anything. Why, sir, you must know his son. Do you not recollect seeing him at Mrs. Bats-eyes' once last winter?" There are those who will ask even strangers and travellers questions of this kind, not considering that they must be very ignorant of them and their friends. It is an imprudence to ask any one, within earshot of others, whether he knows individuals of doubtful character, whom he is quite ashamed to own as acquaintance.

Nor should we begin by making promises, as, "Let me tell you an anecdote which is very amusing," or "Hear a happy hit," or "I just now call to mind a retort which I think remarkably fine," or "I will tell you a thing that will surprise you." As the narrator, by such a proem, makes pretensions he is not able to act up to, so he disappoints his hearers, and meets with a cold reception.

After a recital which has produced an effect, we should not repeat it for the purpose of raising a second burst of applause. Neither should we repeat an anecdote which did not appear to be understood the first time, or attempt to explain it or point out the ludicrous part of it.

What are properly called *stories* may occasionally be told in society for their own sake. In circles that are formed for a whole evening, and forbidden to break up before a certain hour, though every rational entertainment should run dry, recourse is sometimes had to story-telling. There are stories, though they are scarce, which are replete with moral instruction, and seem to be all but incarnations of morality. When we tell one of this nature, we should eschew moralizing as we go along, or at the conclusion: the listeners will naturally wish to say something about its moral. As to long stories, we need not say a word; so we pass on to observe that,

Mimicry is to be shunned; particularly the mimicking of bad habits and constitutional defects, as lisping, stammering, and limping. A burlesquing of national or provincial peculiarities is sometimes warrantable; but it is never meet to make the manners and foibles of individuals a subject of mimicry. This is not, however, to be construed as forbidding a respectful imitation of others with a view to give a correct idea of their characters or manners.

In this connection we must protest against the too common practice of burlesquing the characters, events, doctrines and language of the holy scriptures, or the recital of anecdotes that go to set Christians, as such, in a ludicrous light.

Before undertaking a narration of any kind, we should consider not whether it is interesting to us, but whether it is likely to be interesting to others. Personal affairs, family history and local incidents, are not often entertaining to any but the narrators themselves. The same holds true of repeating in one circle the colloquies of another; in which often recur the expressions "said I," and "said he." Still, after all, we are justified in talking on subjects which would otherwise be hardly passable, when the company is threatened with a long silence, which is more to be dreaded than the worst piece of prosing.

It is wise not to set ourselves to tell an anecdote or story unless we are familiar with it. To stop in the midst for the purpose of recollecting some point, or of asking another to assist our memory; to forget the very word or sentence in which is hid the whole force of the anecdote, is a mortification both to narrator and listener. Nevertheless, if the latter is well-bred, he will listen with respectful attention to such tongue-tied confusion, particularly if the narrator is an aged person or has a frail memory.

The Christian who has at command a variety of religious anecdotes, possesses a means of great usefulness. By their help he can make the most spiritual subjects entertaining to the ungodly themselves: by accompanying a principle with a pertinent fact, example or illustration, he plants it in their minds so firmly, that it can never be rooted out. Anecdotes engage the feelings. It is not easy to press any abstract truth, however practical in its bearings, home to uncultivated minds, so as to touch their sensibilities, and make them the springs of prompt and powerful action. But these living manifestations of truth, by giving it form, complexion, motion and voice, effect this more readily than general arguments and exhortations.

Another use of anecdotes and stories is to give a profitable turn to talk when it is taking a wrong direction. A skilful anecdotist will beguile noisy debaters from their contested ground, triflers from their prattlings, musers from their gloomy silence, and detractors from their prey.

The judicious *narrator* is generally well received in society. He runs little risk of wounding the pride of others, since he does not strive to silence or outtalk them. He aims not to send along the line of the company the running fire of a titter, but simply to afford it a rational and beneficial diversion. As he only tells what he has heard or read, so he does not bring upon himself the charge of oracular wisdom, and the blame that commonly attaches to moralizers and wranglers. He agreeably engages the attention without fatiguing it, and by carrying our minds back to the past, withdraws them from the frivolities of the present; the virtues that are afar off are made to hide the faults that are at hand: the history of a nation or the biography of a hero is made to take the place of the scandal of a coterie or the vaporings of inane pretension.

CHAPTER XV.

WIT AND PLEASANTRY.

"My wife's judgment agreed with mine," says Richard Baxter, "that too much table-talk and too often, of the best things, doth but tend to dull the common hearers and harden them under it as a customary thing; and that too much good talk may bring it into contempt, or make it ineffectual." Those who confine their discourse to the subject of religion and other solemn themes, may preserve a reputation for consistency with those who mistake the nature of the Gospel system, imagining it to be little else than the exaction of penances and austerities; but the attempt which some professors make to adapt their religion to the false notions of such people, only makes it the more forbidding to them. The truth is, that the Christian religion, beyond any other whatsoever, makes the soul that is conscious of a personal interest in it, joyful and jubilant. Christ came down to this world, not to give us a revelation of sin, guilt, death, and hell,—this we had already; but to prepare and proclaim a way of deliverance from them. This train of dark realities was led into the world by the first Adam, not by the second. It was these things indeed that moved the Son of God to come to our rescue, and to send the Holy Spirit into the world to finish the work of redemption; but they properly make no part of the Gospel revelation. The cross was erected on Golgotha "the place of a skull," but it was not itself a skull. The man of the world tells us that our religion is one of terrors; not considering that it is his sins that make him view it in this light. He ascribes to Christ and his servants terrors which are the peculiar portion of Satan and his dupes. Melancholy, sorrow and remorse, always have been, are now, and eternally must be, the cup of those who will not receive the glad tidings of salvation.

There is in some pious minds a mistaken persuasion on this subject. It appears that Baxter was induced occasionally to enliven his familiar talk with secular subjects, not as much by his prevailing temper and frame, as by motives of expediency. The Nonconformists of his time, as well as the Puritans of an earlier period, were characterized by an austerity and solemnity of deportment not strictly answerable to the gentleness, cheerfulness, and sweetness, which mark the highest order of piety. There was no doubt good cause for this type of character. The levity, ribaldry, and blasphemy that overran the palace and the ale-house, the theatre and the drawing-room; the sports and revelries that broke the silence and the sanctity of the Sabbath, were well calculated to drive all pious people to the other extreme of frowning sullenness. And when the general dissoluteness was set over against their habitual sobriety, the contrast made them seem more sanctimonious than they really were. Pure was the flame of devotion that arose from their hearts towards heaven, and brightly did it glare athwart the moral darkness of the earth. It warmed the soul, and yet it did not always gladden it. The conversation of the Puritan was decent and scriptural. His lips were sanctified like those of Isaiah, by a live coal off the altàr, and like those of that prophet, often uttered words of admonitory and presaging eloquence; but they were not like those of the evangelist John, which had been equally hallowed by the society of his Master, and poured forth not only the testimonies of truth, but preserved also evermore the law of kindness.

Yet it is to be doubted whether, taken all in all, the mass of modern professors have altered the manners of their fathers much for the better. For while a few examples of puritanic gravity are still to be seen among us, we have in general backslidden into levity and frivolousness. We might have wisely ameliorated in some degree the ancient preciseness, but that we should have quite cast it off is a fact that calls for regret. The frequenters of the church and those of the ball-room; the worshippers of God and the devotees of Mammon; the children of faith and those of fashion, now assemble on common ground, and gyrate in the same circles. Those laying aside the offending cross, and these investing themselves in their best moralities, contrive to form a confederation which is tolerable to both, but consistent in neither. And while each class sacrifices some peculiarity to the other, the people of the world are allowed to give the tone to the company, and to select the themes of conversation. The talk which is so much in fashion in these companies, is light, grovelling, equally devoid of piety and intellect. It seems as if this empty prattle were invented, that rational and accountable beings might find a decent way of disowning their nature, and an easy method of murdering time. It gives no beneficial employment to the mind, and answers none of the ends for which the human kind should congregate.

In these assemblies, the Christian is led off his guard unawares. Holding converse with people of respectable lives and engaging manners, who pay an exterior deference to religion, and shock none of his moral sensibilities, he is enticed away, step by step, from habits of devotion into dissipating mirth, and held captive to the ruling spirit of worldliness. Were his associates persons of avowed impiety, he would not hesitate to forswear all conformity to their principles and practice; but in these companies of elegant moralists, he is solicited to sinful compliances so gently and gradually, that he is overcome before he is aware of having so much as consented to a parley. When the traveller in the old fable was overtaken with the north wind, he drew his cloak closely about him, but when the wind died away, and the sky cleared up, the genial beams of the sun caused him unwittingly to drop it. Of such a conformist to the world, we may say what the prophet said to Ephraim: "He hath mixed himself among the people. Strangers have devoured his strength and he knoweth it not." Samson has consented to be shorn of the Nazarite locks wherein lay his might, and is to hold himself repaid for the sacrifice he has made, by the Babylonian garment with which his new friends have clad him.

The most pious persons are especially exposed to

occasional bursts of mirth. When once their wonted seriousness is broken, it would seem as if their words, so long held in check, being now let loose, are resolved to make amends for past restraints. Some, at times, give themselves up to jollity, from a fear that their severity would be a hindrance to free conversation, or make piety repulsive to the sons and daughters of folly. Even if they do not carry their merriment so far as worldlings do, still it attracts more attention. Their piety makes their gayeties conspicuous, just as the golden spikes on the top of Solomon's temple owed some of their radiance to their elevation. This fact is too often overlooked. And, we might add, though a certain degree of joyousness is sanctioned, and even fostered by our religion, let us not forget that actions, which are innocent in themselves, are to be omitted when others are likely to be wrongly influenced by them.

Incessant efforts to amuse, though they are always unpleasing, are never more so than when they are put forth in skirmishes of witticisms and jokes. Those who engage in them, soon exhausting what little pure wit they have, are forced to resort to an affectation of it, and to require us to applaud each sally by a laborious laugh. One may very well seek the society of those who are too entertaining when he is too happy; but, surely, he who goes into company in quest of pastime should not look for it among those who are vainly taxing their ingenuity to make him merry. This desire of amusing is a chief cause of the many frivolous confabulations we hear in society. To this divinity are sacrificed good sense and decorum, and even wit itself. Nobody is content to please—to shun whatever is inelegant, and to pursue whatever affords a calm and lasting satisfaction. And since trifles and fancies are the staple of amusement, those who can originate them are amply prepared to meet all the demands of these circles. It commonly happens, however, that the fund of trifles is soon exhausted, so that the entertainment is eventually reduced to a mere round of repetitions.

But shall not the mind be allowed some relaxation? On this point there can be but one opinion. The mind is not capable of unceasing labor; and if, when in the intervals of toil, instead of giving itself up to restless idleness it be employed in diversion, it shortly recovers from its weariness, and returns, with augmented energies, to vigorous thinking. Everybody remembers how Æsop[26] apologized for his playing with children, by alluding to the unbent bow. Cicero justified an occasional relaxation from the business of the forum, by bringing forward the example of birds, which, when they have finished their nests, fly about sportively and at random; and if tradition is to be credited, the evangelist John unbent his mind by playing with a tame partridge. Nature herself teaches us to renovate our enfeebled powers by passing from a severe to a lighter exercise of them; but every amusement that does not so recruit the mind as to prepare it for serious and profitable thinking, is worse than none. The mischief of levity is not that it merely unbends, but that it unstrings the bow of the mind, destroys its elasticity,

[26] Some attribute this action to Agesilaus; the old legendary writers, to St. John: Phædrus says it was Æsop—no matter who it was.

and altogether unfits it for service. Beyond this, it leaves the mind a prey to lassitude, discontent, and disgust. The victims of toil, disease, and sorrow are happy in comparison with those of excessive amusement. A man miserably afflicted with a hypochondriacal complaint consulted Dr. Tonchin. "You want amusement, sir," said Tonchin to him, "go and see Carlini, the harlequin; he will make you laugh, and do you more good than anything I can prescribe to you." "Alas! sir," said the patient, "I myself am Carlini." This disease is almost past cure when it is caused by inordinate joy and hilarity, for it is attended with an exhaustion of those animal spirits which are its best remedy. If one makes that a business which should be only a pastime, whither shall he turn for recreation? He can find relief in no kind of amusement. He must either endure, as best he may, the disaster he has brought upon his jaded faculties, or be driven to this alternative: either to betake himself to the healing of evangelical grace, or to commit suicide in the vain hope that by destroying his body, he will put an end to the miseries of his soul.

The judicious Christian indulges a pure and moderate playfulness, not allowing it to make up the substance of his talk, but only its seasoning. He makes use of it to enliven tediousness, to drive away the melancholy of his friends, and to light up with hearty smiles the faces of his enemies. Yet he is not resolved on amusing at all times and in all places. He does not covet the reputation of a humorist so eagerly as to seek it at all hazards, even if it should force him to sing an epithalamium at a funeral. Grace has not extinguished his natural wit. It has only refined and dignified it, and his newly-tuned sensibilities inform him when, where, and how far to give it utterance. It was, we believe, the remark of Madame de Stael, when, during her visit to England, she had been much in the society of the great philanthropist, that she had heard, before knowing him, of Wilberforce as the *best* man in England, but that she had not been prepared to find him also the *wittiest.* A man of saintly innocence may have a refined and sportive wit.

We do well to consider that wit is an untractable faculty. Unless it is well bridled, it will overleap the lines of propriety. Most of the keen darts of wit that one hears whizzing by, have been pointed, barbed, and poisoned by envy and malignity, and fix on some person the stigma of vice, folly, or weakness. For this reason kind-hearted conversers have little to do with them. Pascal, himself, by nature one of the keenest of wits, has some such remark as this in his "*Thoughts*," that "To have the name of saying *good things*, is a *bad character:*" he means of course one little befitting the lowly and kindly disciple of Christ. The wit can hardly prevail on himself to withhold a gibe for the sake of affection. He falsely presumes that his friends will not smart under the thrusts he gives them; or if they do not, they will forgive the offence since it is committed by him. So he goes on, putting their patience to the proof, till he has provoked them past endurance. He who would be a wit must be content to boast few friends. A joke is "an air-drawn dagger," from which our flesh instinctively shrinks. We see not the hand that grasps it, and cannot divine how deep it will strike: should it prove harmless, we do not thank it for startling us.

There is a kind of banter or persiflage which consists in playing upon foibles that are not accounted real blemishes by those who laugh at them, but are taken to heart as serious charges by the person who is the subject of them. Though this is commonly thought an innocent sort of humor, it is many times far from being such. Besides exposing a worthy person to shame or contempt, and perhaps rousing his anger, it is calculated to lessen our horror of vice. How often, for instance, do we hear people rallying their friends on their intemperance, or indolence, or pride,—rallying men on their too great freedom with women, or women on their too great freedom with men, and the like—people, too, who profess to believe these sins to be among the greatest scourges to society, and the most heinous offences in the sight of God. He who can make sport of such sins, has defective notions of their enormity, and leads others to think too lightly of the guilt of committing them. Again, the habit of humorously setting good qualities in a bad light, as calling zeal, fanaticism, or beneficence, prodigality, and ridiculing persons for vices from which they are known to be remarkably free—this habit is open not only to the abuses before stated, but to this additional one, that what is said in raillery often passes current among slow-minded people as a well-attested fact.

It is scarcely ever wise to repay a joke or repartee in kind. In most cases it is better to make no answer at all; or if any, to answer without vulgarity or unkindness. To a humorous but indecent sally no other than a grave and decent answer is allowable. To indulge even humor in reply would be a degrading condescension. It is often best rebuked by a compassionate silence.

It was the opinion of Luther that Satan himself cannot bear contempt; it is certain that man cannot. No creature is more dreaded in society than a sneering, satirizing, disdainful one. If we cannot avoid feeling an inward contempt of another, we can at any rate avoid showing him any mark of it. The betrayal of such a feeling will offend without reforming him. We should never heed what we cannot help.

Let the Christian wholly refrain from making any part of the holy Scriptures matter of ludicrous comparison, allusion, quotation, travesty, or anything of the kind. He is so familiar with them that he is easily tempted to clothe a facetious thought in their quaint and forcible language, but he ought to feel such a reverence for them as will ever keep him back from speaking of them in a sportive vein. May he not, then, it will be asked, relate some of the instances of pious blunders in discoursing on, reading, or quoting them? Hardly ever; for the ludicrous ideas which they attach to particular words or passages, break in upon us whenever we read or meditate on them. He who thus, in some sort, writes in the margin of my Bible, humorous comments, illustrations, and references, greatly hinders my religious improvement. It is like the old grotesque style of illumination adopted by some of the monastic artists, both in their transcripts of devotional manuals and in the architecture of sacred edifices. The border of the door to the house of worship, and the margin of the manual of prayer is made absolutely to grin with the antic postures and visages of apes, mules, and fiends. Satan does not dread a decalogue which he is allowed thus to ornament and illuminate; and few readers could use it with safety much less with pious edification. Such a man casts hellebore, causing madness, among the daily manna which my soul eats, and into the fountain whence I drink the waters of immortality.

The Christian is also to be cautioned against starting, or taking part in a burlesque dispute on any moral or religious question. For while some trifling matters may be innocently handled in a jocund way, it can hardly be doubted, that if Christians who are solicited to join in the sport, would first consult their consciences as to their duty in the case, few of them would ever consent so to banter about any serious question.

Jests on sacred subjects are not only indicative of very little wit and less taste, but they are oftentimes proofs of the insincerity of the jesters. As servants who feel no respect for their master, will make wry faces at him when his back is turned, so these persons do not scruple to make merry with their religion when it has ceased to work upon their fears, or when they think it more to their present interest than it would be to pay it a hypocritical reverence. If some of those who indulge this species of low wit are sincere—and some of them undoubtedly are—they have, to say the least, too evanescent and superficial a piety

"Foolish talking and jesting," says Paul, "are not *convenient*," or to use a more modern word, *becoming*.

The Apostle must be understood to forbid all badinage and jocularity. Were a heathen, who was wholly ignorant of the Gospel, to enter almost any circle of Christians, and listen awhile to their conversation, so far from inferring the above to be one of our sacred precepts, he would be likely to conclude the contrary to be the case. From the regularity with which we introduce foolish talking and jesting on all occasions of familiar intercourse, he would not unreasonably set them down in his own mind as among the most imperative duties of our religion. And what would be his surprise, when told that Christians had so far yielded to the thraldom of fashion, as habitually and practically to regard the apostolic injunction as a nullity.

It is scarcely worth while to say, that boisterous laughter does not comport with Christian gravity. It is every way improper. Laugh we may at seasonable times, and in a moderate manner. "A fool," saith the son of Sirach, "lifteth up his voice with laughter, but a wise man doth scarce smile a little." It is natural to be cheerful when we or others are happy; and he who puts on airs of surprise at the temperate merriment of others, is further removed from sympathy with his own species, than to make himself morally useful to them. We must, above all, abstain from laughing at our own smart speeches. Whatever may be the physical uses of the laugh, it certainly is not expressive of any high moral feeling. Were we to analyze the habitual laugher, I am afraid we should find him chiefly composed of vanity, scorn, and dissimulation.

As for him who sets up for a wit, he does his own

mind a great mischief. He so accustoms himself to view every object in a quaint light, that in lapse of time, he comes to be unable to contemplate the most solemn things in any other. He is forced to burlesque every subject he talks upon. When he would be serious, you think him joking, and when he would be joking, you think him serious. So long has he abused the faculty of speech, that it has ceased to perform its proper offices. Add to this, that uncommon sagacity and alertness of mind are apt to be regarded as not compatible with probity; the generality are prone to cast a suspicious eye upon those who exhibit powers they do not themselves possess. And yet they do not consider wit as a mark of a high order of talents, but rather as inseparable from a light and superficial mind. The greater number of distinguished wits appear to be wanting in every higher quality, and in none more than in piety.

CHAPTER XVI.

THE STYLE OF CONVERSATION.

The colloquial style is natural, easy and idiomatic. It is the free and animated expression of salient thoughts, lively feelings, and a sportive fancy. It is made up of the words and phrases in familiar use among the generality of those who speak the same language, and abounds in those arbitrary turns and forms of expression which are peculiar to a nation. It is as clear of the jargon of the foreigner and the cant of the vulgar, as it is of the preciseness of the pedant, the verbosity of the declaimer, and the daintiness of the sentimentalist. It is the language of unstudied but elegant simplicity, on which rules are formed—not hampered by them. But if it is simple, it is not necessarily the vehicle of trivial and commonplace ideas. It is capable of giving utterance to original and sublime thoughts, and yet it sometimes makes them pass for old and intimate acquaintance, by reason of the ease and familiarity with which they enter the mind. The scholar, or the philosopher, is welcomed into the conversational circle, so he only speaks in its plain and unassuming language. By deigning to use the vernacular idiom of the conversers, he touches a chord that vibrates in all their hearts, and draws them nearer to him and to one another.

No style is so difficult to master as the conversational. In order to attain its peculiar excellences with no admixture of vulgarities and conceits, we must practise long in the companies where it is spoken. Women of cultivated minds are oftener adepts in it than men of the same class.[27] Few pure specimens of it are to be found in print; the best, perhaps, in the published letters of our classical writers when they forget themselves and their craft. For good examples of the courteous address which becomes disputants, and the phraseology of graceful, kind, and respectful discussion, the learned reader will call to mind the works of Plato, in the Greek, the philosophical works of Cicero, in the Latin, and Il Cortegiano, by Castiglione, in the Italian; and the English reader will remember Joseph Addison's Dialogue upon ancient coins; Berkley's works; and Rev. James Hervey's Theron and Aspasio. We must not be understood, however, to recommend all these authors, in respect of their sentiments or their general style, but only as affording examples of gentlemanly debate. Affectations of the conversational style are to be met with in abundance. They are in great part a medley of styles, consisting of occasional fragments of beauty, in so disjointed a union however, as to produce all the effects of deformity. Not a few imagine that its ease is easily acquired,

[27] Few orators cultivated the art of speech more assiduously than Cicero; and we are expressly told that he resorted to the society of noble and refined Roman matrons to perfect his mastery of the Latin tongue.

and when they hear an accomplished converser, they straightway conclude they can easily learn to talk like him. Those who despise this style would respect it, did they know the difficulty of their becoming proficients in it; and those who think it vulgar, have yet to learn that it calls for the highest exertions of the best taste and the best sense, to select the phrases and expressions of which it is made up, from the language of the common people among whom they originate, and to make them of a piece with the diction of elegance.

It is hardly ever compassed by those who aim at ease or even correctness, while they are talking. Some emulating Johnson by trying to do their best on all occasions, or Mackintosh, who always spoke with faultless elegance, become declaimers or purists, or perhaps both by turns. They do not consider that gracefulness must needs have a certain negligence about it, and that the incautious mood which lies open to mistakes ever attends the truest beauties of diction. In truth, the blunders themselves become excellences when tact and gracefulness are displayed in recovering from them. As to the choice of words, most people never speak so well as when they speak at a venture. Many a stately discourse has been delivered in a circle of friends, in no part of which was a single tittle misplaced or omitted, and yet, viewed in the gross, it was but one carefully wrought error throughout. The correctness and elaborateness of written language is quite out of place in parlance. Here what is irregular often gives force and vivacity, and always naturalness to what is said. Here much is left to subaudition—

what is obscure is explained by the accompanying look or gesture, and what is hinted at in the unfinished sentence, is understood by the hearer, whose thoughts outrun the tongue of the hurrying talker. It is a peculiarity of most good conversers that they deal in happy strokes of thought, delivered the moment they were conceived—in sentiments which come pulsing from the heart or sparkling from the fancy—in observations suggested by a slight occurrence, perhaps; and in off-hand discussions started suddenly and without premeditation. It is then, if ever, that they give us their best specimens of this style. They succeed because they speak just what they mean, and utter their thoughts just as they rise in their minds. Absorbed with the subject, and unmindful of art, their ideas are brought forth by the unregarded operations of nature.

The practiced converser makes clearness his first concern. He makes no apology for using an obsolete or new-coined word that exactly expresses his idea, or is best understood by his hearers. "He chooses," says Delille, "words that are in common use, if they are not vulgar, and keeps equally clear of a labored elegance and an obscure niceness. He occasionally commits a solecism perhaps, which marks his own modes of thought, or gives a happy turn to a sentence. He strews his talk with modest and broken flowers; and though he shows no art, he outdoes all the arts of the rhetorician. Many of his sentences may be stumbling-blocks to the grammarian or the logician, but they are the delight of all who are alive to the beauty and grace of naturalness."

Nevertheless, it is possible for these negligences, if numerous and great, to become untoward. While the talker should not make great ado in conveying his thoughts, still he should not allow his words to rattle on too far ahead of his ideas. Few things are more annoying than the nonsense that vents itself in a profusion of words—than a whirling of the tongue long after the stream of thought that drove it has run dry. There is here and there one who willfully corrupts the language. Presuming on his real or fancied rank in society, he abandons himself to vulgarity or ribaldry, or obscenity of speech. In rebuke of such a one, it is useless to say one word; his own language would correct him, if anything could.

We should guard ourselves against the use of cant epithets. The adjectives "fine," "tremendous," "capital," etc., are nowadays applied to all persons and things indiscriminately. "Some folks," says Coleridge, "apply epithets as boys do in making Latin. When I first looked upon the falls of the Clyde, I was unable to find a word to express my feelings. At last a man, a stranger, who arrived about the same time, said, 'How majestic!' It was the precise term, and I was turning round and saying, 'thank you, sir, that is the exact word for it,' when he added in the next breath, 'Yes, how *pretty!*'"

We should so express ourselves as not to force affirmatives or negatives from the listener. Such phrases as "You know," "You see," "Don't you see?" "Do you understand?" should be avoided. Those who are always saying, "I don't understand you," expose themselves to the retort, "It is your own fault if you do not;" say, rather, "will you please repeat," or "pardon me, I am so obtuse as not to understand;" and instead of saying, "You don't understand me," say "I don't make myself understood." *In conversation* avoid great formality of expression; it is better to say "I can't tell," "I don't know," than "I cannot tell," "I do not know." A lady should not say, My husband—she should call him *Mr.* It is equally good breeding, when she is alone with him, to designate him by his Christian name. A young lady, if the eldest of the family, is entitled to the surname, as Miss *Smith*, while the younger sisters are called by their Christian names, as Miss *Mary*. Do not say *merely* "Ma'am" or "Miss" in addressing ladies of your acquaintance.

The vulgar are ambitious of using what they call "big words," and of multiplying euphemisms. Once he was the rustic who spoke Saxon, now he is the rustic who shuns the Saxon, and will speak only the affected Norman. To use such words as "perspiration" instead of "sweat," "pantaloons" for "breeches," "an eructation" for "a belch," is growing to be decidedly vulgar.[28]

A principal fault in the conversational diction of Christians, is the indiscriminate use of scripture phrases and idioms. A free seasoning of scriptural sentiments beseems the conversation of saints; and even the frequent quotation of Biblical language is

[28] It is in most cases not only lawful, but also expedient, to pronounce all foreign *proper names* according to English rules as applied to syllables of like orthography. Proper names claim the privilege of being naturalized in all languages by receiving, upon their first introduction, the pronunciation of native words.

beautiful in the aged pilgrim. It comports with his wisdom, venerableness, and spirituality. But for others to form a habit of quoting Scripture in talking on all themes is very objectionable. It engenders an irreverence towards the most awful subjects ; and though many of those who treat Holy Writ with this kind of familiarity intend in this way to make their secular affairs a part of their religion, it frequently happens that they only make their religion a part of their secular affairs. Men of taste do not dislike the style of our version. They join in admiring and quoting it. What excites their disgust, is to hear it quoted without judgment; to hear Oriental idioms and the most obsolete parts cited on improper occasions, and with as much freedom as if they were the most poetic portions, and to hear such passages quoted in an abrupt and whimsical manner, in talking with all sorts of persons, at all times, and in all places. And even this disgust comes almost as often of ignorance as of taste. Some of the reporters of Whitefield's sermons, preached in London, were so ignorant of the scriptures, as not to know that what they took for his language and ridiculed as his, was the quoted word of God. Mrs. Hannah More speaks of a gentleman who cited to her, as an exceptional sentence in a sermon he had heard, this declaration of Paul, "There is, therefore, now no condemnation to them which are in Christ Jesus, who walk not after the flesh, but after the Spirit." Whoever has held any intercourse with people of fashion, or even with unevangelized men of letters, must have been often struck with their wretched ignorance of Divine Revelation. Christians ought, therefore, when they quote scripture in their hearing, at the same time to notify them, in some way or other, that they are quoting.

In the received version, the Hebrew and Hellenistic idioms are sometimes not translated, but only transferred. To translate an idiom is not to render it literally, but to substitute for it a corresponding idiom, or if the language affords none, words which convey to us, as nearly as possible, the idea that the words in the original bore to those who spoke them. The idioms in question do not, as they are rendered in our version, make the same impression on the minds of English readers as they did, in the original, on those of the people of the East. Forms of language which were used in the refined court of Solomon, and are now in vogue among cultivated Orientals, are fastidiously shunned by the most ignorant Europeans and Europo-Americans of the present day. This is to be attributed less to a difference in virtue, knowledge, and taste, than to a difference in usage. Accordingly, there are words and phrases in approved use in the most refined circles of London, which are unseemly to the same class in New York, and the reverse holds equally true. The one is not, perhaps, displeased with the idea of the other, but only with his mode of expressing it. The same terms of language have varying shades of signification in different places, so that it becomes necessary to substitute other words in order to give utterance to the same idea, and nothing beyond it.

Occasionally we hear persons making some scripture expressions more offensive than they would otherwise be, by quoting them out of their connection.

The most elegant things may become indecorous when they are out of place, while, on the other hand, things that are indecorous in themselves are made decent by the circumstances in which they are spoken. Words which are not unpleasing to the ear when they are spoken by the aged or the uneducated, may be so when spoken by the young or the refined. The phraseology of the original scriptures is, to a great degree, that of unsophisticated nature. Those who first used it in the East were plain men, dwelling in tents, and, when we read what they said, we bear in mind that they lived in the remote past, and in other regions, and feel that there was a strict accordancy between their character and their language. And so we can easily understand how our Saxon forefathers, living in a ruder age than our own, could use the language of our version without impropriety. But when we, who live in this dainty age, adopt as our own the same simple and unadorned expressions, the incongruity is at once manifest. It is true, that when they are read or quoted on occasions of public or family worship, we do not disrelish them, because we are habituated to hear them on such occasions; but if we hear them in the drawing-room or at the place of business, they do not sound well. Modesty does not turn away abashed from the partial nakedness of the Indian, as he is seen in his native wilderness, but she would blush to see his scanty vestures adopted by the citizens of the metropolis.

Christians, and those who have been religiously educated, do well to bear in mind that some parts of the scriptures which, by reason of long familiarity, do not offend their ears, may not be the most euphonious to persons who are not habitual readers of the Bible. Hence, they should frame their speech less by their own notions of decorum than by those of their fellow-talkers.

Still, it must be owned that we may go absurd lengths out of tenderness for "itching ears," and the mawkish tastes of the world's denizens. Some refined Christians, in their religious utterances, take a deal of trouble to keep aloof from certain words, because vulgar use has, in their estimation, tainted them, not considering that the vulgar cannot taint a word by any abuse of it, so long as people of taste do not consent to disuse it. Though it is with great difficulty that we can bring ourselves to find fault with any member of that persecuted body of men, the clergy, we would respectfully ask leave to suggest whether some of them are not coming to be quite nice enough on this score. Some divines, in quoting this scripture: "Martha said, Lord, by this time he stinketh," would fain say, "by this time he emitteth unpleasant effluvia." Instead of "Be not drunk with wine," they would say, "Be not intoxicated with wine." In describing our Saviour's passion in Gethsemane, they would say, "He *perspired* as it were great drops of blood." The Rev. Dr. Griffin used to tell an anecdote of a clergyman who said, in the course of a sermon, "My dear hearers, unless you repent of your sins and turn unto God, you will go to a place that it would be indelicate to name before so refined an assembly."[29] Few things are more unbecoming the sacred office than an affectation of gentility. When John Wesley told his preachers they had

[29] In President Dwight's satire, "The Triumph of Infidelity,' al-

no more to do with being gentlemen than they had with being dancing-masters, he meant that they were not to affect extreme delicacy in the pulpit. We should make a difference between the official and the private address of the clergyman, just as Shakspeare does between the bearing of the courtier when in the palace and when he is on the field of battle.

> "Courtiers as free, as debonnair, unarmed,
> As bending angels, that's their fame in peace;
> But when they would seem soldiers, they have galls,
> Good arms, strong joints, true swords, and Jove's accord:
> Nothing so full of heart."

Those little elegances of speech which do not misbecome the drawing-room, do not sound well coming down from the pulpit. The preacher who is careful to mould his words to fastidious ears, or to curve his gestures to the admiration of the graces, betrays a want of earnestness. Ezekiel, when he had seen the visions of God by the river of Chebar, would have

ready quoted in an earlier part of this work, a kindred character is happily described:

> "There smil'd the smooth Divine, unus'd to wound
> The sinner's heart, with hell's alarming sound.
> No terrors on his gentle tongue attend;
> No grating truths the nicest ear offend.
> That strange new birth, that methodistic grace,
> Nor in his heart, nor sermons found a place.
> Plato's fine tales he clumsily retold,
> Trite, fireside moral seasaws, dull as old;
> His Christ, his bible placed at good remove
> Guilt hell-deserving, and forgiving love.
> 'Twas best, he said, mankind should cease to sin;
> Good fame requir'd it; so did peace within:
> Their honors, well he knew, would ne'er be driven;
> But hop'd they still would please to go to heaven."

made a very unseemly change, had he next been found adjusting his locks by a curling iron, or taking lessons of a posture-master. A sacred, grave simplicity, is the only fitting adornment of a grave message, deeply pondered, and passionately urged. If the preacher only makes his hearers understand and obey the gospel, he effects the great object of his ministry; if he does this, let some exquisite listener make him an offender for a word if he must. He may answer him in the spirit of Demosthenes, when he said to a snarling critic: "The fate of Greece does not depend on an ill-chosen word." These remarks are to the full as applicable to the laity as to the clergy. Let them take heed, lest in their prayers and exhortations they refine away the dignity and force of the sacred Saxon by the unnecessary use of words of Greek, Latin, or French extraction. Our religion does indeed require us to be true gentlemen, but it requires infinitely more—it binds us to the faithful performance of duties vastly more serious and noble than any the mere gentleman, commonly so called, can or will perform.

But we are wandering from our subject. Some occasional turns of expression in our version are now obsolete, in what is misnamed "good society," and were a new version to be made in the nicest adaptation to modish refinement, its language would, in no long time, be equally obsolete there. Many of the phrases current in the circles of giddiest Fashion, in Chesterfield's time, took no root in the language, and would now sound more uncouthly than the phraseology of Shakspeare's time or Milton's. Had a version been made by some purist or euphuist of those circles, what he would have meant for refinement, would seem to us, in the present time, the height of brainless affectation. In double-refined circles, not only are all scriptural ideas avoided, but the very words in which they are wont to be clad. Evangelical religion, with all its accompaniments, always must be as it always has been, obsolete, antique, and in bad fashion among them. We must venture to say that were we to strip the sacred volume of the venerable garb which it has so long worn, and, pranking it in a suit of modern coxcombry, to introduce it to the fashionable circle, to make graceful obeisance, and speak to fine ladies in polite circumlocutions, it would soon lose cast there, and become as impolite as ever. What of heaven was left about it, in its new guise, would be enough to chill and repel the fashionable patrons it sought, and it would be voted, like a waning beauty, to be "*a little faded.*"

When Col. Gardiner, after his conversion, carried amid his old associates his finished courtesy and dignity of manner, they did not save him from being counted unfashionable. His new love for prophets and apostles, his attachment to the Decalogue and the Sermon on the Mount, were sufficient to forfeit for him the smiles, the sympathies and the plaudits that once awaited him. The world hated him, because it hated his new Master. Whilst Christians, then, are sedulously to avoid giving to the world aught of needless scandal, they are not to flatter themselves that anything short of God's regenerating grace can abate and annihilate the old "OFFENCE OF THE CROSS."

We should aim in our intercourse with society, to

convey religious ideas in a vehicle as finished and comely as fidelity to the truth will admit. Yet propriety does not require us to keep clear of those scriptural words and phrases which, though the vulgar and the vicious have prostituted them, have not essentially any offensive signification. It is decidedly improper to turn aside from such a word, where from the connection its utterance is expected, or to manifest any misgivings or confusion in pronouncing it. It is silently informing the hearers, that we are no strangers to those vile people who defile the privileged vernacular of every child of God, and he informs those who would otherwise never have known it, that the word has a bad sense. If we are not to use any of the words that have, at sundry times, been vulgarized, we must refrain from speaking English altogether. With a view to guard the language against such spoliations, all who, by any sad accident, have heard words used in a low signification, should be careful not to betray their degenerate knowledge in respectable society, and so leave others in holy ignorance of the corruptions of human speech. Men of taste take this course; and it is a significant fact, that there are many words and expressions very freely used in the most cultivated circles, which are scrupulously shunned as indecent by the rude and vicious, on occasions of formal intercourse with the more refined orders, and with one another.

Besides words which, originally or in a secondary sense, have no indelicate or vulgar meaning, but which have received such significations from persons of depraved taste, there are others which were originally significant of gross and material ideas, but are often used figuratively to denote spiritual operations or other moral or religious notions. Words of the latter class are, for the most part, to be avoided, for though some of them are very expressive and forcible, they almost always lead the mind of the hearer from the figurative and becoming, to the literal and indecorous import.[30]

John Foster, in his third and fourth letters on the aversion of men of taste to evangelical religion, condemns the free use of certain words of the received version which are obsolete, and recommends the substitution of current synonymes. He would also have us avoid words which belong to the theological dialect and religious cant, allowing us, however, in speaking on religious subjects, to use all such scriptural words and technical terms for which equivalent words and terms cannot be found except in the form of definition or circumlocution. But grave changes in the *language* of religion have generally heralded, and have universally occasioned a desertion of the true *ideas* taught in the language so relinquished. It is a significant fact, that the great innovators in religious phraseology have been, nearly to a man, innovators in doctrine, and some of them notoriously and fatally heretical. In the ancient church, the

[30] We need not cite examples of this class of words. They will readily occur to every reader. On this subject Cicero remarks: "Fugienda est omnis turpitudo earum rerum, adquas eorum animos, qui audiunt, trahit similitudo. Nolo morte dici Africani *castratam* esse rempublicam: nolo *stercus* curiæ dici Glauciam: quamvis sit simile, tamen est in utroque deformis cogitatio similitudinis. *De Oratore*, l. iii, c. xli. The adjective, *pregnant*, is one of the least exceptionable of this class.

Alexandrian school of Philosophy, Syresius, the Platonist, the Gnostics, and the Rationalizing branch of the Mystics, are exemplifications of this remark. Such substitutions create a *chasm* instead of a *bridge* between the *secular* and the *inspired* mind. And further, as to what are called the obsolete words of our version, they are not and never can be obsolete in the sense in which those of a mere secular work are so; and the current of the best writing is at present rather in favor of restoring to the ordinary dialect than of removing some of these old, dishonored, but honorable words.[31]

In attempting to express religious ideas with plainness, precision and force, Christians sometimes venture to coin words and form unlicensed alliances of words. Thus have many awkward forms of speech crept into evangelical literature, and received the sanction of the best usage. It may at times be necessary to coin a word for immediate use, and ones taste is put to the test by such extemporaneous inventions. Butler accuses Hudibras of a want of judgment in this particular.

> . . . . "he could coin or counterfeit
> New words with little or no wit;
> Words so debased and hard, no stone
> Was hard enough to touch them on;
> And when with hasty noise he spoke 'em
> The ignorant for current took 'em."

The words which are sanctioned by good usage fail in many cases to give full expression to the feelings

[31] Robert Hall, fastidious as he was, made some just animadversions on the opinions advanced in the letters above mentioned, in his Review of Foster's Essays.

of the pious soul. None but those who have undertaken to write on religious subjects, can know how meagre our language is in approved materials for the elegant treatment of them. This meagreness is nowhere more manifest than in the department of Christian experience,—here a distinguished man of letters, himself an author of the first rank, pleasantly checks my pen with the remark; "I trespass upon your good nature; but have you read what Macaulay has written on the range, richness, and power of John Bunyan's dialect as it is unfolded in a book strictly and exclusively of *religious experience*—'The Grace Abounding?' I am ready, sir, to pit that book for power and compass of expression, against nearly any classic of the language—*meo periculo*, as Bentley said." "Thank you, sir, for the suggestion," I reply; but with submission, I must ask whether even Bunyan, mighty in the Saxon as he was, never felt that his graphic words gave his readers very insufficient notions of his wonderful experience? If I happen to understand myself, the idea I would be driving at is, that every writer, be his command of language what it may, must feel his poverty whenever he attempts to clothe his ideas of experience in an elegant garb. But let that pass; every human language must of necessity be defective here, though none perhaps is less so than our own. The various feelings of the renewed heart can be indicated only by the most vague expressions. Many of these states of mind must ever in this life remain unknown to all but the soul itself. As soon as a man is regenerated, he becomes, in many respects, a stranger and a foreigner in these lower regions; while his mind has undergone a radical change, its medium of communication with other minds remains the same. He must then, while here, be content to use the language of idolatrous Egypt, and to hold converse with his fellow-mortals by broken accents and rude signs, till he goes up to the celestial Canaan, where he will find a language copious enough to answer all the demands of his ever-growing faculties.

Christians should, in general, address one another by the appellative "brother" or "sister" only in religious assemblies, and in secular companies which are mostly composed of fellow-disciples, and in talking on religious subjects. These terms of address are most properly used among those who are nearly equal in age, office and honor. The fact that we are "all one in Christ" does not annul those laws of courtesy which require us to address people by their civil and ecclesiastical titles. It is true that, among Protestants, when one who is our superior has no such title, we are compelled to call him "brother" unless we style him "father," which we have high authority for doing, even though he be not our superior as to *age*. A marked superiority in piety, wisdom, learning or usefulness, is sufficient to license the use of this appellative, and a convert may properly use it in speaking to or of the man by whom he was led to believe. In conversing with those who erroneously confine the appellation to *aged* Christians, we do well to conform to their usage. It is a safe rule to apply it to those aged persons only who are thus addressed by general consent. A clergyman calls another clergyman "brother," but if the latter bears the title of "Bishop," "Doctor of Divinity," or "Professor," he addresses him by these titles. We should not call any person "father," "mother," "brother," or "sister," who has not been formally recognized as a Christian by a church: neither can we with any propriety give these endearing titles to those who do not belong to evangelical denominations.

It is not advisable, in ordinary cases, to use the phrases "God willing," "*Deo volente*," "By Divine permission," "With leave of Divine Providence," in publishing a *religious* meeting. It is to be presumed that God is willing that men should worship him at any time. True, it may be objected that He may *not* be willing that announced speakers should live to fulfill their published appointments. But it remains to be proved, that so far *as divine worship* is concerned, God is not willing his servants should live to engage in it. He may have other reasons for calling them out of the world before the anticipated service; yet surely he would be willing they should live *to praise* him, were there no other reasons for their departure. If any one quotes against us these words of Paul to the Corinthians, "I will come to you shortly, if the Lord will," we reply, that had Paul intended to go from Ephesus, where he was sojourning at the time, to Corinth directly by sea, he would have needed at least sixteen days; but if, as is more probable, he intended to take the land-route, he would have consumed full thirty days in the journey. And when we consider the dangers and hardships to which a traveller, and especially an apostle, was in that age exposed, we must conclude that it was no small undertaking—equal to that of a modern voyage from New York to Corinth. But inasmuch as he was not certain that he could visit them at all, it is likely that the phrase, "If God will," refers to the time either of his setting out on, or of his ending his journey, rather than to the perils of the way. The use of the adverb "shortly," favors this interpretation. In either case, the language of the apostle is no precedent for the usage in question, nor, we may add, for its being used in speaking of our ordinary vocations or engagements. The use of these phrases on all occasions sounds too much like cant. The proprietors of the stage-lines in England, used formerly to advertise that "they would be through by such a time, *God willing*"*!* The language of the Apostle James is, "Go to now, ye that say 'to-day or to-morrow we will go into such a city and continue there *a year*, and buy and sell and get *gain*.'" These phrases are properly employed only in speaking of a very important undertaking, whether religious or secular, the results of which are quite remote and uncertain; such as a voyage, a journey, or a new and very hazardous enterprize of any kind.

This direction of James, however, was designed, not so much to guide us in *speaking* as in *thinking* of God's providence. We ought, no doubt, habitually and at all times to feel that we and all our projects and works are in an Almighty and Allwise hand; but where is the propriety of formally alluding to the fact on all occasions? Those who scrupulously use the phrases in question, as multitudes do, without any wonted realization of their meaning, come farther short of the requirement than those who continually cherish a sense of the Divine Sovereignty, while they are less punctilious as to forms of speech.

N

CHAPTER XVII.

PHYSICAL HABITS IN CONVERSATION.

Distinctness of pronunciation is desirable in familiar talk, though it is not so needful in conversations as in orations, lectures, and sermons. Here we are occasionally allowed "to speak trippingly on the tongue" while "mouthing," and a laborious coining of syllables, are the sure marks of bad sense and bad taste. To talk without effort, either of thought or tongue, is charming, especially on gay themes, so it be not attended with heedlessness and thoughtlessness. Nothing is more vexatious than precipitancy and abruptness. These faults, it is true, often result from the nature of the sentiment expressed. On this point, Sir William Temple has a good idea. He says, "Good breeding is as necessary in conversation, to finish all the rest, as grace in motion and dancing. It is harder to dance a *courant* well than a *jig;* so in conversation, easy and agreeable sentiments are more difficult than points of wit, which, unless they fall of themselves naturally and not too often, are disliked in good company, because they pretend to more than the rest, and turn conversation from good sense to wit, from pleasantry to ridicule, which are the meaner parts." The tongue should commonly dance the *courant*, so it does not dance all night.

Lord Bacon has the following wise remarks on speaking leisurely: "In all kinds of speech, pleasant, grave, severe, or ordinary, it is convenient to speak leisurely and rather drawlingly than hastily; because hasty speech confounds the memory, and oftentimes, besides the unseemliness, drives a man either to stammering, a nonplus, or harping on that which should follow; whereas a slow speech confirmeth the memory, addeth a conceit of wisdom to the hearers, besides a seemliness of speech and countenance."

It is a valuable fact that we can keep our temper equable and pleasant by attending to the key in which we speak. A low tone is best when we are angry. By addicting ourselves to speak in a subdued and melodious voice, we can greatly improve a hasty and imperious disposition. There is a singular and useful speculation on the Music of Speech in the second volume of the Philosophical Transactions. The tenor of the writer's article here follows: "Sitting in some company," says the writer, "and having been but a little before musical, I chanced to take notice that, in ordinary discourse, words were spoken in perfect notes; and that some of the company used eighths, some fifths, some thirds, and that those were most pleasing whose words as to their tone consisted most of concords; and where of discords, of such as constituted harmony; and the same person was the most affable, pleasant, and best-natured in the company. And this suggests the reason why many discourses which one *hears* with much pleasure, when they come to be *read* scarcely seem the same things. From this difference of music in speech, we may also conjecture that of tempers. We know the

Doric mood sounds gravity and sobriety; the Lydian, freedom; the Æolic, sweet stillness and composure; the Phrygian, jollity and youthful levity; the Doric soothes the storms and disturbances arising from the passions. And why may we not reasonably suppose that those whose speech naturally runs into the notes peculiar to any of these moods, have a corresponding disposition?"

Accordingly, we must beg to recommend that some ladies and gentlemen put themselves under the discipline of a singing-master, and devote a few evenings to the gamut before they venture more to rasp the ears of their friends and foes at home and abroad. What a millenium would it be if spinsters could only be persuaded to spend less time in biting their lips, and more in seeing that they be the channels of a clear, bland, and mellifluous speech! Would that young ladies would occasionally lay aside the harp and the guitar, to chant the prose they are used to speak so untunably in the ears of their parents, and brothers and sisters. Would that Madame Whiner might exchange her eye-glasses, or her gold watch, or her gold cross, for a pitch-pipe, and especially send her dear poodle to the shambles, whose squeaking noise she is in great danger of copying. I will leave "the music of the spheres" to aeronauts, if you will only give me the music of a kind and good-natured human voice. But we must also guard her against speaking in too soft and languishing accents, as if she were ever on the point of expiring.

A natural or affected hissing is sometimes produced by striking the tongue against the edges of the teeth, particularly if they are artificial. Besides being rather disagreeable, it makes one throw out saliva. Too large a tongue will produce this habit, while too small a one may produce stammering. Whispering and reading aloud with a view to these faults, if persevered in, will generally correct them. The pronunciation may be made thick and indistinct by too much saliva in the mouth. In this case, it should always be swallowed before beginning to speak, and at intervals while talking. Attention to these trifling hints would greatly improve some people's elocution.

We frequently meet with loud laughers and talkers, whose whole aim is to draw off the attention of the company from what they are engaged in, and fix it upon themselves. This is the common artifice of vain young ladies and dandies, whose highest enjoyments in society consist of laughing, stamping the feet, and clapping the hands. Nor can I pass over the set of whisperers who, when any one comes into the room, duck down their heads, and inquire who he is, or tell all they know about him; at the same time staring him full in the face, or, in a tone just audible to the bystanders, speak about private affairs, and ask, "How is *that* matter coming on?"

Beware of indulging in too many and extravagant gestures. Be not so cautious, however, as to put your hands into your pockets, and, when standing, swing your body to and fro like the dancers in a seraglio. Dr. Johnson once, in company, laid hold of the hands of a pantomimic little Frenchman, and held them fast. He disliked gestures. His opinion on the subject is given in his life of Dr. Watts, who thought they were of little use even in preaching.

But an avoidance of all gesture is affectation, unless a man has been smitten with a palsy. Some sanguine and volatile people toss about their limbs in conversation as nimbly as they do their tongues. To witness their actions for five minutes is enough to make one resolve never to lift his finger again. They remind one of the old actors in comedies: when they said *memini* they would point to the back part of their head; when they said *video*, they would put their fingers in their eyes.

Some deem it a mark of respect ever to eye those whom they are talking with. It is a good practice in general, but it is a bad one in particular. There are those who will watch your eye intently, that they may ascertain the effects of their discourse, or keep their necks awry when they are seated at your side. It is a mark of modesty in children to turn their faces towards, but not to look at a stranger who is speaking to them. Then, there are shy and nervous people, who do not like to be continually confronted by the visage of the talker. Nevertheless, if a person be not deaf, it is an incivility for him to keep his ear steadily turned towards the speaker.

CHAPTER XVIII.

PREPARATION FOR CONVERSATION.

Preparation for talking should, for the most part, be indirect. The observation, thought, and reading of years, on a wide range of subjects, are a more reliable aid than special preliminaries for talking on a particular subject or at an appointed time. Most conversations are of a rambling and desultory character, so that it is not often practicable to put forth a prepared opinion, or to bring others to take sides on our favorite question. The attempt sometimes has an air of malapropos and abruptness; it opposes the general mood, and makes the circle formal and unfree. It is said that William Wilberforce used to note down the topics to be started; and this, perhaps, is all that is allowable to one who is expected to lead off a talk. Johnson, who was mighty in conversation, said he wished one day's notice if he was to meet Lord Thurlow. It would imply, that in that case he intended to make some preparation, and that in other cases he did not reject all "cramming" for the rencontre. Little reliance, however, is to be placed on themes previously chosen, inasmuch as it often happens that he who is expected to take the lead can only do so by adapting himself to the spirit and character of the company. Still, he must not be so complaisant to the ruling tone as to start indecent topics; like the elder Walpole, who said he always talked bawdry at his table, that all might be able to bear a part. The chief converser is, in a great degree, answerable for the spirit of the company, and has it in his power to turn it into a high and useful channel. And, by-the-bye, every one should go into society with a purpose to turn subjects broached there to good account; he will, in this way, be more useful than by a direct aim to converse on none but serious topics.

Themes of general interest are preferable to all others. Among these are religion, morals, politics, education, nature, art, science, literature, health, and the weather. Next to these must be ranked those which are of a purely local kind, and interesting only to certain coteries. Lastly, those which concern only private individuals. The latter are admissible only among relatives and friends.

The themes generally current in town differ from those in the country. This holds true among almost all ranks. Religious people in the country talk more frequently and intelligibly on scriptural and moral subjects. People of fashion in the country talk more intellectually than the same class in town. Horace says that the conversation in Rome ran on the villas, families of foreigners, and the theatre; while, in the country, the questions discussed were whether riches or virtue more becomes man; whether utility or rectitude more influences us in forming our friendships; what is the nature of good, and what is perfection. The same distinction, in the main, exists to this day. The variety and interest of events in town are unfavorable to meditation, philosophizing, and discussion.

Objects of the senses are more talked of than those of thought, and matters of taste in preference to those of utility. In general, there is less of what is local and pedantic in town talk, and more of books and human nature in rural discourse. In town, the scandal is chiefly confined to the newspaper; in the country, it is circulated by the drones of the village. It is a propensity of the ignorant, in all situations, to allow trivial matters to engross their talks. A rumor, an accident, or a neighborhood quarrel, or a family feud, a trial before the justice of the peace, or the freak of a school-boy—these are enough to keep their tongues in perpetual motion. So vacant is the life of the illiterate, that the slightest occurrence is magnified into an event of vast importance, even as, to travellers in a desert the smallest shrub which lifts its head above the unbroken waste, awakens an interest which a forest would not in one who was passing through a fertile region.

Reading adds to one's stock of ideas, and consequently to the subjects of discourse. Histories, biographies, books of travel and of the natural sciences, reviews, newspapers, narratives of recent events, and an extensive correspondence, furnish the best matter for general conversation. To those who would be qualified for the company of the educated and the refined, some knowledge of the art of painting, sculpture, music, poetry, eloquence, the sciences, professional information, and current literature, are highly valuable. The Christian and all others indeed, should add to these an acquaintance with ecclesiastical history general and denominational, missionary intelligence, reports of benevolent operations, and evangelical literature, especially biographies of pious persons.

But above all, the converser should have a thorough knowledge of the Bible. He should make its pages his daily study, and read such commentaries and other works as serve to illustrate its truths, clear up its obscurities, and discuss its doctrines. Its theology, morals, laws, history, poetry, and eloquence, should be familiar to him. Such a knowledge will give him a great advantage in all companies; for there are few books of which the generality live in such miserable ignorance, as of the book which reveals their eternal destiny. It is no despicable acquisition to be versed in a book which has for thousands of years been fixing the fate of other books, either lending them its protection, or sinking them in oblivion in the calm shadow of its reprobation—which has set up and cast down thrones, appointed the bounds of empires, and marked out the track of civilization, given wisdom to the sagest lawgivers, furnished models even for the highest secular eloquence and poetry,[32] and is now putting to the proof all creeds and all deeds. But its crowning merit has

[32] The Lake Poets, as they have been somewhat vaguely called, Wordsworth, Coleridge, and Southey, dwellers for a season or permanently beside the Lakes of Westmoreland, have exercised a strong influence on English literature. De Quincey, himself a high proficient in the language, and in literary criticism, traces a part at least of their power to their admiration and use of the scriptural dialect. Fisher Ames, in his earlier time, the great orator of New England, was wont to recommend the Scriptures as a fountain of style; and the yet higher son of New England, who has recently gone to the grave amid the regrets and gloom of the nation—Daniel Webster—was an earnest admirer and student of the same Divine Volume, as a repository of great images and phrases, no less than of great and peerless facts.

not been mentioned. It was the sole guide of multitudes of pilgrims who are now reposing in paradise: on it rest the hopes of all the excellent now on earth, and is to be the trust of all saints in all the ages which are yet beyond us.

It may not be amiss here to say, that though conversers cannot too highly prize the Bible, some of them may be in danger of mistaking its design and province. It was intended to give us light as to religion and morals alone, and those who continually refer to it as authority on other subjects, do, in the estimation of unbelievers, lessen its authority within its own sphere. Though the oracles of God contain much scientific knowledge, it was not to instruct mankind in this that they were given to us.

The converser should ever be pursuing a course of reading. He cannot at any time lay aside books, without leaving a void in his mind, which he can only fill by subsequent diligence. He who neglects the news of a single week, may be ignorant of the one event on which those of a whole year, nay, century, shall turn. And he who omits glancing at the new publications of the passing month may overlook the one book of the age, the last miracle of genius. And as the converser must be continually parting with his knowledge, so unless he is continually adding to his store, he is driven either to seek new society, or to afflict his old acquaintance with repetitions. It is a very simple precept, yet one so valuable that it is thought worth being ascribed to an ancient philosopher, that "If you wish your lamp to emit light, you must feed it with oil."

We frequently hear it said that the prevailing rage

for reading, leaves the people little leisure for conversation, and less for meditation, which alone can make conversation a solid advantage. In some cases, it is to be feared, it has wrought this result; as to the mass of the people, however, it would seem to be otherwise. How can there be less thinking than formerly, when the present habit of reading must suggest a thousand subjects of thought and discourse, where there was but one before; how can there be, when the attention, perception, judgment, and imagination, which are necessarily exercised in most sorts of reading, are thereby better fitted for application to any subject whatever, than they would have been without such exercise? And inasmuch as those who are considered great readers, are left to their own thoughts for some part of every day, they lack neither leisure for thinking nor preparation for it, as regards discipline and matter. Nor does much reading necessarily put an end to independence and originality of thinking. Ignorance is quite as destructive of these qualities as knowledge; prejudice, popular opinion, and common sense, as it is vulgarly understood (i. e., the mind's first thoughts and first feelings), are Goths and Vandals, that trample down all intellectual freedom and power. It is only the great reader that can know when he is engaged in original thinking; it is by his researches alone that he can ascertain what regions of thought lie untraversed; and not being in doubt as to whether he is tracing an old path or a new, he presses forward with all the self-reliance and enthusiasm of an explorer.

Another means of preparation for conversation is the hearing of lectures. It is complained that a rage for lyceum lectures encroaches upon conversation-meetings; not so much because it disables the mind for preparatory reflection, as because it consumes the time which would otherwise have been devoted to conversation, and begets a race of smatterers in superficial and second-hand knowledge. As to the question of time, were people to go to lectures every evening, or were they to spend the whole of every evening in hearing them, then might we make our moan over the imaginary desolations of conversation-rooms; but extremely few have gone so far mad after lectures as to run to them every evening, and those who have, contrive to find time enough before and after lectures to open and canvass their opinions on all sorts of subjects. The hearing of lectures, so far from laying the tongues of people to rest, always drives them to greater activity; and we have scarcely ever known a single tongue to move any long time in public, that did not set a good many more going in private. There is more occasion for the other lamentation, to wit, that mere lecture-going diffuses among the generality second-hand and superficial knowledge. All kinds of lectures, save those that are upon subjects which need illustrating by experiments, do not fix in the memory so large an amount of information as the same time improved in reading would do. The lecturer pushes forward to the conclusion, all along taking for granted that hearers are not wanting in attention, perception, and memory; hence, the many who are wanting in one or more of these faculties, fail to profit by hearing a lecture to the same degree that they would by reading it at their leisure. In that case they could read the more weighty or abstruse parts repeatedly, or if their attention flagged in other portions, they could go over the ground anew. Greater evils are, in my poor judgment, hatched out of the *forbidden* knowledge, than out of the superficial knowledge taught in popular lectures; the stealing of such knowledge was the killing sin of our first parents, and repetitions of this primal theft are likely to be the killing sins of all generations of their children; but let that pass. We fear that the mischief growing out of superficial knowledge is very generally supposed to be greater than it really is. Those lines of the poet, so incessantly quoted, beginning, "Drink deep, or taste not the Pierian spring," are too often construed into ill advice, inasmuch as a little of a good thing is better than none, and as intoxication from shallow knowledge is better than drunkenness from deep ignorance, though both are bad enough, for that matter. So far as the masses of the people are concerned, the question to be decided is not whether they shall acquire much knowledge or little, but whether they shall acquire little or none at all. There are multitudes who at nightfall find their minds so jaded with the business or dissipated with the pleasures of the day, that they have no heart to bend down to the earnest work of reading, but can muster attention enough to listen to what a tolerable lecturer has to say on a passably interesting theme. Such people will make better conversers by hearing a lecture occasionally, than they would were they to spend the same time in idleness or in the vain endeavor to read. Another thing; it is not absolutely necessary that they should be thoroughly acquainted with a subject in order to *take part* in a conversation about it; if, however, they would take a *prominent* part or *take the lead*—they do well to arm themselves at all points. Those who are not made better talkers will be made better listeners by the bits and ends of facts and principles which they in this way pick up; they will not listen with the blank stare and confused manner of those who have yet to dream their first dream concerning the subject of talk. But the indirect benefits flowing from lectures are the largest tributaries to conversation; the lecturer exciting in many of his hearers a literary curiosity, sets them upon a long and useful course of reading if not study, and so leads them away to distant and sequestered sources of information: exhibiting to them a few specimens of the ore of knowledge, they go and dig for themselves, and bring back a large amount of the same precious metal, and make it a circulating medium in the trade of conversation.

Habits of careful observation also add to the treasures of the converser. The books of nature, animate and inanimate, spiritual and material, lie open before every man, but one dozes over them, another gives them a hurried reading, and another makes them a careful study; the same may be said of the arts and sciences. The difference as to knowledge between one who observes and one who does not is immense: it is almost the difference between the living and the dead. Lock up the one in a dungeon and he will compose a system of mental philosophy; lock up the other and he will merely ascertain that he is in the dark. The one, after a short excursion into the country, returns full of interesting accounts of his discoveries; the other, after circumnavigating our planet, returns home only to tell us that he has voyaged round the world, and perchance brought home the scurvy.

Again, he who would talk judiciously must add meditation to reading and observation. This will enable him to form correct judgments concerning the ideas with which reading and observation have supplied him. A man of thought makes the notions of others his own, by what he adds to or takes from them, by weighing them so as to stamp them with their just value, and by the feelings they rouse and the conduct they actuate. The reader who talks without previous meditation, is only a retailer of second-hand thoughts, which have cost him nothing but the storage, and have perhaps become mouldy by the keeping. If at any time he embraces a new doctrine—and every novelty takes with him—he can offer no reason for adding another article to his creed. He forms his opinions amidst the hurry of talking, and of course often makes assertions in this circle which he contradicts in that. As he never ponders a subject, so his feelings are not proportional to its importance; he talks now fervently on the most paltry themes, and now coolly on momentous ones. Or, if he is of a cautious turn, he is at a loss to decide on the plainest question, or speaks so guardedly that his mind seems always hovering on the dusky confines of light and darkness. He is so near the domains of Error, and is in so remote a province of Truth, that the latter is not proud to call him her own.

Meditation will prepare the Christian to talk profitably on the subject of Christian experience, enabling him to separate gracious affections from feelings which have been induced by the temperament, or by disease, or sympathy, or animal excitement, and bringing him to look with suspicion on all experiences which do not result in some practical virtue. He will be profited by a discriminating and cautious reading of such works as "Augustine's Confessions," "Bunyan's Grace Abounding," and "Halyburton's Memoirs." It is from a want of due reflection and study on the subject of their experiences, that Christians make it so small a part of their conversations; a subject which, if properly handled, has the wonder of a miracle, the thrilling interest of adventure, and the enchantment of poetry, blending together the highest excitement of perils incurred, and the most dazzling splendors of hope newly risen and never to set.

Let the Christian also think of the attributes and government of God—the character, offices and mission of our Redeemer—the person and work of the Holy Spirit—our disobedience, misery and obligations, the history of churches, missionary operations among heathens, Mohammedans, Jews, Romanists, and others—Bible, tract and educational societies, especially the relation of these societies to ourselves and the church to which we belong; the best plans for bringing evangelical truth to bear upon the community in which we live, by means of Sunday schools, prayer meetings, and tract distributions. Though words can never evangelize the world, yet, if these enterprizes occupy our hearts and our hands as much as they ought, they will naturally claim a share in our conversations. One of the vast and urgent problems of our time is the relief of pauperism, and the mediating reconciliation of government between the oppressions of Capital and the anarchy of Labor. In a high civilization, the clefts and rifts of want and vice seem deepening and darkening towards the abyss of Brutalism and Despair, as the heights of Luxury and Refinement still ascend and tower higher and higher into the freezing regions of Heartlessness and Pride. In what manner the unfailing Gospel shall be brought most directly and vigorously to bear against the evils of this contrast and dissonance, becomes to the lover of that Gospel a question of the highest interest from its bearings alike on polity, charity, and religion.

The Christian converser should also reflect on the dealings of Providence with nations, churches, and individuals. If in every event and in the most common occurrences may be discerned the hand of God, how comes it to pass that so little is thought or said of this important truth by those who believe that they are themselves led by that hand? And how does it happen that they are used to call only unaccountable and extraordinary events "providences," as if we were always unmindful that the Lord reigns, except when we are startled by some great stroke of the Divine policy? Though the heathens err in *making* a god of everything, they are wiser than some Christians in this, that they *see* God in everything. Let the pious converser regard it as a becoming duty to notice those unobtrusive instances of the Divine superintendence which are too often overlooked by historians and philosophers.

Finally, let the converser contemplate the works of Creation with a view to provide his mind with matter for talk. Here he may range at large; those who will not converse with him on other subjects will on this. Let him then contemplate the garden, or the prairie, either the flower which a lady's fingers rear, or that which the ploughman's foot crushes to the earth; the field of grain waving in the west-wind and shadowed with the passing cloud, or the dark primeval forest; the sands and oases of the desert, the mountain with its mantle of snow and its girdle of clouds, or the valley where dwells perpetual spring; the lake, the river, the cataract and the ocean—the earth with all its living and departed tribes: its modern and ancient changes, organic and inorganic—the heavens with their old and new worlds, all that the naked eye beholds around, the microscope beneath, and the telescope above us. Let him behold in the works of nature the wisdom and goodness of God. But these alone? Nay, verily. God's severity also is seen in the black cloud and the storm-wind; the mountain-wave and the water-spout; the thick darkness and the thunder-clap; the quaking earth and the flaming volcano. And it is He who sends the piercing cold, and the damp, misty, and lowering day; that instead of always looking abroad, we might betimes turn our thoughts back upon themselves, and that we might believe his word when we cannot see his smiles. He causes the thunder to be heard along with the falling rain, and darts the lightning athwart the bow of promise, that we might remember that he is a God of justice as well as of love.

Some advisers would have us conceal our ignorance in conversation, so that if we know little or nothing of the subject broached, we may yet discourse on it with confidence and seeming intelligence. Now, we cannot counsel any one to make a show of knowledge he does not possess. Such an action deserves no better name than dissimulation, and often amounts to falsehood. Let us never be loth to own our ignorance whether it be avoidable or unavoidable: he who is thus ingenuous, will gain the friendship and the confidence of all wise and learned men. If he is not already knowing, he eventually will be. The rod with which he chastises his ignorance will goad him on to knowledge.

The last preparation for the *conversazione*, which we shall mention, is self-conversation. Whatever knowledge we may derive from the above mentioned sources—to which we might add, an intercourse with the world—it cannot stand us in stead of an acquaintance with our own obliquities and failings. And let the tone of the companies we frequent be ever so devout, and the spiritual benefits we receive from them be ever so great, if we do not join self-communion with such conversations we may be quite sure that we are not making them in the highest degree beneficial to us.[33]

[33] "He that would teach man's heart must learn his own.
Up with thy torch then in that cavern drear,
Nor shut thine eyes when hideous forms appear;
By the red flare from fearful darkness thrown,
To thee must passion's motley brood be known,
Dark elves of thought, foul imps of guilty fear,
Keen judgment's flash, which shows the vast and drear,
Threatening in hideous ruin to come down.

Self-discourse aids us in gaining a knowledge of human nature than which nothing is more valuable to the converser. The whole race is formed after one archetype, and all are alike in the main lineaments. To be sure a great deal is to be learned by studying men as we find them influenced by a variety of circumstances. The multiform temptations to evil and encouragements to good which are set before them, bring to light many principles which might else have remained in the dark. While this is to be granted, it must not be overlooked that we may possibly be versed in human nature as it is in other men, and yet be ignorant of human nature as it is in ourselves. It is this latter that is especially advantageous to us in the commerce of society. The homely remark, often made respecting any one who has tact and address, that "he understands himself," is literally true, if it be true at all; for such a one will be found to owe more or less of his skill to self-knowledge. He who is ignorant of his own character is in danger of neglecting the proprieties which are due to others; he who should so mistake his own stature as to think himself a pigmy, would be in continual fear of being trod upon, while he who should fancy himself a giant, might think he could tread upon others with impunity.

Unscared through gloom of conscience thou must grope,
Through passages of tortuous self must wind,
And keep undimmed thy light, untorn thy clue.
So shalt thou learn to sound thy brother's mind,
So minister to faith, so help to hope,
So teach to shun the false, and seize the true."

Rev. Robert Wilson Evans.

There is, perhaps, no precept in the sacred writings which should be more frequently practised in conversation than that which is called the golden rule; and yet no one can duly observe it, who does not also observe the golden rule of the Greeks, namely: "Know thyself"—words which were blazoned in letters of gold over the door of the temple of Apollo at Delphi. The former rule presupposes an accurate acquaintance with our own master passions, prejudices, preferences, and antipathies. Without this, we can behave neither justly nor pleasantly towards our fellow-conversers. In all our talks, and especially when we have parted from the circle, and the music of the tongue has ceased to enchant us, it is wise to ask ourselves questions like the following: "How would I feel were I addressed on that subject or in that manner? How would I be likely to interpret such a remark, or bear such an insinuation concerning myself or my friend? How would I endure such an exposure of my ignorance or folly?" Nothing short of a profound self-knowledge can prepare us to answer such questions aright.

As the thoughts which we entertain in retirement are apt to disclose themselves in the unguarded intercourse of society, we should daily ask ourselves what are our habitual ones, and take care that they always be of such a character as will prompt kind, ingenuous, and cheerful discourse. If we do not wish to betray enmity in our talk, we must not suffer it to rankle in the breast; or if we would avoid boasting, we must keep clear of self-flattery when we are left to our own reflections; as fondly recalling our strokes of wit or anecdotes, or thinking how much more ably we could have handled a subject than another did, how triumphantly we might have answered the opponent of another; but it is not possible to specify all the recollections on which a vain mind dwells with fondness.

Frequent self-discourse will keep our talks from growing tedious and trite. People who always harp upon the same topics, or repeat the same anecdotes, do well to form a habit of calling to mind all their talks, and of marking to whom and where they exhibited their darling thoughts. Those who have had the honor of forming an acquaintance with themselves, and of faithfully cultivating it, do not ride a hobby a great while, or if circumstances call them to talk on the same subject frequently, they do not, on all occasions, mount to the same pitch of vehemence, nor use the same phrases and illustrations; by occasionally changing the caparisons of their hobby, they make it pass for no hobby at all. In this way they get the advantage of that tribe of critics who go into society on purpose to find fault, or else to brand people with absurd or scandalous names indicative of their foibles. When a wise man learns that these persons have so stigmatized him, he says nothing to anybody but himself, and immediately begins to reform his manners, so that, should the *name* continue to be applied to him, the *thing* may disappear, and his enemies be proved unjust for any longer reproaching him with it.

The tongue is, of all our organs, the most ready interpreter of the mind. It sends its roots far down the throat towards the heart, as if to declare, by its very situation, its close connection with "the inward man." It is to be governed only by governing the mind, whose will is its law. In the work of self-conquest it is the last to leave the service of a rebellious heart; and when it has been gained, there is nothing more to be won: "if any man offend not in word, the same is a perfect man, and able also to bridle the whole body." It is, therefore, only by the practice of introspection, and by often taking our minds to task, that this little and nimble member can be controlled.

It will be a help to self-inquiry to consider what opinions others are likely to form of our words, and how they would sound were they to fall from the lips of another. One of the resolutions of President Edwards was, "Never to do anything which, if I should see in another, I should count a just occasion to despise him for, or to think any way the more meanly of him." We are such adepts in the art of finding out the faults of others, that we can detect our own most easily when in imagination we impute them to another; by this means we are able to discover many blemishes which before escaped observation, as by the help of a mirror we can survey parts of our persons which we could not see by direct vision.

Whoever has recalled at evening the conversations of the day, or the talk of a single interview, and has thought of the probable consequences of one misspoken word, must have wished that he had either said less, or else had said nothing at all. Such a self-recollection will convince him that, in general, it is more wise to hold the tongue than to talk, and teach him to guard his lips with ceaseless vigilance. "Suppose," says Richard Baxter, "you were to write down the idle words of a day—your own or any other prattler's—and read them over at night, would you not be ashamed of such a diary of vanity and confusion. Oh what a work might one thus write from the mouths of idle talkers! What a shame would it be to human nature! It would tempt one to question whether he be a reasonable creature, or whether all be so, at least. Remember that all your words are recorded by God and conscience, and that all this medley must be reviewed and answered for." Who has not cause to tremble at the thought, that every unprofitable word he has spoken, is noted down in the books which are to be opened in the day of final adjudication—when will be brought forward records not only from the archives of heaven and of conscience, but also from those of material nature. It is the opinion of Laplace, that the curves which are described by a single molecule of air, are subjected to laws as certain as those of the planetary orbits, and it has been shown that the movements of our tongues give an impulse to the air, the results of which will be forever discernible by an All-seeing Eye; so that to use the words of Mr. Babbage, "the atmosphere we breathe is the ever-living witness of the sentiments we have uttered." We may add, that the Omniscient Being who will behold all the effects on the material universe, of one vibrating atom, will also be witness to the effects on the moral universe, of the pulses of every communicated thought, which, in obedience to a higher law, is to be received and registered by myriads of minds throughout eternity. "Weigh well thy words," is the solemn warning which both spirit and matter whisper in the ears of every man.

> "O words! not from immortal mind alone
> Immortal are ye sprung; let heaven and earth
> Receive you, standing witness to your birth,
> And send you back when many years are flown.
> Not swallow comes more surely to its own,
> Nor nightingale renews her last year's mirth,
> Than ye return, in plenty or in dearth,
> Changed, yet the same: echo, yet living tone.
> From weeping hearts where ye have brooded long,
> From bosoms festering with deep offence,
> From minds that on your promise full have fed,
> To him that sent you ye return, all strong
> In ancient sound, and doubly keen in sense;
> Nor will ye take repulse, O things of dread."
>
> REV. R. W. EVANS.

CHAPTER XIX.

ACCOMPANIMENTS OF CONVERSATION.

In large mixed companies, as they are commonly arranged, free and familiar conversation is out of the question. There will be present strangers, whom we do not feel at liberty to talk with on every topic, and unconversable people who will not talk at all, having, as said the despondent Frenchman of some taciturn companion, a singular talent for silence. None but the most general and commonplace subjects can safely be started, and even these we are forced to touch upon with extreme caution and brevity. The knowing person must sacrifice his pleasure to ignorant people, or else they must sacrifice theirs to him; and if a profitable conference is commenced, it is soon broken off by bringing forward something else. That the talk may be as unrestrained, and generally engaged in as possible, a large company should part off into small groups. Thus the separate circles will be able to entertain themselves, being so small that each person will have courage to say something, and each easily hear what others say. Conflagrations act in circles, and the fire of conversation seems to act in very small ones. These groups do away the diffidence which is apt to prevail when people are arranged along the walls like chairs in a hall. De

Foe's solitary mariner, finding that he could not tame his kids, or catch them by hedging them in a field two miles in circumference, altered his plan, and diminished the area of the enclosure fourteen-fold.

Eating, as an accompaniment of talk, has something to recommend it. By this act various sorts of people declare that they have common wants and gratifications, and that they are so near an equality as to warrant mutual affability. At dinners we should not talk too much during the first course; it discommodes the speaker and annoys the listener. If we ever say anything, it should be something that requires no reply, much less a refutation. It is not honorable to attack our opponent when his mouth is so occupied with masticating, that he cannot defend himself. If he hesitates or seems confused, the party may think he is nonplused by the arguments of his adversary, when he is only nonplused by some delicious morsel. Mrs. Gore pleasantly argues thus: "as nature has allowed but one organ to perform the functions both of talking and eating, it is clear to me that she never intended man should speak and feed at the same time, but the contrary. These two excellent faculties of our nature should act separately, for when a good thing going into the mouth meets a good thing coming out thereat, they are almost sure to run foul of, and mar each other." Above all things, do not start a vexed question as soon as you have taken your place at the table. People are pugnacious when they are hungry, and will, in all likelihood, deal severely with you if they are called out at that time; besides, you run the risk of bringing down upon you the displeasure of the hostess, for preferring the debate to the dinner, and for allowing it to grow cold while some gormand must sit and be tantalized by the dishes which are brought on. Yet the solemnity which is permitted to reign from first to last at many tables, is, to say the least, altogether unscriptural: "Eat thy bread with joy, and drink thy wine with a merry heart." (Eccl. ix. 7.) The host and hostess should aim to lead their guests into conversation, and not engross it all to themselves. In "the feast of reason" they are best entertained who are permitted to entertain. The host and hostess should, in due season—and the sooner the better—be lost among their guests. "If," says the son of Sirach, "thou be made the master of the feast, lift not thyself up, but be among them as one of the rest; take diligent care of them, and so sit down. And when thou hast done all thy office, take thy place, that thou mayest be merry with them, and receive a crown for thy well-ordering of the feast."[34]

[34] Tobacco smoking, as an accompaniment of household talk, is now principally confined to vulgarians, and the Camanche Indians. Cowper, in his admirable poem on Conversation, makes a launch upon those smoking colloquists who

" . . . with solemn interposing puff,
Make half a sentence at a time enough;
The dozing sages drop the dozing strain,
Then pause and puff, and speak and pause again.
Such often, like the tube they so admire,
Important triflers! have more smoke than fire.
Pernicious weed, whose scent the fair annoys;
Unfriendly to society's chief joys,
Thy worst effect is banishing for hours
The sex whose presence civilizes ours."

Conversers who use narcotics, and stimulating and exhilarating

As an interlude to conversation, and as a suggester of a fresh theme, *reading* is occasionally allowable, especially in small circles; supposing always that it be with the consent of all, and the book be one of common interest. The reader should allow others to interrupt him with questions, objections, and remarks. The listener should give close attention, and not break in upon the reader with observations foreign to the subject. When the book opens a rich vein of talk, the reader should cheerfully lay it aside, and take a part in the colloquy. When the subject is exhausted, and the conversation flags, or is taking a wrong direction, the reader may return to his task, being careful not to continue it so long a time as to weary the group. We could not advise an author to read his own works, or a composer to sing or play his own pieces for a whole evening, going on without interruption, and locking up the lips of the circle in perpetual silence. Persons who are urged to contribute their own productions to the common entertainment, should reflect that none are likely to be so great admirers of their performances as themselves; and that how warmly soever the party applaud and cry *encore*, brevity is a merit they will value more highly than they will venture to express.

Another and more common interlude to conversa-

drinks, are often betrayed into words and actions which would come with better grace from those who are stark mad. Whoever consumes more tea or tobacco, opium or wine, than the majority of his company, falls out of tone with them, and unwittingly commits a thousand indiscretions which surprise and disgust them. Total abstinence ought to be the virtue of the conversationist who has any character to establish or support in society.

tion is music. A long intellectual talk jades and exhausts the mental faculties; a hymn, a song, or a tune, exhilarates and reposes them, so that they may return to animated and improving conference. Goethe's "fair saint" in her "confessions," speaking of the effect of devotional songs in parties, says: "They sat like jewels in the golden ring of a polished, intellectual conversation; and without pretending to edify, they elevated me and made me happy in the most spiritual manner." But Christians should refuse to fill up the intermissions of talk with the light and amatory songs which are so fashionable. A great moral degeneracy in musical composition has been going on of late. Many of the recent contributions to sacred melody are of the artificial, theatrical, and voluptuous kind. We may admire the ingenuity of the composition and the skill of the execution—nay, and be filled with certain inflating sensations, but our souls are not drawn heavenward by the solemn and heart-moving tones of true devotion. Would that there might be a speedy return from this captivity, which is, in some respects, literally Babylonish, inasmuch as it causes those who are held captive to hang their ancient harps upon the willows, and disqualifies them for singing the songs of Zion. Such music is allowed not only to mingle its strains with the praises of the congregation, but to ascend with the incense which curls towards heaven from the family altar. Indeed it is on the family hearth that this strange fire is first kindled, whence it is borne to the altars of religion. If Lycurgus forbad the Spartans all luxurious music, and if Plato would exclude from his model state all Lydian and Ionic airs, as being too sensual, should not every Christian parent, guardian, and teacher consider well the moral tendencies of the music, which is daily thrilling the hearts of children, and, as an authorized censor, deny his imprimatur to every song which ministers to a refined sensuality? It is no wonder that those who have spent years over the pages of this class of Italian, French, and German composers, should long to see them received into the fellowship of Christian music, and should lose all relish for the artless but full-souled and spiritual notes of our forefathers. While the Christian is not to be against musical innovations which are improvements, let him not cast aside those spiritual songs which have so long been the delight of all devout assemblies; if heartily sung, even the man of the world will occasionally prefer them to those amatory ditties which he hears so often that their very name grates upon his ear. Let him not engross a whole evening with these ditties, so that, when the hour of prayer has come, he can only slur over a hymn in which the heart's voice of melody is not heard. Neither let him admit into the *conversazione* an alternation of sacred and profane pieces. Such an ill-sorted fellowship were worse than an entire exclusion of serious music. Let not the harp and the psaltery of David be heard blending their strains with those of the pipe and viol of ungodly revellers. This were not only to profane holy things, but utterly to destroy them by allowing sacred harmonies to be swallowed up and drowned amid the demoralizing melodies of the world.

We would not here be understood to condemn those songs which, though they have a high moral bearing, do not avowedly aim to assist devotion. There are occasions when such songs may more properly be sung than those of a more solemn kind. Collections of a deep moral and religious tone, adapted to the drawing-room, are greatly needed, and it is hoped that pious poets and composers will in no long time supply this deficiency.

The last, but not the least important accompaniment of conversation which we shall mention, is prayer. Aside from its higher designs, it is one of the best of mental recreations. The celebrated Haydn was accustomed to resort to prayer as a restorative to his mental energies when they had been exhausted by long application to his musical studies. How becoming, and yet how uncommon it is for Christian circles to invoke the divine blessing on their conversations. When Christians meet together, though it be for an object not directly religious, let them not so far forget the adorable Redeemer or themselves as wholly to confine their communion to one another, having not a word to say to Him who has promised to be among those who meet in his name. And though it is not always convenient to open parties with prayer, they may be closed with it; and in some cases short prayers may properly be interspersed among the parts of conversation. What if an address to the throne of grace should check awhile the blitheness of those who are strangers to their Divine Benefactor? Even these will afterwards, in their moments of sober reflection, approve the action as honorable to the actors. Were a person of distinction present, all would think it uncourteous not to accost him nor allow him to take any part in the conversation. If we are not practical atheists, or at least those who believe that God has nothing to do with his own world, we must feel that it is treating him with great effrontery not to acknowledge his supremacy, presence, and grace in all collections of Christian people. Thrice happy will be "the celestial nobility" when they shall aim to make each of their assemblies a levee of King Immanuel.

CHAPTER XX.

A HISTORY OF CERTAIN CONVERSATION-CLUBS; WITH SKETCHES OF THE CONVERSATION OF JOHNSON, HANNAH MORE, COLERIDGE AND OTHERS.

A FULL history of conversation-clubs would embrace an account of the groups of talkers that used, in the patriarchal time, to gather under the shade of the vine and of the fig-tree, and in the gates of cities; of the story-hearing crowds at Arabian caravansaries; of the *symposia* of philosophers and the parties of Aspasia at Athens; of the table-talks of Lucullus, Lælius, Atticus, Cicero, and Mæcenas at Rome, and her suburban villas. It would also tell of the dinners of the mum and chattering monks and nuns in religious houses, and of knights recounting their adventures in hospitable castles during the middle ages; concluding with the principal talking-societies of the following centuries. But for fear we should fall into the error of them that when they have a short story to tell must needs begin with the foundation of the world, we make haste to say that it is our design only to take sketches of such of the modern notable conversation-clubs and conversationists as fall within the scope of a practical work, and yield some useful lessons.

We will begin with that literary circle at Paris, which, from various causes, became more celebrated than any other, ancient or modern—that of which Madame de Sévigné was the brightest ornament. Madame de Rambouillet assembled at her house a company of wits, among whom were Voiture, Balzac, Chapelain, Benserade, Cotin, Desmarets, Vaugelas, Ségrais, Bussy Rabutin, Rochefoucault, the mother of the great Condé, Mademoiselle de Scudéri, Madame de la Suze, Madame de Grignan, and Madame de Sévigné. The greater number of these personages designated each other by anagrams, and the mistress of the house was christened variously Arthénice, Eracinthe, and Corinthée. This society has been accused of bringing into fashion that double-distilled jargon and insipid gallantry of which Mademoiselle de Scudéri has given an example in her romance called Célie. Here they composed enigmas, madrigals, *bouts-rimés*, sonnets, and rondeaus; and if we may believe some writers of that time, those verses were best received which were the farthest removed from everything natural in style.[35] La

[35] "All was done by rule—all adapted to a system. The lover entered on his amorous journey, knowing the stoppages he must make, and the dangers he must pass through on his way to the city of Tenderness, towards which he was bound. There was the village of *Billets-galans*, the hamlet of *Billet-doux*, the castle of *Petits soins*, and the villa of *Jolis Vers*. After possessing himself of these, he still had to fear being forced to embark on the sea of Dislike, or the lake of Indifference; but if, on the contrary, he pushed off on the river of Inclination, he floated happily down to his bourne. When 'an innocent accomplice of a falsehood' was mentioned, a *Precieuse* (they themselves adopted and gloried in this name) could, without a blush, understand that a night-cap was the subject of conversation; water with them was too vulgar, unless dignified as 'celestial humidity;' a thief could be mentioned when

Bruyére has, with some exaggeration, described the conversationists which met at the house of this lady: "They surrender to the vulgar the art of speaking in an intelligible manner. When anything is said that is scarce understood, it is followed by something else which is still more obscure, on which they improve by downright enigmas, which are always followed by a long clapping of hands. By the help of all that they call delicacy, sentiment, and elegance of expression, they succeed in not being understood, and in not understanding themselves. He who would be furnished for these conversations needs neither good sense, nor judgment, nor memory, nor the least capacity, but wit only, and that not of the best sort—merely that false wit in which the imagination bears sway." Molière dared to attack these absurdities in his *Precieuse Ridicules*, a farce which was first played on the 18th of November, 1659. It pro-

designated as 'an inconvenient hero;' and a lover won his mistress's applause when he complained of her disdainful smile as 'a sauce of pride.'" This account of these circles by Miss Shelly, is drawn more from Mademoiselle Scudéri's novels and Molière's comedy, than from any authentic chronicle. The following extract from her biography deserves more serious attention. "Purity of feeling, however, was the soul of the system. Authors and poets were admitted as admirers, but they never got beyond the villa of *Jolis Vers*. * * * Their style of life was as eccentric as their talk. The lady rose in the morning, dressed herself with elegance, and then went to bed. The French bed, placed in an alcove, had a passage round it, called the *ruelle;* to be at the top of the *ruelle* was the post of honor; and Voiture, under the title of *Alcovist*, long held this envied post beside the pillow of his adored Julie, while he never was allowed to kiss her little finger. This folly had its accompanying good. The respect which the women exacted, and the virtue they preserved, exalted them, and in spite of their high-flown sentiments and metaphysical conceits, wits did not disdain to put a soul into the body of nonsense."

duced an extraordinary sensation;[36] at the second representation the price to the pit was raised from ten to fifteen *sous*, and the price for the other places was doubled. The piece was acted at Paris four months without interruption. It was equally applauded at court, which was then held at Versailles.[37]

The leading characters in this farce are two ladies, whose principal faults are preciseness and coquetry. They make a free use of pomade, think it vulgar to call persons and things by their right names, and insist that they will not marry until after an eventful courtship conducted after examples set forth in romances, and according to the code of gallantry. They talk in the mock genteel style, and vainly endeavor to make their servants adopt the same. They are ambitious of the society of men of rank and letters, and belong to a literary circle where the burden of talk is, that one has written a madrigal on happy love; another has composed stanzas on unfaithfulness; Monsieur last night wrote a *sexain* to Mademoiselle, to which she sent him an answer at eight o'clock next morning; this author is at work upon the third part of his romance, and that has put his

[36] Manage says, "I was present at the first representation. Mademoiselle de Rambouillet, Madame de Grignan, M. Chapelain, and others of the Hotel de Rambouillet, were there. The piece was acted with great applause, and for my own part, I saw at once the effect it would produce. Upon leaving the theatre, I took M. Chapelain by the hand and said, 'We have been used to approve all the follies so well and wittily satirized in this piece; but believe me, as St. Remy said to King Clovis, we must burn what we have adored, and adore what we have burnt. It happened as I predicted, and we gave up this bombastic nonsense from the time of the first representation."

[37] See Molière's Biographers and Editors.

works to press. Such are the topics of gossip, without a knowledge of which, in their opinion, all wit and genius are not worth a pin. Two suitors of rank whom they have discarded, resolve to avenge themselves, and to convince these conceited finical ladies of the folly of their tastes and pursuits, by dressing up two of their valets in the guise of noblemen, and sending them to make the acquaintance of these ladies. The one who is to pass for a marquis affects the man of genius and condition, and looks down with disdain on other valets, calling them unrefined. He feigns surprise that the porter should demand his dues of a gentleman of his rank. He introduces himself to these ladies, and meets with a very cordial and flattering reception. They exchange compliments, and talk in a style of the most superfluous elegance. Our marquis is of that favored class who take all the arts in the natural way without the slightest application to study. He boasts of having in his day composed two hundred popular songs, as many sonnets, four hundred epigrams, and more than a thousand madrigals, to say nothing of enigmas and portraits; but his impromptus are wonderful—he lets off one which throws these fair creatures into raptures, one of them declaring of his interjections, that she had rather be the author of "that *oh! oh!*" than of an epic poem. The marquis introduces the other valet to them as a viscount who had been his companion in arms, and has received a wound in the back part of his head. In short, these noblemen take captive the ladies' hearts, and while they are dancing with them they are surprised by their masters, who expose the whole plot, to the great mortification of their mistresses; and offer the lackeys liberty to continue their gallantries, and at the same time declaring that they will not be at all jealous of them. This farce needs to be read by those who would gain any tolerable estimate of it. As a description of the assemblies that met at the house of Madame de Rambouillet, it is to be received with many grains of allowance. It is the aim of comedy, according to Aristotle, to exhibit men worse than we find them; and this literary circle was represented to be worse than it really was, not only by Molière, but by La Bruyère, Voiture, Ménage and others. Even Hannah More, in her zealous defence of the Blue Stocking Club, has hardly done justice to the Hotel de Rambouillet. After singing of its affectations, she adds:

"Nature of stilts and fetters tir'd,
Impatient from the wits retir'd;
Long time the exile houseless stray'd,
Till Sévigné received the maid."

Now, when we have pardoned something to poetic license, these lines would seem to imply that Madame Sévigné did not belong to this very company of wits, and that she had no tastes and sympathies in common with them. When, therefore, Mrs. More laments;

"No votive altar smoked to thee
Chaste queen, divine Simplicity!"

she seems to have forgotten that there was in the temple of Rambouillet such an altar, of which Madame de Sévigné herself was the priestess. Another and much-thronged altar to Affectation no doubt there was; but in a circle composed of the most polite and ingenious persons in France, there must have been not a few of the votaries of simplicity. Madame de Sévigné was more of a formative genius than not to have exerted a favorable influence in these companies. Some who have ridiculed in their writings this forced conceit and labored refinement, were themselves frequenters of these gatherings, and must by their own example have done, or at least were capable of doing, not a little to counteract any faults of this kind. We have a reliable tradition that it was not unusual for those persons of purer tastes who frequented these assemblies to come away so weary of absurd and labored wit, that they used to express the comfort they felt in their emancipation by saying: "*Allons! faisons des solecismes!*" "Come! now let us go to blundering!" Could these persons have abandoned themselves to the absurdities which they so much disliked? And then we are not to think that this quaint and superfine wit was always indulged in as a serious employment, but often to give a lively and playful zest to the usual bill of literary amusements; and, as generally happens, what was at first only seasoning became at length the food which sickened all, and could not be restored to its former use. Besides, there prevailed in those times a merciless prejudice against women of wit and learning—a prejudice which still occasionally shows itself among the unlettered classes; so that the language which would now be expected from the lips of a tolerably informed woman, was then sneered at as impertinence, pedantry, and a craving after the prerogatives of the other sex.

However prejudicial at first the houses of Rambouillet and of Longueville may have been to a taste for the natural and the true, it appears upon the whole that the farce of Molière wrought a speedy reform in these assemblies. It is true many women sought to avoid the ridicule which had been inflicted upon wit and genius by taking refuge in philosophy and classical learning. Thither Molière pursued them, and thirteen years after, in his comedy *Les Femmes Savantes*, made an attack upon female pretensions to superior knowledge and pedantic fondness for the philosophy of Descartes, at the same time showing that he held his old grudge against feminine geniuses by transferring the war against sonnets, puns, and madigrals to the higher grounds of classical literature and metaphysical science. Altogether this comedy drove out of society a little refined jargon, some pedantry, and nearly all taste for intellectual discourse.

About a century later we find the literary assemblies of Paris altered for the better as to affectation, but for the worse in regard of intellect and morals. In the rival coteries of Madame du Deffand and Mademoiselles Lespinasse, Geoffrin and Boufflers, wit and infidelity, learning and lust, blasphemy and gayety, formed strange but congenial alliances; Voltaire, D'Alembert, Helvétius, Raynal, Marmontel, Carraccioli,[38] D'Holbach, Galliani, and Vanloo, were among the distinguished persons who were in the habit of resorting to these parties. Hume, who was but coolly welcomed to the best literary circles of Lon-

[38] It may be well to remark, that Carraccioli was a believer in Christianity.

don, was affectionately received into the bosom of these assemblies.

Of all the Parisian literary coteries of this period, that of Madame du Deffand for a time took the lead. This lady had been married, but the match being an ill-suited and unhappy one, issued in a separation. Left with a moderate fortune, and a great reputation for wit and conversation, she gave up her hotel and retired to apartments in the convent of St. Joseph, where she continued to receive, almost every evening, whoever was most distinguished in Paris for rank, talent, or learning. She possessed great vivacity and strength of mind, a ready wit, clear conceptions, and superior reasoning powers, to which she gave utterance in words of the most lively and simple eloquence. She was the author of that proverbial *bon mot* about St. Denis carrying his head under his arm, "*Il n'y a que le premier pas qui coûte;*"—"It is only the first step that is difficult;" "a saying sufficient," as one observes, "to make reputation in France." But with all these shining qualities she was egotistic, cold-hearted, selfish, given to detraction, and subject to frequent fits of anger, ennui, jealousy, and moroseness. She was wont frankly to own that she could never bring herself to love anything, though in order to ascertain whether it was possible, she had several times attempted, with little success, to become a Romish devotee. We find her, in her old age, in her correspondence with Horace Walpole, still speaking of religion with too much levity, and confessing her scepticism as to many points of Christian faith, and apologizing for it as involuntary, and arising in part from her education, thus denying her native depravity, like Reynard the Fox, in that old Teutonic story so true to human corruption, who, when led to the scaffold for his crimes, said in his speech to the crowd, that rapacity was no natural inclination of his, for in his youth he had been accounted as virtuous as any one breathing. In her youth she was greatly given to gallantry, and her faithlessness and disregard of all moral principle were such as could never for a moment have been endured anywhere but in the society of infidels to which she belonged. President Hénault was her lover in her youth, and though he afterwards refused any longer to sustain that character, he continued to be her friend as long as he lived. His character of her has come down to us, and is the least flattering of any that flowed from the pens of her admirers; it ends as follows: "In order not to betray too much prejudice, and to obtain more confidence for what I say, I will add, that age, without diminishing her talents, has rendered her jealous and suspicious, yielding to her first impulses, and awkward in managing the men whom she might have easily controlled. In a word, she is of irregular humor, unjust, and ceases to be amiable to those persons only in whose society I have been most happy, and most unhappy, because it is her whom I have loved most." The following anecdote of Madame du Deffand and Hénault, is said to be perfectly authentic, and the moral of it is so good that we cannot refuse it a place. The incident which it relates occurred in their youth, before their mutual alienation had sprung up. They were both complaining one day of the continual interruptions which they met with from the society in which they lived.

"How happy would we be," said the Marchioness, "to have a whole day to ourselves." They agreed to try whether this was possible; and at last found a small apartment in the Tuilleries, belonging to a friend, which was unoccupied, and where they proposed to meet. They arrived accordingly, in separate conveyances, about eleven in the forenoon, appointed their carriages to return at midnight, and ordered dinner from an eating-house. The morning was passed entirely to the satisfaction of both, in expressions of love and friendship. "If every day," said the one to the other, "were to be like this, life would be too short." Dinner came, and before four o'clock, sentiment had given place to gayety and wit. About six the Marchioness looked at the clock, "They play Athalie to-night," said she, "and the new actress is to make her appearance." "I confess," said the President, "that if I were not here, I should regret not seeing her." "Take care, President," said the Marchioness, "what you say is really an expression of regret; if you had been as happy as you profess to be, you would not have thought of the possibility of being at the representation of Athalie." The President vindicated himself, and ended with saying, "Is it for you to complain, when you were the first to look at the clock, and to remark that Athalie was acted to-night? There is no clock for those who are happy." The dispute grew warm; they became more and more out of humor with each other; and by seven, they wished most heartily to separate. That was impossible. "Ah!" said the Marchioness, "I cannot stay here till twelve o'clock, five hours longer, what a punishment!" There was a screen in the room; the Marchioness seated herself behind it, and left the rest of the room to the President. The President, piqued at this, takes a pen and writes a note full of reproaches, and throws it over the screen. The Marchioness picks up the note, goes in search of a pen, ink, and paper, and writes an answer in the sharpest terms. At last twelve o'clock arrived; and each hurried off separately, fully resolved never to try the same experiment again.

It is proof enough how utterly a stranger to these connections was every deep and holy affection, that the very evening Hénault died, after an intimacy with Madame du Deffand of twenty years, she went out to Madame de Marchais's and supped with a great company; and when her friends there spoke to her of her bereavement, she replied: "Alas, he died this evening at six o'clock: had it not been for this you would not have seen me here." "These were her very words," says La Harpe, who was present, "and she ate as usual very freely; for she was a great gormand." The moment of final and awful separation caused her no sorrow, and in one of her letters she gives an account of his death with the most appalling indifference; and there cannot be a darker or more faithful comment on the fiendish fruits of infidelity, than the letter of condolence which Voltaire addressed to her on this occasion.

In her fifty-fourth year, Madame du Deffand lost her sight, and in order to made up as far as possible for the loss of this sense, she adopted Mademoiselle de Lespinasse, the illegitimate but well-educated daughter of a man of rank, as her companion, to read and write for her, and to assist her in doing the honors of her *conversazioni*. For awhile she was greatly delighted with the young lady; by-and-bye however, she discovered that she who had at first been employed in the drudgery of reading her asleep, possessed an originality of thought, a maturity of judgment, and an easy and copious eloquence, that bid fair to engross the attention and admiration of the coterie. As Madame du Deffand, to whom day and night were the same, did not usually present herself till six o'clock in the evening, she often found that her *protégé* had been entertaining the guests for an hour, and that they had come early to enjoy her conversation. She took the alarm, and drove from her house the fair rival whom she thenceforth regarded as a traitor and a usurper. Far from being a homeless wanderer by the dismissal, she was immediately supplied with a house and furniture by her friends, who obtained for her a pension from the crown, so that she now opened her own doors to a society not less brilliant than that of her patroness; indeed she attracted to herself a greater part of the blind Marchioness' circle. The blind clear-seer, *aveugle clairvoyante*, as Voltaire was used to call her, told D'Alembert, that if he countenanced the new idol, he must bid farewell to his former patroness; he did it, and lost no time in joining the party of the young aspirant, and became her most obsequious suitor—nay, the lackey of his jilting mistress in carrying to her from the post her billets from another and preferred rival.[38] Soon,

[38] Mademoiselle Lespinasse had resolved to raise her position by a distinguished marriage. With this view she endeavored to entangle

however, the health of Mademoiselle Lespinasse gave way before her inflammable and ambitious spirit. Yet while her heart was consumed with the fires of more than one passion, and she was wasting away with coughs and spasms, agitated with opium, and her thoughts were turned hourly on suicide, she dined out and made visits every day; and within a few weeks of her death she still had her *salon* filled twice a day with gay company, and dragged herself out to sup with all the countesses of her set. She died before she had attained middle age, and it is said that the mortifications caused by her alienation, followed

the affections of M. Mora, a young Spanish marquis then at Paris. His family hearing of it, and recalling him to Spain, D'Alembert fraudulently procured for her a certificate from an eminent physician of his acquaintance, to the effect that a return to the climate of France was essential to his safety. M. Mora set out for Paris but died on the road. "Thus crossed in her designs," says Marmontel, "she was no longer the same with D'Alembert, yet he not only endured her coldness and caprice, but often the bitterness of her wounded temper. He brooked his sorrows and complained only to me. Unhappy man! Such was his devotion and obedience to her, that in the absence of M. Mora, it was he who used to go early in the morning to ask for Mora's letters at the post office, and bring them to her to read when she awoke."

Yet she was all this while attached to a third person, M. D'Gilbert, and in her letters addressed to him, she did not hesitate to declare that she was most ardently in love with both at the same time. In the very letter in which she addresses M. D'Gilbert in terms of the most passionate adoration, she makes him the confidant of her unspeakable devotion and unalterable love for M. Mora; and when M. Mora died, she continued to love his *memory* just as ardently as she did the *person* of his living successor: her letters are divided between expressions of heart-rending grief and unbounded attachment—between her desire to die for M. Mora, and her delight in living for M. D'Gilbert. Such was the brutish confusion and sneaking meanness of these Luciferians in the Pandemonium of Infidelity.

by grief for her death, broke the spirit of D'Alembert, and embittered and enfeebled his latter days.

Madame du Deffand survived her four years, and continued to preside in her own circle till extreme old age, and died in 1780, after a long life of eighty-three years. Her house had been, for fifty years, the resort of many of the most eminent literary men of the age, where they unbent their minds, and talked easily and familiarly to their female friends of their own works, and made and repeated all sorts of jokes upon them with unfeigned gayety and indifference. Yet, during her long and festive life, Madame du Deffand knew not one happy day. Her jealousies and antipathies were continually fanned to a flame by the many factions which then divided the fashionable and literary societies of the French capital. Courted and flattered as she was to the last by the great and the gay, she was daily devoured by *ennui*, and her own discontented spirit. She did little else but importune her gallants, and annoy them with her murmurs and self-commiserations. A stranger to that active kindness and generosity which can make the worst condition delectable, she lamented that she had ever been born; she complained of existence as an irreparable evil, and yet, as well she might, confessed her unwillingness to die.

An equally brilliant though less formal and exclusive coterie of the time, was that of Madame Geoffrin. This lady was the daughter of a *valet de chambre*, and the widow of a glass manufacturer. She was ignorant not only of syntax, but of orthography as well. She laid the foundation of her reputation by making herself the centre of a circle of artists and men of letters. She had been much in the confidence of Madame de Tencin, and, on that lady's death, succeeded in attracting around herself those who remained of that illustrious circle, dimmed as it was by the departure of Montesquieu and Fontenelle. By activity and energy, she widened the circle till it embraced many of the first literary men in the nation. She never made visits herself—was absolute in her admissions and exclusions, bold in her sarcasms, free and blunt, often to rudeness, in her opinions and observations; and severe or kind to all by turns, as her caprice suggested. Having once gained her high position, she did not assume the subdued and cautious tone of one who felt she was in danger of breaking the social rules of a fastidious aristocracy. A simplicity and freedom accompanied all her actions, and she courageously adopted what she regarded as becoming to herself rather than what seemed fit in the eyes of others. She delighted in lively discussion and in the paradoxes which always provoke people to it, as the following incident will show. The Marquis de Saint Lambert, the author of a poem entitled *Des Saisons*, once introduced to her Galliani, known as the author of several works on political economy. Madame Geoffrin received him kindly, as she did every one presented by the Marquis. The economist was punctual in his visits to her for many months. One day, when he was entering her mansion, a domestic stopped him, and said, very gravely, that his mistress could not receive him. "What! has she gone out?" "No, but she cannot receive you." "But is she sick?" "Monsieur, pardon me," replied the servant, "I can only repeat what I before said:

Madame cannot receive you." This, of course, was not to be resisted, and Galliani bowed to the domestic, and departed. He went immediately to seek his friend—told him he had been discarded, and asked him what indiscretion he could have been guilty of, to produce such coldness on the part of Madame Geoffrin. Saint Lambert took out of his pocket a letter which he requested his friend to read. It was from Madame Geoffrin, and was written thus: "I shall shut my doors upon your learned acquaintance, dear Marquis. His society is insupportable. He states too many facts—makes assertions which are undeniable, and is always in the right." These few words enlightened, all at once, the learned man; and Saint Lambert took the opportunity to caution him against wearying his hearers by constantly and methodically dwelling upon facts without advancing disputable opinions. Accordingly the political economist adopted a new system for the barter of thought, and, by advancing paradoxes and singular propositions, was restored to the favor of Madame Geoffrin. In fact, he became one of the most entertaining and delightful conversationists in that coterie from which he had been so harshly expelled.

Delille, at the conclusion of his poem, *La Conversation*, has given us a delineation of Madame Geoffrin as the president of the literary society that met at her house on Wednesday evenings—a delineation which has received an overwrought coloring from the partiality of friendship and the demands of rhyme. He says it was not till the decline of her glory that he became a member of her coterie. The brilliance of her powers was not obscured by years. In old age she drew around her easy chair a triple circle of admiring visitors from all parts of Europe. She exercised a firm, artless, and gentle supervision in her *salon*, stifling contradiction in the birth, but encouraging the wrestlings of free opinions, chiding with good humor, and praising with judgment, assuring the timid, and calming the fierce, comforting the ugly, and warning the beautiful; in a word, if we may credit Delille, uniting in herself all the qualities that go to make up the corypheus of a conversation meeting. Delille was introduced to her acquaintance at a period when age would naturally have given some check to her offensive energy and independence; causing her to appear to better advantage than she had done in early life.

Benevolence was a strong trait in her character. The poor were fed and laborers encouraged by her liberal bounty; and many were the poor authors and artists that were gladdened by her patronage and generosity: she would confidentially inquire into wants of youthful talent, and as confidentially supply them. When she was no more, Delille burst forth in an affecting apostrophe of gratitude to her for the offer of relief which his proud poverty had declined.[40] Yet this great leader of conversation, who harbored in her house some of the principal deists of her time, the friend of Hume, D'Alembert, and D'Holbach, was sneered at as weak enough to have a turn for secret devotion. She had an apartment in a convent of nuns, and a gallery in the church of the Capuchins. But her devotions were kept in such deep mystery as not to be annoying even to infidels; they

[40] See close of *Chant III. La Conversation.*

were pleased that she did not carry her piety into social life, and amused themselves with her inconsistency and superstition.[41]

It was at this time the rage to hold entertainments at private houses, according to the arrangements and etiquette of a public *café*. Among the amusements then fashionable were pantomimes and acted *tableaux*, in which each took a turn. At one of these routs we find Hume seated in the character of a sultan, between two obstinate beauties, as if intending to strike his own bosom, but really aiming a blow at theirs, and accompanying his acting with characteristic exclamations. Not all their meetings, however, were scenes of such contemptible fooleries; some were chiefly devoted to conversations in which, however, scepticism, credulity, and presumption found free ex-expression; while flattery went beyond all bounds. When poets despaired of flattering any one by their verses, it went hard with them but they would contrive, in some way, to puff up his vanity. Madame le Page du Bocage, a rival of Madame Geoffrin, desired to be reputed a poetess. Voltaire labored long to write a *quatrain* in praise of her miserable verses; but the muse, refusing to obey his call, he overcame the difficulty by twisting some laurel twigs into a wreath, and placing it on her brow.

The French ladies of that age, passing a great part of their time in public, had no relish for the sweets of domestic life, and were consequently denied all

[41] See the works of Grimm, Marmontel, Bauchemont, and La Harpe, Also, Edinburgh Review, article on Memoires de Marmontel, vol. vii., p. 358, on Deffand's and Lespinasse's letters, vol. xv., p. 409, and vol. xviii., p. 290; Life and Correspondence of Hume, by J. H. Burton, Esq., vol. ii., p. 207.

the solid happiness to be derived from household tastes and attachments. Their affections were scattered among many competitors, and their attention occupied with an incessant variety of amusements. They talked with a kind of soulless gayety, not only of the follies of their associates, but of their greatest misfortunes as well: knowing no true friendship, and no devoted love, they were incapable of feeling any deep sympathy for the sufferings of their most intimate companions, whose sorrows they made a jest of, whose calamities they condoled in epigrams, and whose deaths they witnessed or applauded as capital comedies.

Let us now cross over to London, and look in upon the famous "Literary Club" which had, about this period, reached its highest prosperity. This society, which numbered among its membership the brilliant names of Johnson, Burke, Reynolds, Goldsmith, and Garrick, was at first not to exceed the number of the muses; but, from 1763 to 1777, it increased to twenty, at which time there was an addition of six more. In one of his letters, Johnson writes: "It is proposed to augment the club from twenty to thirty, of which I am glad; for, as we have several in it which I do not like to consort with, I am for reducing it to a mere miscellaneous collection of conspicuous men, without any determinate character." But it has always continued to be essentially a literary club. In 1791, the number of members was thirty-five. The club, as it stood in 1829, enrolled on its records, among the names of other distinguished persons, those of Professor Buckland, Francis Chantrey, Dr. Copleston, Sir Thomas Lawrence, Sir James Mackintosh, and Sir Walter Scott. At first it met at some tavern one evening in every week at seven o'clock, and generally continued its conversations till a pretty late hour—so late that Sir John Hawkins, one of Johnson's biographers, seceded from the society on account of its interfering with his domestic arrangements. About three years from its institution, it was resolved, instead of supping weekly, to dine together once a fortnight during the meeting of parliament. At the meetings of the club, the chair was taken by the members in alphabetical rotation. A unanimous vote was necessary to the admission of a new member, a single black ball excluding a member. The talk was miscellaneous, but chiefly literary, politics alone being excluded. Boswell has, in only one instance, ventured to give in any detail the conversations of the club.[43] He has recorded other talks which seem to have passed in the club; but as he usually suppresses the name of the society, and gives the remarks of Johnson, and his own, the foreground, even where it is evident that others took a prominent part in the conversation, it is not always easy to decide where the colloquy took place. Both felt a lively interest in its meetings. Johnson regarded the hours he spent in them as the happiest of his life, and he would often plume himself on his sagacity in selecting its original members. Johnson was so constant at its meetings that he never absented himself. He came late, stayed late, and was often the last to go home. Boswell rejoiced to learn that Johnson pronounced him "a clubable" man, and

[43] See Boswell's Life of Johnson, (Crocker's Edition,) vol. ii. April 13th, 1778.

seems to have thought his admission to this society the greatest of mortal honors. In their tour to the Hebrides, they beguiled the tedious stages of their journey by fondly recalling the high character of the club. "I started a thought this afternoon," says Boswell, "which amused us a great part of the way. I said, 'If our club should come and set up in Saint Andrews as a college to teach all that each of us can, in the several departments of learning and taste, we should rebuild the city, we should draw a wonderful concourse of students.'" They then fell to distributing the offices among the members.

At a club Johnson was in his element; his love for such institutions is seen in his definition of the name: "an assembly of good fellows meeting under certain conditions." Besides the literary club he belonged to others less intellectual, at which he delighted to preside as symposiarch. A gentleman once venturing to say to him, "I wonder sometimes that you condescend so far as to attend a city club," he replied: "Sir, the great chair of a full and pleasant club is, perhaps, the throne of human felicity." In opposition to some, who, having wives and children, said they preferred domestic enjoyments to those which a tavern affords, he made the following confession: "As I enter the door of a tavern I experience an oblivion of care, and a freedom from solicitude; when I am seated, I find the master courteous and the servants obsequious to my call, anxious to know and ready to supply my wants; wine there exhilerates my spirits, and prompts me to free conversation, and an interchange of discourse with those whom I most love; I dogmatize and am contradicted, and in the conflict of opinions and sentiments I find delight." In the pursuit of pleasures like these, Johnson was too often drawn into the society of epicures who did not improve his morals and keep him mindful of the great purposes of life. At club meetings, as, indeed, he did everywhere, Johnson led the conversation, though he was far from being a monologuist. He would allow himself to be interrupted, and his assertions were of a nature to call out all the intellectual forces of the circle, instead of keeping them down: yet, when he had once called them out, he gloried in putting them to rout by the blows and "whiffs of his fell sword."

Johnson usually spoke in a coarse, bow-wow tone, which was now and then relieved by mutterings, puffings, gruntings and growlings, while his mouth was tortured with convulsive twitches, and his gigantic and ungainly body rolled like an elephant. His address was often rude and occasionally ferocious; yet in certain points he insisted upon being very ceremonious, and always exacted the most polite treatment from others. Few men were better versed in the etiquette of the court and the drawing-room, or could turn a more delicate and graceful compliment, yet no man outraged conventional forms with so little compunction. He would insist upon a whole company's rising when a lady came into the room, and five minutes after, perhaps he would drive her out by his personalities. He was vain of the society of ladies, and could make himself agreeable to them when he chose; and few indeed were the fair frequenters of the assemblies where he was the oracle, who did not one time or another carry home with them some piece of flattery, on which they set a high value, as an offset to the abuse which had crimsoned or blanched their faces. He criticised Mrs. Montague's Essay on Shakspeare without mercy, and then dealt out to her strains of the most fulsome panegyric, telling her she was little inferior to queen Elizabeth. To Miss Monkton, who insisted that some of Sterne's writings were very pathetic, he said: "Why, that is because, dearest, you're a dunce." When she sometime afterwards mentioned this to him, he said: "Madam, if I had thought so, I certainly should not have said it." He would flatter Hannah More in no measured terms, but when she quit scores in the same coin, he begged she would consider how much her flatteries were worth before she choked him with them. He drove Dr. Percy out of the room by his animadversions, and went on discoursing without taking any notice of it. He even boasted of having spoken to Mr. Melmoth so roughly as to make him whistle with surprise. He was hard-hearted enough to send Goldsmith home wounded in spirit, without taking any pains to beg his pardon at the time. There was scarcely one of his friends that he did not affront, and there was but one person who could bear his insolence and rage; this was Dr. Mayo, a man of calm temper, who, because he never flinched under the strokes of his satire, received the epithet of the "Literary Anvil." Of his inattention, he sometimes made his boast. "When," says he, "Mr. Vesey talked to me one day concerning Catiline's conspiracies, I withdrew my attention and thought of Tom Thumb." On one occasion, at least, he made no bones of uttering double meanings, which set a bevy of ladies tittering and blushing, and made Hannah More slyly hide her face behind a lady's back who sat next to her. Ever generous and humane towards bodily pain and discomfort, he made nothing of wounding pride, shocking modesty, and torturing envy.

As a reasoner he was ready in exposing the false testimony, and detecting the fallacies of an opponent, but his own arguments were too often crippled by some vulgar prejudice or some superstitious scruple. There was in his mind a singular compound of credulity and scepticism. When any one related to him a plain matter-of-fact, the likelihood was that he would say in his haste all men are liars; when told of marvels and miracles that bore the fabulous on the face of them, he commonly listened agape with childish wonder. This grew in part out of his love for paradox, in which feature he bore a strong resemblance to the wits of Madame Geoffrin's *salon;* to this source is to be attributed the strange lack of uniformity and consistency in his opinions; it being his custom to be in the *opposition*, to whichever side of the question he might be driven. At one time good, and at another, evil was predominant in the moral constitution of the world. Now he would deplore the non-observance of Good Friday, and now deny that there was any decline in the observance of religious festivals. He would sometimes contradict self-evident propositions, such as, that the luxury of the country had increased with its riches, and that the practice of card-playing was more general than formerly. He would meet a sound argument with a "What then, sir?" or a "You do not see your way through the question, sir;" or, "Sir, you talk the language of ignorance;" and when he was compelled to give his assent, which he always did reluctantly, he would preface it with a "Why, no sir." His dogmatism gave great animation to his talks. In companies where the presence of great lords, ladies and *literati* tended to freeze the current of fellow-feeling into hard formalities, and where pedantry and a conceit of infallibility would else have chilled the whole social atmosphere—in such companies there was needed a man who spoke out roughly and aloud—who received not any man's opinions, and trusted not to any man's reasonings, though he put forth the boldest sophisms himself. He contradicted for victory rather than truth, and his constant aim to get the better of his adversary vitiated his mode of argumentation. In attaining his low purpose he endeavored to set the character of his antagonists in a bad light; fearing, as he said, that if he gave them a good character, auditors would conclude that they were engaged on the right side. And then people undoubtedly felt a kind of savage pleasure in hearing his personalities and witnessing their effects: fine ladies saw him wound and kill his man with much the same sensations that their Roman sisters felt in seeing the combats of bloody gladiators.

Nevertheless, we shall lose our clue to the character of Johnson as a conversationist, if, as many have done, we allow it to escape us that he was a great humorist. As those who noted down his talks could not transcribe his humor, and have not always told us with what air and tone he spoke, much that, viewed apart from his singular address, seems fiendish to us, did really overwhelm the company with gusts of laughter. Some persons are surrounded with nitrous oxyd—with a kind of laughing gas. They exercise a strange lordship over your risible faculties ; you cannot approach them without a smile, and their gravest remarks make you laugh outright. Of this sort was the humor of Johnson. It dulled the edge of his sarcasms, and blunted the point of his rebukes; it made even his rudeness pleasant, and gave an air of mock-heroic to his maddest onslaughts. In buffoonry he knew no match, though he did not often indulge himself in it, and when he did it was for the purpose of burlesquing false wit. When Warburton would on one occasion have passed with him for a man of pleasantry, Johnson aped his manner so exactly that he put him quite out of countenance.

He aimed to talk his best on all occasions, and never brought out his thoughts in an undress. The language that fell from his lips, so unlike that which ran from his pen, was plain, pointed, and forcible; what time his mind was stirred, as if by some spirit of inspiration, his thoughts flamed up into the most lofty and splendid eloquence. Like most great conversationists he excelled in recitation, though he rarely repeated pieces of any great length; mostly limiting himself to a few English or Latin verses that naturally fell in his way.

Such were some of the characteristics of Johnson's conversation. To describe them is little more than to enumerate bad qualities. He combined in himself the worst faults of all other talkers, with not a few that were peculiar to himself, and yet was he the greatest conversationist of the time. His reasoning powers, his ready and finished eloquence, his humor, his memory, having at its command large acquisitions in many departments of human knowledge, seem first to surround and then to cover his defects with a flood of glory. Albeit his intellectual powers, in which his pre-eminence consisted, cannot be appropriated by imitation, and so far as the *proprieties* of conversation are concerned, he should be looked upon rather as a beacon to warn, than as a chart to follow.

The moral tone of his conversation in his earlier days, when judged by the standard of the age, was high; when judged by the standard of the gospel it was low. Though he often condemned impiety, injustice, and vice, the ethics of his conversation was at this time a singular medley, never much higher than that of Plutarch or of Seneca, sometimes that of the trickster, the epicure, and the quibbler. He carried his love of paradox, where it ought never to be carried, into his discussions of moral and religious questions; and stickler as he was for certain theological tenets, he felt little concern about reducing them to practice. Though he liked to sit down and talk with Wesley, and spoke in high terms of the self-devotion and zealous labors of his preachers, he had little sympathy with the dissenters in general, and was more charitable to men of bad morals who would receive his creed than to evangelical men who would not admit his interpretations of the Thirty-nine Articles. At one time he had no higher notion of Christianity, than that it was a revelation of the immortality of the soul and of the atonement, than that it was merely designed as an exhibition of the Divine hatred of sin. As the infirmities of age began to creep upon him, and as the companions of his prime one after another dropped off, his piety grew to be more consistent and fervent, though to the last it was clouded with melancholy and superstition. Religion was always rather an awful than a pleasurable matter in his mind: till his dying days he seemed to be under the law and not under grace, occupying himself more with the forms and minor observances of religion, than with its principles and inward workings. Neglecting the root of piety in himself and others, he pruned the branches and then complained that little or no good fruit was borne. He now frequently spoke out in censure of the levity and dissipation which prevailed among many of the clergy of his day; he once reproved Dr. Maxwell for saying grace without mentioning the name of our Lord Jesus Christ. When Boswell was about to embark for the Continent, Johnson took him into a church and said to him, "Commend yourself to your Creator and Redeemer." Once delighting in companions where oaths were frequent and loud, he now would not allow any one to swear before him: when a libertine, but a man of some note, was interlarding his stories with oaths, Johnson said, "Sir, all this swearing will do nothing for our story; I beg you will not swear." The narrator went on swearing; Johnson said, "I must again entreat you not to swear." He swore again—Johnson quitted the room. His death-bed conversations were truly evangelical. When he took leave of Mr. Windham, he said with great fervor, "God bless you, my dear Windham, through Jesus Christ. May we share some humble portion of that happiness which God may finally vouchsafe to repentant sinners." He often said to his servant, "Attend, Francis, to the salvation of your soul, which is the object of greatest importance." He persuaded Sir Joshua Reynolds to promise he would not paint on Sundays, and read the Bible whenever he had opportunity, and never omit it on Sundays. To Dr. Brocklesby he said: "Doctor, you are a worthy man, but I am afraid you are not a Christian. What can I do better than offer up in your presence a prayer to the Great God that you may become a Christian in my sense of the word?" After a fervent prayer, he added, "My dear Doctor, believe a dying man—there is no salvation but in the sacrifice of the Lamb of God." When we think how intent he now was upon the salvation of his friends, we cannot help regretting that more of his long and influential life was not spent in conversations like those of his last days. His *conversazioni* would have become "spiritual routs," as Whitefield used to call the drawing-room congregations to which he preached; and his words would have fallen like the dew, as they did along with it, reviving many a drooping and dying soul. He would have drawn the children of Nicodemus to his house by night, to inquire into the mysteries of the kingdom. He would have established in many of the gorgeous halls of London the principles of the Nazarine, and at last gathered around his grave many sons of glory, at whose new birth he had assisted, to mingle tears of sorrow and gratitude over their common loss.

In close correspondence with the "Literary club," was the famous "Blue Stocking Club," which met on the same day that the "Literary Club" dined together at Turk's Head, or some other tavern. In the evening, the members of the Literary Club were invited to Mrs. Montague's, Mrs. Vesey's, Mrs. Garrick's, or Mrs. Boscawen's, or wherever else the Blue Stocking Club assembled. The origin of the name of the club was this: One of the most eminent members of this society was Mr. Benjamin Stillingfleet, the author of a poetical essay on Conversation, which is to be found in the first volume of Dodsley's collection. His dress was remarkably plain, and he always wore blue stockings. He was an excellent converser, and his absence was felt to be so great a loss that it used to be said: "We can do nothing without the Blue Stockings," and thus by way of pleasantry this title was established. A Frenchman of distinction, whose name is hid in the deepest obscurity, supposing this to be the real name of the party, innocently called it *Bas Bleu*, the corresponding appellation in his own language, and now given to women who are devoted to literary pursuits. These gatherings were composed of persons of distinguished rank, talents, and respectability, who met for conversation, and were different in no respect from other parties, but that the company did not dance, and did not play at cards. They had no supper, but refreshed themselves with tea, milk, lemonade, and biscuits; and when the Literary Club adjourned to meet with them, they had sour crout. Hannah More has given some account of this club in her *Bas Bleu*, a poem, in which several members of the Literary Club are introduced, as

Johnson, under the name of Cato; Garrick, under the name of Roscius, and Burke, under that of Hortensius. The poem is addressed to Mrs. Vesey, a lady distinguished more for her good sense, taste, and amiability, than for learning and conversational skill. These gatherings were often at her house. She had the good-natured fault of sending out too many invitations; at one of her parties almost every nation of Europe was usually represented. Her companies were so large and variegated as not to be the most favorable to conversation, and so Miss More, Mr. Walpole, and Mrs. Carter were chosen a committee to invite or exclude at pleasure; but the benevolent and sweet-tempered Mrs. Vesey could not help inviting every agreeable creature that came in her way. She was remarkable for her skill in breaking up the formality of a circle, by inviting her parties to form themselves into little separate groups so that all might join in the conversation, and persons coming in could peep into the various circles, and fix upon that which they liked best; and when new circles were formed in the course of the evening, they could if they desired join a new group. Hannah More has celebrated this lady's talent this way in the following lively lines:

"Small were the art that would insure
The circle's boasted quadrature.
See Vesey's plastic genius make
A circle every figure take;
Nay, shapes and forms that would defy
All science of Geometry.
The enchantress wav'd her hand and spoke!
Her potent wand the circle broke;
The social spirits hover round,
And bless the liberated ground."

When Dr. Johnson or Mr. Stillingfleet came in and took the great chair, the whole company would collect around him, till they sometimes became no less than four, if not five, deep; those behind standing and listening over the heads of those who were sitting before. The conversation would for some time be carried on by two or three distinguished persons, and if at length the talk became more general, the company would fall away into separate groups.

Mrs. Elizabeth Montague, the founder of the club, and at whose splendid mansion in Portman square it frequently met, had acquired some celebrity as the author of an Essay on the Genius of Shakspeare, was a childless widow of ample fortune, and one of the finest ladies of that day. Her mind was active and well cultivated, with strong reasoning powers, and her conversation was a constant stream of valuable thought—a very river flowing with golden sand. She lived in a style of generous hospitality, and for many years her house was open to the literary and fashionable world. She was sometimes honored with visits from the queen and other members of the royal family. Miss More makes honorable mention of her in the verse:

> "Boscawen sage, bright Montague."

Conspicuous among the constellation of Blue Stockings, shone the lady first mentioned. She was the widow of Admiral Boscawen, and is thus panegyrized by Mrs. More, in her poem called "Sensibility:"

> "'Tis this whose charms the soul resistless seize,
> And gives Boscawen half her power to please."

Her sensibility was probably refined by her afflictions, of which her life was a continual series. The death of her husband left her in great opulence; she rode in a gilded chariot with four footmen. The friend and patron of literary men and women, she was not insensible to their flatteries; when Miss More's *Bas Bleu*, in which her name is mentioned, came out, she dreamed that she was requested by a very large company to set it to music and sing it before them. Nevertheless she was polite, humble, learned, judicious, and a very brilliant conversationist withal. Boswell says her manners were the most agreeable, and her conversation the best of any lady with whom he had the happiness to be acquainted.

The Blue Stocking Club was often misrepresented. It was generally thought that it revived the absurdities that had a century before been attributed to the Hotel de Rambouillet; Miss More, in her *Bas Bleu*, defends the club against the prejudices that had gone abroad concerning it: she declares that the members were free from all the censurable errors that had been laid to their charge, such as those of pedantry, bad taste, levity, and detraction. She also exposes the vulgar error that learned ladies are doomed to be second-rate in literature, and worthless in domestic life, insisting that the ladies of the club were not of that character, but

> "Ladies who point, nor think me partial,
> An epigram as well as Marshall;
> Yet in all female worth succeed,
> As well as those who cannot read."

All the members of the club were not the most select; in a society where there was no fixed rule of admission, it was of course impossible to keep out all improper persons: and then some who would merit admission for one quality, would deserve exclusion for another; and some unworthy characters would be introduced by the favor and partiality of their friends. They could not keep out some such men as Boswell, who, just come from dinners, where the bottle had circulated too freely, would talk loosely; and there were some such men as Dr. Mounsey, who was frequently seen at Mrs. Montague's. He was a coarse humorist, swore and talked loudly, and at his death, directed in his will, that his body should not suffer a funeral ceremony, but undergo dissection, and after that treatment, be thrown into the Thames or wherever the surgeon pleased.

Horace Walpole, in one of his letters, describes an attempt made by Lady Miller about this time to call back the customs of the Hotel de Rambouillet. There was held at her house near Bath, every Thursday evening, a "Parnassus Fair," where, among other ancient sports, *bouts-rimés* were revived. Themes and rhymes were distributed among the people of quality then at Bath, who, by making verses to match them contended for the prize of honor. A Roman vase, decked with pink ribbons and myrtle, received the poetry which was drawn out on every festival. Six judges decided the merits of the compositions, and the successful competitor kneeled before Lady Miller, kissed her fair hand, and was crowned by it with myrtle. The collection thus made was superbly printed and published. Here the nobility of that generation read *bouts-rimés* on a buttered muffin by her Grace the Duchess of Northumberland, and receipts to make them by Corydon. Dr. Johnson held the collection very cheap. "*Bouts-rimés*," said he, "is a mere conceit, and an *old* conceit *now*. I wonder how people were persuaded to write in that manner for this lady."

"A gentleman of my acquaintance wrote for the vase," replies one.

"He was a blockhead for his pains."

"The Duchess of Northumberland wrote."

"Sir, the Duchess of Northumberland may do what she pleases; nobody will say anything to a lady of her high rank. But I would be apt to throw ——'s verses in his face."

Johnson was the last man that would have allowed the queen of such a farce to usurp his colloquial throne. He foresaw that if he should give way to this "Parnassus," it would prove a Vandal as desolating to conversation as quadrille or whist. Walpole called Lady Miller as romantic as Madame Scudéri; and the Blue Stockings generally were of simpler manners and purer tastes than to regard it with any favor.

There was another association of poetasters, which grew in part out of Lady Miller's coterie, called "The Della Crusca Club," from one Robert Merry, who adopted the signature, Della Crusca, in the printed effusions of his muse. The members of this confederacy flooded the newspapers and periodicals of the day with verses, in which the sins of tawdry affectation and false feeling were but poorly atoned for by occasional gleams of imagination and pathos. Besides setting themselves up as literary dictators, they were in the habit of heaping the most fulsome flattery upon each other. Their bad taste, self-conceit, and absurd conduct, called forth William Gifford's "Baviad," a paraphrase on the first satire of Persius, abounding in personalities towards the ladies of this club. Fairer game for satire could not have been found; still, it has been questioned whether these harmless but foolish creatures deserved to be so severely lashed; and Gifford has been accused of betraying a want of chivalry in this affair, and of not behaving as courteously as was to be expected, considering the company he kept. Mrs. Piozzi, Mrs. Robinson, Robert Merry, Miles Peter Andrews, and Mr. Parsons were the penny candles among the farthing rushlights of this strange association.

It was in the meetings of the Blue Stocking Club that Hannah More began to unfold her powers as a conversationist. At this period, however, her intellectual and social, rather than her moral faculties, found eloquent expression. Literature was now her all-absorbing theme. Her talks were refined, modest, and benevolent, but they wanted a high purpose, and were too strongly seasoned with flattery; and, though a high evangelical spirit was wanting, a remarkably strict moral principle always found in her a tongue. Mrs. Garrick called Miss More her chaplain. The death of Johnson and of Garrick seems to have led her to take more sober and worthy views of the objects of life. She now sought occasions in which to speak frankly and pointedly on religious subjects; but in promiscuous circles she did not so frequently start religious subjects, as extract from common themes some useful and awful truth, and counteract the mischief of a popular sentiment by one drawn from religion. This sort of conversation fine people would, in a degree, endure; and it was her opinion, that if she did any good in general society, it was in this way. Sometimes, however, she was bold to proclaim before the children of pomp and pleasure, what she considered duty and truth, even at the risk of being discarded; but her personal reproofs were always mild, and she ever avoided personalities. She was even too charitable towards the excesses or failures of her acquaintance; and kept up intercourse with some persons of kindred intellectual tastes, with whom, as a Christian, she had nothing in common. Though flattery was one of the great sins of that age, after making all allowance for peculiar temptations, she was always a little too fond of bestowing compliments on her friends; but when they made a liberal return in kind, she was too wise to be deceived by them. Notwithstanding her success as a writer, she always had a low opinion of her literary productions, and if she ever patiently heard them praised, it was because she felt the need of encouragement. She listened to criticisms on her own works with a candor and good humor that astonished the stranger, and in her strictures on the works of her contemporaries she showed none of the meanness of envy or of resentment; and took peculiar pleasure in pointing out their merits. She hated detraction with a perfect hatred, and this drove her to such an excess of generosity as made her blind to the moral qualities of actions. Well-defined as her opinions on most important subjects certainly were, she was indulgent to all parties in the church and state; it is a significant coincidence that Edmund Burke, Dean Tucker, and Mrs. Macauley called upon her the same morning; fortunately in *succession*, as they were all at that time writing against each other. She had received, both from nature and grace, a tender sensibility, and she could not always help betraying it even in the most stately companies. The feeling expressed itself not only in smiling and laughing, but in weeping as well. The only jewels she wore were the tears that upon occasion adorned her eyes; nay, her heart also, for they were full of its sterling sentiment: they were those legendary tears of Eve, which hardened into pearls as they fell.

Mrs. More was never guilty of ostentation and forwardness, faults than which few others are more unwomanly. Accustomed to listen to others with the most flattering attention, she betrayed no anxiety to be heard or approved. Her fluency was not a gibbering loquacity; she had the scarce gift of saying much without seeming to take a leading part in the conversation. Robert Hall once being in company where some one inquired whether there was anything distinguishable in the manner of Mrs. Hannah More's *conversation*, immediately replied: "She talks but little, sir, on ordinary occasions; and when she speaks, it is generally to make some pointed, sententious remark. Indeed, sir, she seems to be always lying in wait for such opportunities. The last time I was in her company, she spoke but once, and then some one complained how long in the summer genteel people remained in London, and how little of it they spent in the country. Another accounted for it by saying they did not leave town, from a principle of loyalty, till after the celebration of the king's birthday. 'Then,' said Mrs. More, 'the wickedest thing that George III. ever did, was being born on the 4th of June.' This, sir," continued Mr. Hall, "was the only sentence she uttered all the evening."[43] If Mr. Hall could here speak of her taciturnity as a disparagement to her conversational gifts, what would he have said had she made any the least seeming attempt to eclipse one who loved to shine unobscured so well as he did? Could Mr. Hall have been so dead to the charms of that beautiful timidity which taught her to listen in deferential silence to the oracles of conscious greatness? Mrs. More could and did speak freely and copiously when she knew that others prefered her discourse to her attention. Still it was a virtue which became her sex, that she could brook a superior in an art in which she was known to excel.

Admirably did she exercise her skill in calling out retired merit and giving heart to the timid; she recognized the social equality of a company by dividing her kind attentions equally, but not officiously, among all, and by giving common sense as full a hearing as genius and learning. She had a turn for anecdote, lively strokes of wit, and particularly excelled in recitation. In her old age she received at her cottage at Barleywood the visits of strangers, who came from all parts of the world to do homage to her genius. At this period her conversations abounded with quotations from the scriptures; with thoughts on experimental religion; on the operations of benevolent institutions; as, the progress

[43] Morris' Life of Robert Hall.

of the gospel in foreign lands and at home, especially through the agency of the sunday school, and bible and tract societies. She showed admirable address in shaping her conversations to the motley sorts of people who came to see her. When two or three of her old friends paid her a visit, aged as she was, she would sit up talking with them till two o'clock in the morning; and all the while the words would fly from one to the other as rapidly "as the bird of a battle-door."

There was a something—call it considerateness if you please—that held her back from hasty and unadvised speeches. Few women have talked as much and as ably as she, and yet as carefully weighed their words and said so few that they could have wished to recall. What was it that kept her lips from evil and her tongue from guile? While the gay and the learned, in every circle in which she moved, plied the scourge of the tongue warmly and on all sides, what was it that forbade her engage in the cruel sport? Why was it that, while gifted and nobly-born beauties were betrayed by their words into life-long sorrows, why was it that upon her lips continued the "law of kindness" and the lessons of virtue? This was it; the grace of God ruled her soul and carried her safely through all the mazes of society: like the heroine of Comus she carried in her bosom a talisman, and all who heard her words and saw her behavior, were compelled to say,

"Sure something holy lodges in that breast."

Oh, ye daughters of winged and winning speech, how dangerous is your gift, unless, like Mrs. More, you possess another and a better that can assist you to use this aright? Without it you may possibly make a little better use of your tongues than did Aspasia or Ninon de l'Enclos: yet you will fail of dedicating this noblest organ of your frame to a holy and worthy purpose.

Were it not too wide a departure from the practical purposes of this work, we would like to sketch some of the features in the conversation of the Rev. Robert Hall and Sir James Mackintosh.[44] Though differently gifted, they were in many respects as brilliant conversationists as the world has yet ever known; neither would such sketches be barren of instruction; but as it is our design to bring forward such conversationists only as may be regarded as types of the principal classes, we reluctantly pass these two great characters by, and dwell awhile on the conversation of Coleridge, one of the most singular and surprising of talkers.

[44] To these names we might add those of Burke, Wesley, Sir Walter Scott, Sir Humphrey Davy, Sheridan, C. J. Fox, Thomas Moore, Miss Edgeworth, Brougham, Dudley Ward, D. Sharp, known in his day as "Conversation Sharp," Goethe, &c., &c. Besides these, which belong to the eastern shores of the Atlantic, there have appeared on the western side, Franklin, Jefferson, John Randolph, Chief Justice Marshall,* President Dwight, John M. Mason, J. C. Calhoun, &c., &c.

---

* Since the name of Washington, as a conversationist, must be omitted here, he being rather deficient in colloquial as well as oratorical gifts, we cannot forbear bringing forward Judge Marshall's testimony as to the attention Washington paid in early life to the formation of proper manners. Writing to Mr. Sparks, the editor of the Washington Papers, he says: "I have read no part of these volumes with so much pleasure as the maxims under the head of 'Rules of Civility, and decent behavior in Company and Conversation.' These rules, of which I had never before heard, *furnish a key with which to open the original character of this truly great man.*"

Coleridge's voice was naturally clear, .soft, and flexible, but in his last years it grew to be a nasal and snuffling tone. His eyes, which were large and hazel, were veiled with a soft haze or dreaminess. His manners were uniformly gentle and easy, and he had the art which few great men possess, of making conscious inferiors serene and tranquil in his presence. He was full of benevolence and sympathy, and could talk with ladies, even children in the most affable mode; and when in the midst of high discourse if a lady, no matter who, entered the room, his tone was softened and his whole manner subdued by the charm of her appearing. Still he had neither taste nor talent for small talk; he might sometimes talk for the sake of talking, and of whiling away irksome hours, but had no genius for that prattle which can glide from one trifle to another for the amusement of the idle; his was a solemnity of spirit which kept away everything silly and gay. Wit he wanted not; but it appeared oftener in sarcasm than in anecdote and banter. When he talked of the common and the concrete, his style was simple and natural; when he came upon philosophy and theology his sentences grew involved, poetic, and occasionally obscure. Howbeit you could not listen to the strains of his metaphysics without being convinced that he was indeed a magician in the use of words; so rare and available was the wealth of his language. He had intermeddled with many kinds of knowledge, had been a man of travel and adventure, had viewed nature with the eye of a philosopher and a poet, and of course took pleasure in opening and exhibiting to all, the princely casket of his thoughts. He loved to dwell upon the subtleties of the Greek philosophies and of the schoolmen, on the freakish and changeful dreams of the German wisdom; and then he had a philosophy of his own. This of course was his bantling; the chief care of his life was to give it to the world, and he harangued upon it with fatherly fondness. In theology he was a Titan, and as he tore up and piled one mountain of speculation upon another, his friends looked on with doubt and dismay; as he clambered up into the regions of ærial abstraction, they trembled for his fate; for he daringly inquired, not why things exist *as we find them*, but why they exist *at all*. In piling up his mountains he sometimes laid the beams of his chambers so deep in the waters that ordinary minds often failed to discover the foundations. In treating political questions he discussed general principles, not often descending to measures, hardly ever to men. His mind loved to rise above facts, events, and evidences, that it might rest in eternal laws, or what he imagined such; hence his conversation abounded in striking aphorisms and shrewd guesses at truth. History was not his favorite theme; he lived neither in the past, present, nor future, but above all time: when he contemplated an old ruin, a celebrated plain, or river, it awoke no historical recollections; he spoke of them as they appeared in the passing hour. If he was walking in the morning down Highgate Hill to London, he would take off his hat and address an impromptu hymn to the sun; when he was looking on a midsummer sunset he would fall into a sort of trance, and with his eyes swimming in tears, lift up his hands and breathe a silent prayer;

then rouse himself, quote some old poet, and break forth in most enchanting utterances of his own. Often there was in Coleridge's conversation great individuality; he loved to wrap the seer's mantle about him, and utter such high and wondrous raptures as made his friends bow down as if blinded and awestruck before him. At such times he would look down upon their objections, and doubts, and attempted interruptions, as the mutterings of sleepers, who knew not what they said; yet they went home wonderfully enlightened, though they could not always tell in what respect: they felt marvellous experiences which they could not describe, and which it was not to be supposed that any but themselves could or ought to feel. On such occasions his thoughts were more logically connected than his sentences; to the inattentive hearer, not a few of his transitions seemed but leaps in the dark; but it was by reason of the immensity of the orbit in which his thoughts circled that he lost sight of them; had he tarried longer, he would have seen them again as they came round on the other side. After he had come to be an opium-eater, if not in rare instances before, he did indeed talk ramblingly; in other words, he would start from well-defined premises, perhaps, but come to no conclusion; or, as was often the case, start from no premises, and come to a conclusion that ought to have been his premises.

Madame de Stael, whom Coleridge visited at Coppet, said he was master of monologue, but that in dialogue he had no skill. There was some truth in this observation. He was known to talk almost incessantly for three or four hours together—sometimes a whole day; pouring forth his accumulated stores of reflection and feeling, and scattering broadcast and wastefully his gathered treasures of theosophy, metaphysics, criticism, and poetry. After fifty, he was confined to his own room many months in every year, so that he was not often seen except by single visitors, who used to listen with deep and unbroken attention to whatever he was pleased to say. He passed so much of his time in solitary thinking, that when any one came to see him, he felt it a relief to think aloud, but without ever breaking the thread of meditation which he still went on unwinding as before; so it was, that he came to be a continuous and rather exclusive talker. Still he did sometimes pause when the listeners desired to throw in a word of objection or inquiry, which was seldom the case however; for they would as soon have thought of staying the waters of the Amazon in their course as of checking the majestic flow of his dissertations; such wide and beauteous regions of thought did they traverse, and such green islands of novel ideas, brilliant metaphors and dreamy fancies did they pass in their way.

Coleridge was more a *reasoner* than an *arguer*, being in the habit of throwing his intellect back upon its own powers, and leaving it to work out its own conclusions, without any help from others. He was not, like Johnson, a conversational gladiator; he disliked the character, and could not often be provoked to enter the lists with any disputant, however honorable; he insisted on being allowed to reason in his own way, and on giving such a turn to a question as he liked best. Yet he was by no means a dry and tedious reasoner. No man, perhaps, was more successful in making his arguments attractive and entertaining to ordinary minds; in his better days he spoke in so musical a tone, so fluently and energetically, and with such apt and striking illustrations, that he delighted even ladies with his discussions of Kant's metaphysics. He endeavored to make his reasonings serve some, though by no means the highest practical purpose. He argued too much like a mere partisan. He once confessed to a friend that he was engaged in undermining at the same time the faith of a Jew, a Swedenborgian, and a Roman Catholic.

Whatever may be our opinions of Coleridge's character or philosophy, thus much must be granted on all hands, that his was an ardent thirst after truth, and a disinterested pursuit of it. Yet he seems to have set a higher value on the *discovery* of truth than on the *applications* of it. He disowned the doctrine of expediency, not only in his philosophy, but in the uses of his conversations also. He often wasted his words, or, as a Hindoo would say, scattered jewels in a jungle. It is a matter of regret that this motley-minded man did not discourse more earnestly on the obligations of practical faith; his talks enlightened the judgment, charmed the imagination, and refined the taste—would that they had equally benefited the heart. He overvalued the uses of a new philosophy, but did not enough consider how superior a Regeneration is to a Reformation, and that to save a soul, something more is needed than probing the depths of human consciousness or filling the imagination with visions of the true, the beautiful, and the good, or offering criticisms on the sacred text, or prying into the mysteries of providence and revelation. He burrowed so deeply into metaphysical science, scholastic erudition and speculative divinity, as to chill the compassionate ardor of his spirit, and remove him from the every-day-work of helping poor sinners up to the top of Golgotha along the steeps of repentance. Coleridge's faith was without works, and his words without actions to match them. We should consider the history of his closing years, and should recollect that even Southey lost all confidence in his moral character at that period, if we would form a true estimate of all his qualities as a man. And when I compare this sketch of his conversation with his general life, I am inclined to say of it, the name being changed, what he once said of Wordsworth's portrait: "It looks more like Coleridge than Coleridge himself."

There is now living in the northern hemisphere, a man whose conversation is so singularly original, learned and elegant, that I am moved to make some mention of it; and though I cannot hope to do it anything like justice, yet to pass it by unconsidered, would be an atheistic disregard of the works of the Lord who made him what he is, and a withholding from the reader that would excel in conversation, one of the best patterns he can set up for imitation.

What first strikes you in his conversation is his modesty, and his reluctance to open himself freely to strangers; and if you have gained access to his parlor with a view to hear him talk, without saying anything yourself, you presently find that he is no monologuist delighting to talk oracularly to large silent circles, or even to one tongueless person; rather, that he prefers to converse with one or two friends who are willing to act the part of interlocutors as well as listeners. If you have come at the wrong time, or merely to gratify curiosity or to amuse an idle hour, the chances are that he will sit and wait for you to take the lead in the colloquy, all the while turning towards you his shoulder, his ear, and his profile. Finding nothing to say worth his hearing, as you stare at him, you call to mind the student that, when Goethe treated him in the same proper manner, had the face to take a candle in his hand and step around the genius, inspecting him as he would the statue of an enthroned Jupiter, then putting a piece of silver on the table, walked coolly out, without speaking a word. But knowing yourself to be the aggressor, you feel no impulses towards such an impertinence in his presence; you remember too that he is naturally affable to all sorts of persons; insomuch that little children come and sit at his feet that they may regale themselves with his talks. What next and ever strikes you, is his deep and broad scholarship, and his accurate and multifarious reading. When he gives you occasional glimpses of his vast stores of knowledge, you seem to yourself to be sitting down before the Egyptian Sphinx, whom some power has bidden to breathe and speak, and converted its vast cranium into a library containing diamond editions of all the principal books that have ever blessed the world; besides not a few rare old scrolls from the Alexandrian library, which you supposed Omar had burnt long ago. There must be there, you are sure, *cunabula* and black-letter rarities in great plenty, but no vacant shelves, and no *succedanea;* and the speech of the Sphynx is so fluent and various that you fancy each leaf of every book is a tongue, uttering all that is upon it. Then, as original thoughts come dancing out to the sound of some low, gentle, and tremulous melody, your fancy enters another apartment of the cranium, and discovers that all this is not a mere talking library; for you cannot number the volumes of original ideas that are here arranged around you in orderly alcoves. When the Sphinx calls up some dim and far-off epoch in civil or ecclesiastical history, cites some never-known or forgotten name—by no means on purpose to make a show of his erudition, nothing further from his thoughts, but as a telling proof or rich illustration of some great principle—when he does this, you think that the spirit of history is in him the spirit of prophecy, and that the bygone is his interpreter of the passing and the coming. But the Sphinx, you observe, has a more comely countenance than the stern, weather-beaten, broken-nosed one you used to marvel at when a boy, in the "Seven Wonders of the World." The intellectually severe is softened by the benevolently mild, and especially by that innocent, good-natured curl at the corner of the lips, which Rubens has given to his young John the Baptist talking with the child Jesus. These, along with the soft, gentle, half-whispering tone that is natural to him, cause you quite to forget the Sphinx, and to feel that you are conferring cheek by jole with some tried and confidential friend. There are times however when, dismayed at his enormous learning, you think you are still sitting under the shadow of the awful Sphinx, and as you cast your eyes abroad, feel that you are stark alone amid the waste howling wilderness of your own ignorance. Then, again, you are gently caught up, and find yourself reclining in some grove of the south, lending your ear to the notes of the good-humored mocking bird; and while he is criticizing contemporary authors, or quoting their best passages, or canvassing current opinions, you mark how skilfully he imitates each peculiar note of the flocks of songsters that are embowered around him, and how he scorns to quote the cawings of the crow, the whistlings of the hawk, and the hateful dialects of other birds of prey, and how he never imitates the notes of even clean birds to burlesque them, but to admire them, and to join you in admiring them. This done, as is said to be the wont of his genus, he strikes up a song of his own, which, in your opinion, though not in his, is more ravishing than all the rest; and you find that his power to sing the notes of the rarest birds abates not a jot of the originality and independence of his own peculiar song—a song which is none other than the free utterance of a soul that is fearless and modest, earnest and refined, poetic and strong. His music breaks through and entangles the measures and bars of other songsters, else it would not be his music. You say of many a *sentence* of his, what Quintilian says of the style of Seneca, *abundat dulcibus vitiis*,—"It abounds with delightful faults." But his *words* are more than faultless; they are full of the poetry of the Saxon: they are as antique as beautiful, as quaint as elegant, as picturesque as bold. You also witness how his mode of reasoning explodes the old precept, that you must first formally convince the understanding before you presume to approach the imagination or pay your addresses to the heart; for he melts your reasoning powers, and imagination, and feelings into one intense co-working; his illustrations at once affect you with the conviction of the most labored arguments, and move you with the persuasion of resistless exhortations. Then you notice with what ease these faculties act together, and yet equally well, and that they are always at command; that in letting off his thoughts, he never hangs fire—never leaves any interval between the flash of the mind and the report of the lips. Yet this alertness does not, as it is apt to do in other men, tempt him to inflict on anybody flesh wounds of raillery, or chance-medley strokes of repartee, or to take part in the lighter game of small talk. Never did you hear from his lips anything of this sort; no never. Only you remember to have heard him once or twice, when the occasion called aloud for it, let fall a pleasant but irresistible sarcasm. In taking leave of him, you detect yourself loitering to pass one word more; and when, much against the will, you drag yourself away, you cannot help fervently repeating to yourself those lines of Cowper, which some suppose to refer to Rev. John Newton's conversation, and others to John Wesley's; but you think they describe him whom you have just left, better than either of the others.

"Oh, I have seen (nor hope perhaps in vain
Ere life go down to see such sights again)
A vet'ran warrior in the Christian field,
Who never saw the sword he could not wield;

Grave, without dullness, learned, without pride,
Exact, yet not precise; though meek, keen-ey'd;
A man that would have foil'd at their own play
A dozen would-be's of the modern day;
Who, when occasion justified its use,
Had wit as bright as ready to produce;
Could fetch from records of an earlier age,
Or from philosophy's enlighten'd page,
His rich materials, and regale your ear
With strains it was a privilege to hear;
Yet above all, his luxury supreme,
And his chief glory, was the Gospel theme;
There he was copious as old Greece or Rome,
His happy eloquence seem'd there at home,
Ambitious not to shine, or to excel,
But to treat justly what he lov'd so well."

"Even these lines," you add, "come far short of conveying a sufficient idea of his conversation. To those only who have heard him is it given to know what it is; and neither poetry nor parables can describe it to them that have not."

Pass we now to the subject of modern conversation-clubs Having already given some account of the most celebrated literary clubs which flourished in the seventeenth and eighteenth centuries, we have forestalled much that might otherwise be said concerning the literary clubs of the present day; inasmuch as they bear a resemblance more or less close to the ancient clubs of Paris and London. Literary conversation-clubs are now as they ever have been, necessarily few in number, and those boasting no very long list of members. They meet regularly during only a part of the year; and the greater number of those clubs that are made up of staid *literati* know but a brief existence. Like the Spectator Club, the members, one after another, drop off till there are not enough remaining to constitute a meeting: Sir Roger de Coverly dies of a defluction, Will Honeycomb marries his tenant's daughter, and Captain Sentry and Sir Andrew Freeport retire to their estates in the country. However, the curse of mortality which threatens them does not prevent their formation, nor keep them from compassing the design of their creation.

The advantages growing out of these societies are almost too obvious to need any mention. They keep up a good understanding and brotherly communion among the members; and afford occasion for mutual counsel and encouragement. Here they fling out their thoughts to air; and if they are blown upon from all quarters so much the better; their aroma is wonderfully improved by these breezes and counter breezes; but where flattery, as it is apt to do, becomes fashionable in literary soirees, it makes the man of letters a Cyclops of one eye, and that in the occiput; looking back with self-gratulation on what he has already done, as he stumbles carelessly over what he has yet to do. In these, though less than in other clubs, there spring up names, signs, pass-words, and cant phrases, which strengthen the bond of fellowship by keeping up confidential recognitions and reminiscences.

> "The language to th' elect alone
> Is like the masons' mystery known.
> In vain the unerring sign is made
> To him who is not of the *trade.*
> What lively pleasure to divine
> The thought implied, the hinted line;
> To feel allusion's artful force,
> And trace the image to its source."

Here *literati* find what they do not always find elsewhere, appreciating ears and tongues that can give a right answer—the two arch-inspirers of social eloquence. Here they may talk with all freedom of the biography of authors, the history of books, and all the jots and tittles of criticism, rising now and then to great national and international questions in literature, religion, and politics; sometimes wandering away from literary topics altogether.

There flourish in great cities clubs of quite another kind; and fearfully permanent and prosperous institutions they are. They meet ostensibly for conversation; but it is understood that eating, drinking, smoking, and gaming, are to come in for the chief share of attention. Wine and strong drink are invoked in songs, doggerels, and rhapsodies, as the inspirers of colloquial wit, poetic genius, and all generous and brotherly sentiments. The chair is taken perhaps by some veteran "fogy," who can remember the time when precedence in the club was given to every man according to his power of drinking a certain quantity of liquor, sitting in an erect position; who piques himself on his skill in ascertaining the exact quality of wines, and on knowing the best way to ice claret, and to make sherry cobblers. Other members attain to fame by an alacrity at low humor, or insipid witticisms, or punning, or badgering, or ribaldry, or blasphemy. A glass or two quickens their tongues, so that they move with astonishing glibness, a few draughts more paralyze their vocal organs; and voices that before ran up to a high key, now fall to mumbling and stammering; their ideas once so clear, grow muddy, till nonsense succeeds, and hiccups and snoring end the conversation. Meeting, as they often do on Saturday night, they go or are carried home drunk on Sunday morning. The Lord's day is divided between sleep, drugging a sick stomach, cooling a heated brain, and quenching a burning thirst. The effects of Saturday night's debauch are, in many cases, powerfully felt even on Monday morning, and relief vainly sought by a return to the bottle. We hope and pray the day will come, when such accounts of the symptoms of drunkenness will not be regarded as repetitions of what everybody knows, but as points in ancient history, which shall excite the wonder and disgust of distant generations.

In vain do the members of these clubs quote to us the rules by which they profess to be governed, so long as they practically disregard them; so long as they notoriously sell themselves to intemperance and its attendant vices, in violation of all laws, human and divine. Nor would a more strict observance of their rules greatly mend their morals; for the rules, to which they appeal with so much confidence, in defence of these societies, if narrowly inspected, will be found to encourage the violation of one another. In proof of this, we will not quote the regulations of any modern club, lest we should lay ourselves open to the charge of exposing to public curiosity laws which were enacted for the initiated alone; we will refer to the rules which were composed by the great moralist, Dr. Johnson, for the Essex Head Club—rules which we are willing to pit against those of any modern club of the kind. Among several rules enjoining decorum, we find one requiring each member present to spend *at least* sixpence; thus *requiring* the systematic growth of the appetites, and *approving* their most unlimited indulgence. Let us go still further back and look at Ben Jonson's *Leges Convivales*, which have for generations been considered the golden oracles of the club-room. He directs wisely and well:

> "Let the contests be rather of books than of wine;
> Let the converse be neither noisy nor mute;
> Let none of things serious, much less of divine,
> When belly and head's full, profanely dispute."

But elsewhere in the same code we have the following admonition:

> "Let no sober bigot here think it a sin,
> To push on the chirping and moderate bottle,"

which if heeded, must, as all experience proves, lead to the infringement of the excellent rules before quoted; nay, and of all excellent rules whatsoever. Apart from the habits of intemperance which these clubs beget and foster, they overrule the attractions of the domestic circle. We have seen in the case of Johnson, that a scholar capable of the highest intellectual pleasures, and strong in his domestic attachments, could forego all the sober comforts of home for the low gratifications of a sixpenny club at an ale-house. What charms then must invest a club-house furnished with every imaginable luxury of life, in the view of a man possessing, perhaps, not a tithe of Johnson's mental resources. We could call witnesses to this, but it is not necessary. These charms however have a dark side. In many cases the wife is left to evenings of solitude, or to society that is worse. Unassisted must she gather and keep the children round the family hearth, and provide for their amusement, instruction, and government. This were nothing for female patience to endure, compared with the soul-piercing reflection that other society has greater allurements for him than that of his wife and his children—that when he comes home, though late, he brings with him each night a worse heart, and a worse intellect, worse manners, and worse health—in short, every faculty and possession altered for the worse. Need we call down from heaven the spirit of one such broken-hearted wife, and bid her tell the story of her domestic woes—of all the tortures which a drunken and alienated husband can inflict on a kind and constant heart; or need we call up from among the wassailers of perdition, the remorseful spirit of her husband himself, and suffer him to howl out his dolors and warnings—need we do these things to convince the club-goer that this his way is his folly and his ruin? No; if he will not believe the evidence of his own senses, neither would he be persuaded though one should rise from the dead. If he would believe the evidence of his own senses—would look abroad in the world, and consider the life and death of the mass of club-goers, and hearken to the unbribed witnesses within, above, and beneath him, all testifying against the institution, sure we are that he would break with his treacherous companions forever, and take up this self-adjuration: "Oh my soul, come not thou into their secret; unto their assembly mine honor be not thou united."

THE END.

www.ingramcontent.com/pod-product-compliance
Lightning Source LLC
LaVergne TN
LVHW020127110826
845151LV00001B/303
9781425540074